TEACHING SCIENCE AT THE SECONDARY STAGE

A.S.E. PUBLICATIONS
of particular interest to readers of this book

SCIENCE FOR PRIMARY SCHOOLS

Four paperbacks

Children Learning Through Science
List of Books
List of Teaching Aids
Materials and Equipment

SCIENCE TEACHING TECHNIQUES

A series of inexpensive booklets on teaching science to secondary pupils of average ability. Nos 8 to 12 are in print. Contributions to recent issues include:

Safe Chemistry; An Astronomy Course; Soldering for the Science Teacher; Worksheets in Science; etc.

HOW TO BEGIN YOUR FIELD WORK

Two workbooks by V. E. Ford, B.Sc. (not necessarily expendable) giving precise yet adaptable instructions on field work.

A full list of A.S.E. publications and details of membership (which includes subscriptions to the two journals, *The School Science Review* and *Education in Science*) are available from:

The General Secretary
Association for Science Education
52 Bateman Street
Cambridge

TEACHING SCIENCE
AT THE
SECONDARY STAGE

A Handbook on the Teaching of
Science to the Average Pupil

PREPARED BY THE

SECONDARY MODERN SCHOOLS
SUB-COMMITTEE

OF THE

ASSOCIATION FOR SCIENCE EDUCATION
\\

JOHN MURRAY
50 ALBEMARLE STREET, LONDON, W.1

Fitz Memorial Library

Endicott Junior College
Beverly, Massachusetts 01915

© The Association for Science Education, 1967

Printed in Great Britain by
Cox & Wyman Ltd, London, Fakenham and Reading
and published by John Murray (Publishers) Ltd

29096

CONTENTS

CONSTITUTION OF THE SUB-COMMITTEE

H. E. Knock (*Chairman*)
Formerly Headmaster, Bellfield County Secondary
Modern School, London

D. M. Chillingworth[1] (*Secretary*)
The Village College, Swavesey, Cambridge

E. A. Box
Portland County Secondary School, Portland, Dorset

W. H. Edwards
Sheffield College of Technology

G. B. Inskip[2]
Redhill Secondary Modern School, Arnold, Notts

H. C. Jenkins
Bessemer County Secondary Boys' School, Hitchin, Herts

F. W. Kaye[3]
South Craven County School, Cross Hills, Keighley,
Yorks

Mrs E. M. Lucia
Furzedown College of Education, London

Miss M. Martinson
Farnborough Bi-Lateral Girls' School, Nottingham

W. G. Rhodes[4]
Department of Education, University of Sheffield

L. J. Rowse
Formerly Headmaster, Goole Modern School, Yorks

R. Thurlow
Chief Inspector, Education Department, Leeds

[1] Secretary from June 1963.
[2] Secretary till June 1963; Chairman from June 1963 to October 1964; resigned October 1964 owing to ill-health.
[3] Resigned from the Committee in July 1964; Chairman till June 1963.
[4] Died in January 1965.

PREFACE

SUFFICIENT time has elapsed since the publication of *Secondary Modern Science Teaching, Parts I and II* to enable the Secondary Modern Schools Committee to judge the impact of these reports on science teaching in secondary schools. Considerable changes are taking place in the organisation and population of non-selective schools up and down the country, and there have been modifications in teaching thought and practice brought about by the formation of comprehensive and multilateral schools. The increasing influence of scientific advancement on the industrial and social life of the country, and the considerable amount of scientific information broadcast by radio and tele-vision, have meant that science education for the average citizen needs a changed content.

The committee therefore felt that it was necessary almost completely to re-write the two previous reports. Some portions of the original books were no longer necessary owing to the changing attitudes towards provision for the teaching of science in non-selective secondary schools. The personal experience of members in the teaching of science to the average pupil during this decade has made possible a more analytical approach in selecting and editing the material in this book. The amalgamation of the Science Masters Association and the Association of Women Science Teachers into the Association for Science Education has meant that a first-hand knowledge of the development of science teaching in girls' schools has become available.

The work of compiling this volume has been shared amongst the members of the committee but the final result has the unanimous support of them all. It is impossible to acknowledge the source of all the experimental work described in this volume but the committee is very conscious of the debt that it owes to those who have gone before.

There are three past members of the committee to whom special reference must be made. G. B. Inskip was an inde-fatigable secretary and a stimulating chairman until ill-health forced him to resign; his enthusiasm for the task was an inspiration to us all. F. W. Kaye, who was the first chairman of the committee when the re-writing of the original books commenced, did considerable work in starting the committee off along the right lines. It was mainly due to his efforts that the Secondary Modern Schools Committee was reconstituted in 1961. W. G. Rhodes, who died in January 1965, gave us considerable help and was a valued link with the original committee which published the previous volumes.

My committee hopes that this volume will prove a useful and a stimulating guide for those engaged in the fascinating and constantly changing task of teaching science to those who will be the citizens of tomorrow.

June 1966

H. E. Knock
Chairman

FOREWORD

MAYBE it is as Chairman of the Education Committee of the
A.S.E. that I am asked to write a brief foreword, and as such I
sincerely welcome this up-to-date addition to A.S.E. publications. Nevertheless I cannot but regard the present volume with
the eyes of a former Chairman of the Secondary Modern Committee, the Committee which got to work in 1950 and in 1953
produced the first edition of *Secondary Modern Science Teaching*. I
reflect on how greatly science teaching has changed since then,
and how much further change is imminent. How, too, a more
informed attitude towards the teaching of science has produced
improved facilities and time allowances: not adequate but at
least they exist unquestioned. Apparatus also: in 1950 perhaps
the best handbook for the secondary modern teacher was
'Steve's' UNESCO publication, *The Teaching of Science in
Devastated Countries*!

The 1953 A.S.E. handbook had its faults: it tried to be new
and different and to fit secondary modern needs, yet the curriculum advocated was still too close to that of the grammar
schools. However it did provide a certain standard of excellence,
a standard against which other methods and ideas could be
measured – like attaining international status by beating Eng-
land at cricket or football: to do so is gratifying though not ex-
cessively difficult. May the present work be as successful now as
its predecessor has been: 'The King is dead, Long live the
King!'

HENRY F. BOULIND
1966   Chairman, Education Committee A.S.E.

I. INTRODUCTION

THIS volume replaces the successful, but now partly outdated, earlier publication *Secondary Modern Science Teaching*, whose two parts were issued by the former Science Masters' Association in 1953 and 1957 respectively. The new volume comes within the scope of the series of publications on science and education which have been appearing from 1961 onwards, first under the auspices of the Science Masters' Association and the Association of Women Science Teachers and then of their successor the Association for Science Education. It is therefore essential that this volume should be viewed against the background of the 1965 general policy statement of the A.S.E., entitled *School Science and General Education*. That statement should be studied in its entirety, though the following extracts provide *partial* indication of the general framework of the principles laid down:

The effects of science on human life and thought have become so great, and are potentially so much greater, that those who have no understanding of them, and of the science which has produced them, cannot be considered properly educated or truly cultured and therefore are unable to participate fully in the life of their time. Present 'scientific illiteracy' is, in part, due to a lack of factual knowledge, but is more the result of a lack of understanding of the basic nature and aims of science.

Science should be recognised—and taught—as a major human activity which explores the realm of human experience, maps it methodically but also imaginatively, and, by disciplined speculation, creates a coherent system of knowledge. As a human quest for Truth —and it is much more subjectively human than is often realised— science is concerned with basic values and is, indeed, one of the humanities.

It follows that schools have the duty of presenting science as part of our cultural and humanistic heritage to be taught in harmony with, not in opposition to, the various arts subjects which alone have hitherto been called humanities. This cultural responsibility is no less important than the duty, already rightly accepted by schools, of providing preliminary training for the minority who will become professional scientists and technologists. We recognise that an adequate supply of scientists and technologists is needed and we believe that our recommendations will help to meet that need, but we stress the cultural aim here because science has not yet been given its proper place in general education. It should be one of the 'core' subjects in a 'liberal education'.

To achieve the ends which are envisaged 'all school pupils should study science in *all* stages of their school life'. In the earliest stage this study will need to be very elementary and very general, but even there the natural interests of children in scientific phenomena can be fostered and encouraged in ways which are educationally valuable. Later, although science in the widest sense may be concerned with the exploration and mapping of all human experience, the school science course must be more restricted in scope in order to allow greater depth of study in the time available. It should lie within the range of a group of the so-called 'natural sciences', each of which is concerned with a limited aspect of human experience.

Pupils should be helped to appreciate the wider range of science as a whole, but their formal course should consist mainly of work involving the sciences of biology, chemistry and physics, with some astronomy and geology if possible, even if the geology is studied as part of a geography course.

The school science course should be based on the following sequence to match the development of children:
A. Primary Stage Science Education (the 5–11 age range)
B. Secondary Stage Science Education (from 11 years upwards):
1. An Introductory Phase, covering approximately the first two years.
2. An Intermediate Phase of two or three years up to fifteen or sixteen years of age.
3. An Advanced (Sixth-Form) Phase.

In this report we are concerned with the first two phases of the secondary stage, the 'intermediate phase' being the *final* phase for those who leave school at fifteen or sixteen. Further, we are planning for the great majority of the pupils in the secondary stage.

Aims
(1) As far as possible the course should be based on the everyday experience of the pupils. This means the pupil pro-

ceeds from the known to the unknown, a method too often neglected in science teaching. For example:

(a) rockets, car engines, guns and atomic bombs can be used to *introduce* the idea of expansion of gases;

(b) observations that iron rusts in a fire grate and in a forge as well as on scratched chromium plated handlebars can raise questions as to the role of water in the rusting process *before* the setting up of laboratory experiments;

(c) the effectiveness of 'mouth to mouth respiration' can cast doubt on the statement that 'we breathe in oxygen and breathe out carbon dioxide'. This doubt can be resolved by laboratory experiments.

General principles should follow from facts. Experience has shown that pupils have little interest in the study of principles if they are introduced *before* the dependent facts.

(2) The course should not omit reference to modern developments in the fields of medicine, space travel, television, atomic energy, etc. These should be clearly explained in simple terms and, if possible, demonstrated. They can often be related to the simpler work done by the pupil.

These subjects may sometimes need a 'lecture-demonstration' approach. This will require very careful planning if it is to teach and not merely to entertain, but omission of such topics on the grounds of difficulty of teaching will mean that much of the vitality of the whole course will be lost.

(3) Whenever possible pupils should do practical work, individually or in small groups. Demonstration is important when the necessary practical work is too dangerous, too complex or too demanding of special skills.

Both individual work and demonstrations should be directed to 'finding out' and not to the verifying of given statements.

(4) At least for the first three years the course should consist mainly of an integrated study of physics, chemistry and biology.

In the early stages the topic method has its uses but a formal approach would be more helpful later. The teacher should be free to follow up new avenues of interest suggested by his pupils.

(5) After the introductory stages emphasis may be given to

3

one or more of the branches, particularly where pupils are concerned with external examinations which qualify for entry to vocational courses.

(6) To offset any tendency to keep subjects in water-tight compartments, therefore, science should be related to other fields of study whenever the opportunity arises. For example:

All branches of applied science have had far-reaching social and economic effects throughout the ages. A study of these effects would link science and *history*.

In *geography* the weather, climatology, soil formation, erosion, plant and animal breeding with its economic applications, all have scientific links.

The study of the physical characteristics of metallic and non-metallic materials, simple chemistry and ideas on work and machines find practical applications in the *craft* room.

The quantitative problems of heat supply and transfer, simple bacteriology, food values, problems of cleaning, etc., can often be dealt with more effectively in the laboratory than in the *housecraft* room.

Examinations

The committee agree that external examinations can form a very effective stimulus to pupils in their last year at school. Similarly a vocational bias can also help to create and maintain interest. The present G.C.E. 'O' level form of examination is not suited to all secondary pupils and the committee deplores the fact that entry into many fields of employment is now dependent upon a minimum number of passes at this level. In the existing circumstances pupils should be allowed to take the G.C.E. examinations, provided that:

(*a*) the whole organisation of the school is not specially geared to this small group.

(*b*) the most competent members of staff are not wholly concerned with this group.

(*c*) these pupils have a reasonable chance of success in several subjects.

The Certificate of Secondary Education with its teacher-controlled examinations is more suited to the needs of the average pupil. With the choice of three modes of C.S.E. examination, teachers are given options which enable them to find the best system suited to themselves and their pupils. If the teacher wishes to work to his or her own syllabus or to the syllabus of a group of schools this may be done with examinations either set by the Local Board or set and marked by the teacher and moderated and assessed by the Board. The Regional Board's syllabus will have been compiled by teachers in the area. These teachers are in contact with the local subject groups in their own area and the ideas and opinions of many teachers should have reached the panel writing the syllabus. Teacher assessment, practical examinations and course work may have their place in this scheme of examinations.

The committee is fully aware of the shortage of science teachers, and also of the lack of science facilities in many schools. These factors affect not only the quality of the science teaching but also the extent of the work done. In some schools lack of science staff results in the inclusion of little or no science in the time-table.

It is advocated that at least one-eighth of the teaching time should be devoted to science subjects and this work should take place in fully equipped laboratories. This means a three-form entry school with a five-year course will have a minimum of two laboratories and two full-time qualified staff. In the interests of safety practical classes should be limited to twenty pupils.

Implementation of these standards will need a large increase in the number of science teachers entering the profession from both colleges of education and universities.

Although many graduate and non-graduate science staff entering secondary schools may have a special field of study they should also have a sound basic knowledge of the three main branches of science. It is also very desirable that they should be interested in extending their boundaries of knowledge over a wide field.

Science has an ever increasing influence on our outlook and philosophy and on our physical environment. It is not a study for the specialist only and unless a knowledge of its effects, methods and limitations is made available to all pupils in secondary schools the educational background and awareness of society as a whole will be incomplete.

2. PRINCIPLES AND METHODS

In the original report issued in 1953, *Secondary Modern Science Teaching*, the discussion of the principles and methods of teaching science in these schools laid much stress on the fact that, in contrast to the other types of secondary school in this country, the secondary modern schools were not geared to the study of one or more sciences in order to give their pupils the opportunity of acquiring qualifications useful for entry into certain careers. Such professional and vocational incentives were then largely absent from the secondary modern schools. In fact, the set-up of many of the examinations stemming from the implementation of the 1944 Education Act was expressly designed to make it impossible for the pupils of the non-grammar school type of secondary schools to enter for these examinations.

By 1965 the situation had changed radically. In a rapidly increasing number of secondary schools pupils are being entered for a number of papers in the examinations of the General Certificate of Education. In many schools there are pupils taking the examinations of the Royal Society of Arts and still more children are now entering for the Certificate of Secondary Education through the fourteen Examination Boards which have been set up to cover the country. The coming into force of the suggestions contained in the *Beloe Report* has thus increased the number of potential examinees.

Many of these examinations are being used by the Local Education Authorities as aids in the selection of pupils for the appropriate courses in Further Education. These examinations are being used to provide an incentive to study as well as to make possible the issue of the award of a 'passing-out' certificate to an increasing number of schoolchildren, especially amongst those not academically brilliant.

There has thus been a complete reversal of educational policy and practice during the decade 1953–1963. By force of circumstances, therefore, most secondary non-grammar schools are becoming at least 'bilateral', even if they do not fall completely into the 'comprehensive' category.

In all institutions of learning, the aim of the education given

6

should be to enable the person taught to accommodate himself to his environment, while at the same time allowing him full scope for the development of his own personality, and his talents.

This is a technical age, in which our environment is dominated by the practical applications of the scientific thought and research of the past hundred years. Each of us, pupil and teacher alike, according to his ability, his acquired knowledge and his inclinations, finds adjustment to the external world and to his own inner self in different ways. There are pupils, relatively few in number, who find their greatest satisfaction in following up the logical development of present knowledge and experience. These are the 'scholars' of the future. They will become research students, technologists and scientists in the years to come. By selection and transfer, most of this type of pupil will have been gathered into the grammar school or into the grammar type of class in the secondary school before the age at which examinations are taken. These pupils present few difficulties provided they have not been deterred by uninspired teaching in the lower school and by excessive cramming in the examination forms. A much greater number of pupils, however, have far wider interests than those in the academic group. They wish to penetrate far less deeply into a broader field and hope to acquire an understanding of an ever-widening range of the inter-relationships of phenomena. Let us never forget that there are also those to whom an intellectual exercise of any kind presents little or no attraction, and for whom satisfaction and a reasonable amount of contentment can be achieved by the mechanical repetition of easy or of more difficult operations.

The non-selective secondary school, taking as it does the bulk of the school population of this country (up to 75 per cent in some areas) is compelled to cater for *all* the classes of pupils mentioned above.

Science is one and undivided in its principles and in its method. The various aspects of science presented to the pupil must eventually be integrated into one coherent whole. Nevertheless, the degree to which any pupil can achieve this, and the control he learns to exert over the 'technical' world in which he finds himself, will vary with his own make-up.

7

For the pupil with the logical mind who can play easily with words, symbols and ideas—not too common in the secondary school—the classical methods of approaching science teaching as exemplified by the usual textbook and by the well-tried methods of approaching science courses at the 'O' level of the G.C.E. are not to be despised, provided the preparation for the examination is confined to the pre-examination year and that it grows naturally out of a course of a more stimulating nature in the lower school.

For the pupils to whom the strictly logical approach is unsuited—and this means the bulk of secondary school children —a much less rigid type of mental discipline is required, not, let it be affirmed most emphatically, as an easy option but as a way of study more appropriate to the kind of mind they bring to bear upon the subject. No matter what branch of science is being studied, it can hardly be called science unless, within the limits of the pupils' ability, it embraces observation, hypothesis, verification and the formulation of a 'general law'.

In general, the pupil with the logical mind can recognise, describe and reproduce phenomena. Later he can make deductions from which further investigations may follow. At the other end of the scale in the secondary school are those who after careful instruction are only able to recognise the activities and the phenomena of the external world. If in course of time and after lengthy instruction these last named pupils can record, and at a later stage, reproduce their observations, the time spent on their science training has been more than justified.

In the secondary school science teaching will have to be carried out with these different categories of pupils, each of which will require different degrees of intensity of activity in depth and breadth of treatment.

Teaching science through a rational, non-academic approach will give the pupils a far less compartmentalised body of knowledge, equipping them to meet the demands of life as they know it and enabling them to adjust themselves to the very different conditions with which they will be faced in the future. The most able of the non-academic stream, in general, will not swell the ranks of the research workers but rather will become technicians upon whom will fall the responsibility of translating in everyday work the findings of the technologist and scientist. Furthermore, these may well become leaders in the social and political life of their locality. There are particular reasons, therefore, for hoping that from their science lessons these pupils will acquire a life-long readiness to examine new ideas critically and impartially—an attitude which, unfortunately, sometimes tends to be stunted rather than developed by the taking of examinations. The great danger confronting the country is that future development in all fields of human activity will be blocked and held up by unenlightened conservatism clinging too firmly to the well-known paths of the past.

From the rapidly diminishing ranks of the non-examination streams in the secondary schools will come those who will not be called upon to make important decisions in industry, in commerce, in social and political life. Nevertheless it is equally possible for such folk to prevent progress by a stubborn resistance to change. It is imperative therefore that such pupils should find the science that is taught in school to be reasonable and that they should acquire a faith in science even if they themselves are unable to work out the implications of current knowledge. For these pupils, the ability to *see* is the goal of their scientific studies. It is, of course, equally aimed at in teaching the other types of pupils even though they are enabled to proceed further in the use of these observations.

For all pupils in secondary schools, particularly in their early years, simple experiments are necessary by which skill in handling apparatus may be acquired. It is a great fallacy to act on the assumption that a considerable expenditure is necessary in setting up a laboratory. Far more true science can be got over to the pupils by the use of homely and common things than by elaborate equipment unlikely to be met with again in later life. Control of the forces and materials met with in ordinary life is much more worthwhile and a far more vital science than one which is concerned with the exotic and the unusual. The major approach to science must always be through a study of everyday happenings and experiences. A feeling of increasing power with an extension of the boundaries of knowledge comes with the rational approach; boredom and a sense of going through the motions and getting nowhere, apart from examinations, is the common return for

9

the conventional academic approach with non-academic pupils.

Schemes which stem from the pupil's own environment and experience can be developed *ad infinitum*: they give an escape from the traditional G.C.E. textbook method of dealing with conventional school science topics, topics which in our rapidly changing world are having decreasing relevance. In such a rational scheme of work, the material studied is related to the child's normal experience and not to some strange piece of magic which the 'teacher does in the lab'. As it should, the method commended starts with observation and relates what is seen to what might be considered a possible explanation, which may be expanded and/or confirmed at a later stage in the course of study. True, it may be, that the less philosophically minded will never get there, but at least they may have had their eyes opened to see.

By this reversal of the logical sequence in the usual courses it is possible to see the truth and the relevance of a 'general law' without going step by step through each individual stage in the argument as it was formulated, in most cases so many years ago that it is now incorporated into our normal experience, thus making proof unnecessary for us. It is too easily forgotten that the present-day schoolchild is the inheritor of the experiences of those who went before and that while recapitulation of the thought processes of the past is a nice philosophical exercise for some people, the school pupil has only a limited time in which to accommodate himself to the world in which all these early discovered facts and ideas are already widely known and taken for granted.

It should be remembered that in the school there will also be those pupils who can observe a phenomenon one day and completely forget it by the next morning. For them, in adult life, doing what to many people is dull and repetitive mechanical work can bring satisfaction or at least absence of aversion. Co-ordination of actions and of ideas is impossible and the attempt to do so only causes confusion. Science for such children can be little more than hand or craft work with an application to objects in which the teacher can see some scientific interest. This 'science with craft' work can be linked with general knowledge lessons illustrated by working models which depend upon scientific principles, which can be pointed out but which the teacher will not expect to be explained back to him when next he refers to the item, though there might be a lingering memory in the child's mind of the relevance of this object, model and idea. For this level of intelligence, it should suffice that activities in nature are recognised as examples of the operation of rational processes which can be studied and which can be made use of for the welfare, or otherwise, of mankind.

While the upper and lower forms of the secondary school seem to be poles apart intellectually, the fundamental principles governing the work done in the science lessons must be applicable over the whole range of ability with which the teacher has to deal. The teacher of science is faced with the necessity of formulating a philosophy of science teaching and of employing methods and techniques which shall be all-embracing over the wide field of the intellectual ability of his pupils—from those who can recognise phenomena and reproduce information about the observations that have been made, to those who with difficulty can be led to observe and recognise activities in the natural world.

The development of the ability to 'observe' is the primary function of the science teacher, no matter in what kind of educational institution he is working. When he has 'opened the eyes of the blind' then he must go on to show how control may be exercised over the phenomena observed.

Science in a secondary school demands the skill of an extremely capable teacher. He must be able to seek material for his lessons from a wide variety of sources. Dependence upon commercial suppliers will never satisfy his needs nor will it give him the material best suited for his pupils. Intellectually he must be more agile than the teacher who depends upon the set syllabus of an examination board to limit and to direct his path. For him, most textbooks are poor guides for the problems he has to face.

It is essential that the most able teachers take over the classes as they enter the school. The science teacher has an advantage over all his colleagues which he should exploit to the full. Children come to a new school expecting to enjoy the thrills and marvels of science. A dull lesson in the first year does untold harm. Combined operations and joint activitiy in science investigations leads to enthusiastic pupils. To arouse enthusiasm and maintain it the science teacher has more than half done that for which he was trained and for which he was appointed to his present post.

3. TEACHING MATERIAL

THIS chapter has been divided into a number of sub-sections, each dealing with one part of the syllabus and giving suggestions for its teaching, including demonstrations and class practical work. The experimental data together with the teaching techniques involved are given in considerable detail so that provided the instructions are followed carefully and accurately success is almost certain. This does not mean, however, that a teacher using these experiments for the first time, as either demonstrations in front of the class or for the pupil's practical work, should not first attempt them alone.

All the experimental data has been gathered from experienced teacher sources and then carefully scrutinised and checked by the whole committee for possible error. Purely for ease of reference by the teacher-reader, the experiments have been grouped under the three main divisions of science and then under the principles, laws, or concepts involved. The teacher using this data will take it and use it in the order which bests suits both his syllabus or scheme of work and his pupils. Whenever the links between the branches of science can be shown, these links should be brought out by using the relative experiments.

In Part I of the original edition of *Secondary Modern Science Teaching* a chapter was given over to a suggested scheme of work together with the associated practical work on the principles, concepts and topics studied. Since that book was published the teaching climate in secondary schools of the non-grammar and non-selective types has changed and it was felt that this approach is no longer so likely to be successful.

The experienced teacher reading this book will quite probably feel that he may already be able to attempt much of this chapter successfully, but he may yet find new ideas and new methods of attack experimentally which will be an improvement of his own. As the full committee have discussed and checked these items we have all learnt new and better procedures and techniques. The less experienced teacher and particularly one whose science knowledge is limited in a particular field will find the information of great value. The members of the committee are all very conscious of the fact that they were themselves novices at one time (sometimes too many years ago) and are all aware of the debt that they owed to their experienced teacher colleagues in those early days. They feel that this is one way of repaying this indebtedness.

As has already been stated in Chapter 2, as far as is possible the apparatus required for performing the experimental work has been kept as simple as possible, but not to the extent of unduly sacrificing accuracy of result nor the understanding by the pupils of the reality of the principles involved. Improvisation for its own sake is never recommended although it is sadly true that there are occasions when finances make improvised apparatus necessary, but the wise teacher will gradually overcome this state of affairs by wise spending of his allowance for the subject.

Finally, the teacher should read Chapter 4 on 'Building the Syllabus' before attempting to use the material in this chapter. The statement in Chapter 1, 'At least for the first three years the course should consist mainly of an integrated study of physics, chemistry and biology', should be kept in the forefront of every science teacher's thinking at all times. The connections and inter-relationships between the man-made divisions of science must be stressed whenever and wherever possible as is indicated by the many examples suggested in Chapter 4.

BIOLOGY

Plants

1. SIMPLE STUDY OF THE SOIL

Practical Work

(1) *Simple analysis* Shake a sample of soil in water in a gas jar or jam jar. Allow to settle. Heavy particles will sink, humus will float.

(2) *Water content* Weigh 100 gm of soil and then heat it in an evaporating dish over a beaker of boiling water. Heat until dry. Re-weigh, loss of weight represents water content.

(3) *Humus content* Heat a known quantity of dry soil in a closed crucible fitted into a pipeclay triangle on a tripod over a Bunsen burner. Continue to heat till the weight remains constant. Weight loss represents the quantity of humus.

(4) *Air content* Push an inverted tin with a perforated base into some soil in the ground. Dig the tin out and cut the soil off flush at the edge of the tin. This gives soil *in situ*. Suspend the tin in a jar or cylinder of water. Rake out the soil and the air will escape. Note the final rise in water level. Compare this with the rise resulting from using the same volume unperforated tin full of water. The difference represents the air content.

(5) *Capillarity* Fill two tubes 2 ft. $\times$ $\frac{1}{2}$ in, one with sandy, the other with clayey soil. Tie muslin on the lower ends of the tubes and stand in water. Compare the rise of water levels in the tubes at intervals, for several days.

(6) *Permeability* Fill two similar tins with perforated bases, with equal quantities of sandy and clayey soils. Add equal quantities of water simultaneously to the tins. Compare the rate of water draining through.

Further experiments on porosity, acidity, micro-organisms, etc., can be found in any reliable biology book.

2. FLOWERING PLANTS

The parts of a flowering plants together with their main functions; root, stem leaf and flower.

Pollination and fertilisation. Dispersal of fruits and seeds.

Practical Work

(1) Examination of plants and flowers (using a hand lens if necessary), examination of pollen grains under a microscope, examination of slices of stems and roots under a microscope (prepared slides may be used).

(2) Fruits and seeds may be collected and their method of dispersal studied.

3. Physiology of the Plant

Practical Work

A. *Photosynthesis*

(1) To demonstrate the evolution of oxygen.

Place a green water plant under a funnel in a beaker of water. It is essential if a good supply of oxygen is required that the water be saturated with carbon dioxide. Invert a test-tube full of water over the end of the funnel. Leave in the sunlight. Bubbles of gas will collect in the top of the test-tube. These can be tested with alkaline pyrogallol or a glowing splint and proved to be oxygen.

(2) To show that carbon-dioxide is necessary for photosynthesis (see Fig. 1).

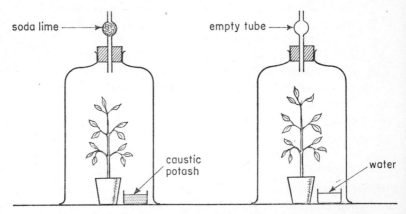

soda lime

empty tube

caustic potash

water

Fig. 1   To show that photosynthesis requires carbon dioxide

Use two pot plants that have been in the dark for twelve hours (thus making them starch free). Place them under

16

bell jars, one containing a small dish of caustic potash and having air entering through a soda lime tube, the other open to the air. Leave both plants in sunlight for some hours then test the leaves for starch. The one where carbon dioxide is excluded will contain no starch.

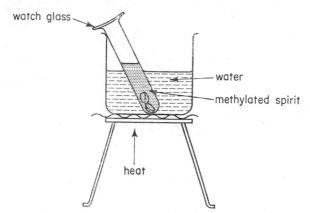

watch glass

water

methylated spirit

heat

Fig. 2   Test for starch

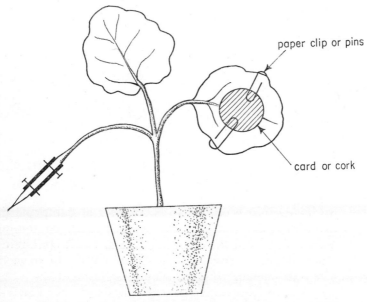

paper clip or pins

card or cork

Fig. 3   To show that light is necessary for photosynthesis

17

N.B. To test leaves for starch (see Fig. 2). First place the leaves in boiling water to kill the protoplasm, then put them in a test-tube of methylated spirit covered with a watch glass. Place the test-tube within a beaker of water and gently heat. Stir occasionally until the chlorophyll leaves the leaves. Use iodine to test the leaves for starch. Keep the spirit away from the flame but should it catch fire, cover the test-tube with a piece of asbestos, this will put out the flame.

(3) To show that light is necessary for photosynthesis (see Fig. 3).
   Pin a piece of cork or black card on either side of a leaf of a starch-free plant. Place the plant in sunlight for a few hours; then test the leaves for starch. Where the leaf has been covered no starch will have formed.

(4) To show that chlorophyll is necessary for photosynthesis. A starch-free plant with variegated leaves should be used. Geranium (Pelargonium) gives good results. Leave the plant in sunlight for a few hours; then test the leaves for starch. It will be found in the green parts but not in the cream-coloured parts.

B. *Respiration*

(1) To show that oxygen is required by plants (see Fig. 4).

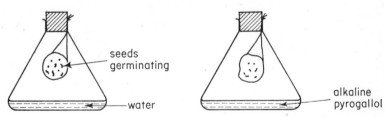

Fig. 4   To show that oxygen is required by plants

Sprinkle moist seeds on to two pieces of damp plastic foam. Suspend one piece in a corked bottle containing a little water and the other in a similar bottle containing some alkaline pyrogallol solution to absorb the oxygen. The seeds lacking oxygen will fail to germinate.

(2) To prove that plants give out carbon-dioxide (see Fig. 5).
   Place a pot plant in a large bell jar, cover with a black

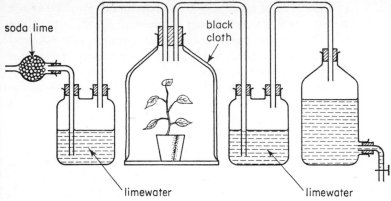

Fig. 5 To prove that plants give out carbon dioxide

cloth to prevent photosynthesis. Using an aspirator or pump draw air first through soda lime to remove carbon-dioxide then through limewater, then through the bell jar and finally through more limewater.

The second bottle of limewater only will turn milky due to the presence of carbon-dioxide, which can only have come from the plant. (All joints in the apparatus should be sealed with petroleum jelly or wax.)

C. *Transpiration*

(1) To show that a plant transpires (see Fig. 6).

Use a pot plant; completely cover the pot and soil with

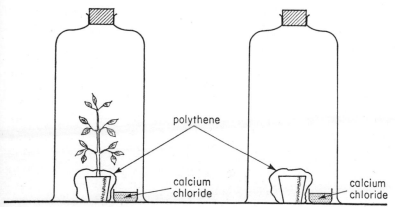

Fig. 6 To show that a plant transpires

polythene, also cover a pot of soil of similar size. Place each pot in a bell jar containing a dish with similar quantities of calcium chloride. Leave for 24 hours. The increase in weight in calcium chloride for the pot with no plant is due to atmospheric conditions. In the other jar it is due to atmospheric conditions and the transpiration of the plant. By subtraction the amount of transpiration can be calculated.

D. *Osmosis*

(1) Wash a potato and cut across to form a base. Cut the other end similarly, then make a cavity in it nearly reaching the base. Remove the peel to about one inch up from the base. Half fill the cavity with strong sugar solution and stand the potato in a dish of water. As osmosis takes place the level of the solution in the cavity will rise. If the experiment is repeated with a dead (boiled) potato, osmosis will not take place.

(2) Tie a piece of pig's bladder, vegetable parchment or cellophane over the mouth of a thistle funnel, greasing the rim of the funnel and making sure the seal is air-tight. Fill the funnel with diluted golden syrup, strong glucose solution or peptone solution and immerse the bulb in a beaker of distilled water (see Fig. 7). Note the

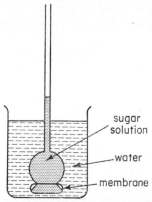

Fig. 7 Osmosis experiment 2

level of the liquid in the funnel tube. After a few hours the level will have risen. By extending the tube a column of water three or four feet high may be obtained. This is explained as the movement of the solvent only through the semi-permeable membranes. (When using cellophane it is advisable to try a specimen first as some types of cellophane, toffee wrappings, etc., act as semi-permeable membranes, others do not.)

E. *Germination*

(1) Soaked seeds of the larger varieties can be examined to show the structure: seeds with one or two cotyledons, seeds with endosperm, etc. The embryo can also be found.

(2) Seeds can be grown in jars between the glass and damp blotting paper, or in dishes on damp blotting paper or the larger seeds may be grown in sawdust or bulb fibre. A wooden box with one glass side is useful. The box should be filled with damp fibre and the seeds planted touching the glass side.

(3) Percentage germination of a sample of seeds can be discovered.

(4) Conditions necessary for growth: attempt to grow seeds
  (*a*) without water,
  (*b*) without heat (in a refrigerator),
  (*c*) without air (totally immersed in freshly distilled or boiled water in a sealed jar). Alternatively, exclude oxygen by having a tube of alkaline pyrogallol in the jar and putting a greased cover over the jar.
      A control experiment is necessary. It will be found that seeds need water, warmth and air (oxygen) in order to germinate.

F. *Tropisms*

Phototropism

(1) Grow mustard seeds in light, in darkness and in a box illuminated from one side only. (Shoe boxes can be adapted.) Shoots will give a positive result.

(2) Grow beans with light from one side only and note the effect on the root and shoot.
      Roots show a negative result.

Hydrotropism

(1) Grow seeds on damp cotton wool on a piece of perforated

zinc. Suspend the zinc over a dish of water. The roots will grow through the zinc towards the water. On removing the water the roots will grow back towards the cotton wool. The roots are positively hydrotropic.

(2) Fill a seed box with fairly dry soil. Place a plant pot with its base plugged, in the box. Fill the plant pot with water. Plant bean seeds in the soil round the pot. When taken out and examined the roots will be seen to have grown towards the pot of water. (Any porous pot may be used.)

Geotropism
(1) The standard experiment to show geotropism requires a klinostat, but an effective demonstration can be made by growing seeds in damp bulb fibre between two similar pieces of glass (3 in × 3 in lantern slide glasses). The glasses should be held together with strong elastic bands. As the seeds grow the position of the glass can be altered.

Region of Growth
(1) Root and shoots of growing beans may be marked out at equal distances with Indian ink. The position of greatest growth can be noted.

G. *Culture Solutions*

For satisfactory growth, plants need the elements: nitrogen, sulphur, sodium, potassium, magnesium and calcium. These are supplied in a normal culture solution.

Practical Work
(1) Use jars with bungs having three holes, one to put the seedling or cutting in, the others to replenish the solution if necessary, and to allow air to enter. Green *Tradescantia* or maize seedlings give satisfactory results. Solutions can be prepared, each one omitting one of the elements. (For chemicals and quantities see Bibliography.)

(2) A culture experiment on a small scale is described by D. G. Mackean in *The School Science Review*, 1963, 153, **45**, 403.

(3) Tomato plants obtained in April or early May can be used to illustrate mineral deficiency. One plant should

be grown in sand and watered with only distilled water, another can be grown in 'John Innes' potting compost. The difference in growth can be noted in six to eight weeks. The plant grown in sand will show improvement if it is watered with complete culture solution or some proprietary brand of liquid fertiliser.

To obtain satisfactory results using culture solutions meticulous care must be taken with regard to cleanliness and to the purity of the chemical used. (Analytical reagent quality is recommended.)

4. DISPERSAL OF FRUITS AND SEEDS
Examples to illustrate the various methods and agents can be collected, e.g.
pepperpot method: poppy.
wind dispersal: ash, sycamore, dandelion.
water dispersal: water lily.
animals, on their coats: burdock, goose-grass.
animals or birds eating the flesh of the fruit and disposing of the seed: cherry.
animals or birds eating the fruit with indigestible seed: bramble, hip, haw, raspberry, strawberry.
explosive mechanism: broom, pea, balsam (touch-me-not).

5. FOOD STORAGE IN PLANTS AND VEGETATIVE PROPAGATION

Practical Work
(1) Examples of food storing organs should be collected and their formation studied. The food stored can be tested for starch or glucose. e.g.
swollen tap root; carrot.
rhizome: couch grass, iris, Solomon's seal.
tuber: potato, celandine.
corm: crocus.
bulb: onion, tulip.

(2) Vegetative propagation may be studied if facilities are available for the taking of cuttings, grafting, budding, etc. Where these facilities are not available tubers should be grown and cuttings taken from house plants such as Tradescantia and various cacti.

6. Flowerless Plants

For example, fungi, algae, seaweeds, liverworts, mosses, ferns. The local environment should be a guide as to which types are studied. Fungi can easily be grown on damp food. It is worth noting that some flour is treated so as to be resistant to moulds.

Animals

As with the study of plants, this work should be of as practical a nature as possible. For convenience in the layout of this syllabus the human biology section has been placed separately but the whole of plant, animal and human biology should be integrated.

The laboratory or classroom should contain as many types of living animals as it is practicable to keep, so that the pupils become familiar with animals and their habits and life histories. The pupils should be given responsibility in caring for the animals; where difficulties arise during the long holidays, there are usually plenty of reliable offers to take them home.

Through observation the pupils should learn for themselves the general characteristics of living animals; nutrition, growth, respiration, excretion, irritability and reproduction.

In some of the practical work the use of microscope slides is suggested, the loss of the three-dimensional effect with the monocular microscope should always be noted. Pupils who find this difficult to understand should not be required to draw diagrams from such slides.

During the course the life histories, structure and special features of the following types of animals should be studied (these types are not in teaching order; frogs, fish or insects often provide a useful starting point):

1. Protozoans, e.g. Paramecium

This is usually the easiest species of protozoan to find and identify. It can be found in stagnant water, or water containing any decaying vegetable matter (water from flower vases). All protozoans need to be studied under the microscope. Study of this group leads on to the study of the animal cell, but this should not be attempted too early in the course.

Practical Work

(1) Pupils should be given the opportunity to examine under a microscope water known to contain the animals. Enough water can be placed in a watch glass or small petri-dish and the microscope need only be low power. The 'slipper shape' of the animal and also the nucleus can be seen. It generally moves with the round end forward. By shining a beam of light to one side of the glass, movement away from light can be noted.

(2) The structure can be seen more clearly using a stained specimen or a prepared slide.

(3) Different samples of stagnant water can be taken and examined for microscopic plant and animal life, a reference book being useful for identification purposes. Even using a reference book it is not always possible to identify all specimens. This work can often be done after pond dipping excursions.

2. COELENTERATES, E.G. SEA ANEMONE, HYDRA

Often this group can be studied in an 'Animals of the sea-shore' topic, together with crustaceans, echinoderms, etc. The work generally fits in better either just before or just after the summer holidays.

Differentiation of tissues and division of labour can be seen in these animals.

Hydra brought from a pond will live in a small aquarium or tank in the laboratory. It is also possible to buy live hydra from a biological supply agency, but it is more useful if they are then kept as pets for a while before they are studied, otherwise the pupils tend to get the idea they are not really 'wild creatures'.

Practical Work

(1) Hydra can be observed using a hand lens. They can be removed from the aquaria using a fine clean paintbrush. Methods of feeding and movement can be noted. When the water is disturbed almost total contraction can be seen. Movement of tentacles can be attracted by adding fine particles of goldfish food to the water.

Hydra can be seen to reproduce asexually by budding,

25

sexual development can also be seen. Sexual reproduction usually occurs in autumn only and not often in captivity.

(2) Cell structure and reproduction can be further studied under a microscope using prepared slides.

3. ANNELIDS, E.G. EARTHWORM

Practical Work

(1) External features can be studied using a hand lens; segments, saddle, spermathecae, sperm groove, chaetae, openings of the oviducts and sperm ducts.

(2) Movement can be watched when the worm is encouraged to move on brown paper.

(3) A simple dissection shows the digestive, nervous, circulatory and reproductory systems. The worm should be killed by chloroforming, then pinned carefully at head and tail on to a cork board or black wax in a dish. The cork or wax is best covered with about an inch of water. The dissection consists of a dorsal cutting starting from a small incision just above the saddle. As the cut is made the body wall should be carefully pinned out on each side.

(4) Habits can be studied by making a wormery. This consists of a wooden box with one glass side. (This can be easily constructed and should be a minimum of 9 in to 1 ft deep.) The box should be filled with layers of soil of differing colour; a thin layer of powdered chalk and a layer of sand may be used. The layers should not be packed too tightly. The worms are put into the soil and the glass side of the box covered with black paper. When the paper is removed the movements of the worms against the glass side can be studied. If the soil is kept fairly moist the worms may come to the surface at night and worm casts can be noted in the morning. The implications of these movements on the fertility of the soil can easily be drawn.

(The wormery when not in use as such may also be used to watch the germination of seeds placed against the glass.)

(5) Worm casts can be found in a garden or on a lawn and when examined under a microscope the fineness of the particles can be seen.

(6) To see worms in coition requires an early morning visit to a lawn or the school playing field; a heavy tread on the ground is enough to disturb them.

(When teaching reproduction in the worm the hermaphroditism and the resulting relationships of the offspring generally arouse interest and amusement.)

(7) Where schools are near the seashore the various 'bristle worms' can also be studied.

4. Molluscs, e.g. Snail

This group of animals illustrates the use of mineral salts to make a protective covering for the animal (the forerunner of a 'skeleton').

Practical Work

(1) Water snails in a fish tank make a useful study, their external features can be seen through the glass of the tank and they frequently breed in captivity. Movement using the foot can be noticed.

(2) On the edge of dry paths the slime trail of land snails can be found. By observing land snails the movable eyes can be noticed.

(3) Interesting collections of bi-valve and uni-valve molluscs can be made. Frequently, fossil molluscs can be found in chalk and limestone country.

5. Crustaceans, e.g. Crabs, Prawns, Shrimps

This group is important for the development of the external skeleton and jointed legs.

It may be preferable to study these animals as a topic.

Practical Work

(1) Using a complete crab, study the structure paying special attention to the various appendages; claws, jointed legs, mouth parts, etc.

For a lesson it is useful to buy one complete (but not dressed) crab and some prawns or shrimps.

(2) Hermit crabs are frequently found in whelk shells and the local fishmonger will often provide specimens.

(3) Small crabs set in a transparent block can often be bought at seaside resorts and these are useful for reference. The best ones are generally made in Belgium or Japan.

(4) 'Beach and Sea Animals', a G.B. film, gives a good picture of crustaceans and their neighbours, also 'Between the Tides' a British Rail film.

6. Insects, e.g. Butterflies, Houseflies, Locusts

The general characteristics of the group should be taught so that the pupils can recognise an insect. Then some selected species should be studied in detail. The species chosen should be ones that are comparatively easy to find in the locality. One or two should be pests, e.g. housefly, gnat; others should be useful, e.g. bees.

Practical Work

(1) Various types of insects can be kept in the laboratory: stick insects are very useful, they feed only on privet, they can be kept in a vivarium, or wooden box with a glass side or just placed on privet leaves standing in a jam jar with a bell jar or toffee jar inverted over them. They breed in captivity but the eggs take some months to hatch. (They do sometimes exhibit parthenogenesis.) Locust eggs can be obtained and their complete metamorphosis studied. (A booklet showing the stages is usually supplied with the eggs.) The larvae will feed on grass and need only a moderate temperature. They can be kept in a wooden box with a glass side or perforated zinc side or top; a 40-watt electric light bulb over the box gives enough heat.

(2) Caterpillars of various butterflies can be kept in vivaria or large boxes but it is important to know the type of food each species requires. Silk moth caterpillars can also be kept, some of these will feed on lettuce leaves as well as the traditional mulberry leaves.

(3) Water insects can be kept in aquaria, e.g. great water beetle, but carnivorous types should be kept apart from other pond creatures.

(4) Aquatic insect larvae can also be collected from ponds. The caddis fly larvae with their protective cases are among the most interesting.

The P.F.B. film, 'The Rival World', is very helpful.

7. ARACHNIDS, E.G. SPIDERS

Practical Work

(1) Spiders can be collected and kept in the classroom. If enough flies are not available for food these can easily be obtained. In order to see the parts of the body of a spider and to compare it with the body of an insect, a garden spider is a clear example.

(2) During field work, the pupils can study the webs. The web of the house spider can be compared with that of the garden spider.

(3) Water spiders will live in an aquarium. They make interesting study as they take bubbles of air from the surface to their underwater nests.

8. FISH

Fish can be obtained both from an aquarium and also by using herrings or other similar fish. Adaptation to environment requires special study. Reproduction in fish forms a useful basis for teaching the principles of sexual reproduction in animals.

Practical Work

(1) Make and keep a balanced aquarium, either cold or tropical.

(2) Trout eggs can be obtained from a hatchery and successfully hatched. They should be kept in a tank, on stones and under running water. A metal dish or box with perforations in the sides is suitable.

(3) Sticklebacks and their nests can be studied during field study.

(4) Using a herring, structure can be studied, gills, scales, stomach, roes, etc.

(5) Movement can be observed in an aquarium.

9. AMPHIBIA, E.G. FROGS

The frog makes a good first animal to study in a biology course. The metamorphosis is easy to study in the classroom.

Practical Work

(1) Collect spawn and keep it in large tanks or troughs containing pond water and some water weed.

After hatching, for a few days the tadpoles will eat the plants but later they will require feeding. They will eat maggots, pieces of raw meat or worm. These should be hung in the water on a string and the remnants removed. The tadpoles will also feed on goldfish food.

The stages in development should be noted. When front legs are developing, partly submerged rocks or stones should be available for the frogs to support themselves while breathing air.

(2) Frogs can be kept in a terrarium. A wooden box with a glass front can be used, the larger the better. The bottom should be covered with turf, a small dish of water being sunk into the turf and rocks and twigs added as shelter for the frogs. Frogs can be fed on small caterpillars or black or green fly. Snails and slugs will survive in the same terrarium as the frogs.

(3) With older pupils a dissection can be made to show the internal organs.

10. BIRDS

The study of birds generally comes as part of field study and the time devoted to it will depend on the environment of the school and to some extent, the interest of the teacher.

Practical Work

(1) Observations of birds of the locality should be made by the pupils. A bird-table should be set up where it can easily be seen, a half coconut or pieces of fat can be hung up to encourage titmice.

(2) Migratory movements can be studied.

(3) During field study signs of adaptation to environment should be noticed: beaks, feet and feathers.

(4) Feathers can be examined to show the structure.

(5) More advanced pupils can study the process of flight (physics, also the Walt Disney film, 'Man in Flight').

(6) A hen's egg can be examined, and slides of its development can be examined using either a hand lens or a microscope. Pupils specially interested in bird study can join one of the junior sections of the R.S.P.B., or a group from the school could enter their annual 'Bird and Tree' competition.

11. MAMMALS

General characteristics of this group should be studied. The choice of individual mammals studied will depend to some extent on the environment of the school and the individual interest of the teacher and pupils. Rabbit or mouse and a ruminant mammal should generally be included. Some study should be made of temperature control including hibernation.

Human biology will form the greater part of the study in this section.

Human Biology

1. THE SKELETON

Its function and general pattern.
Bone under a microscope.
The working of joints.

Practical Work

(1) Examine a model skeleton.
(If the pupils are able to make the model body the skeleton part can be made using cotton reels [see Fig. 8].

(2) Model joints can be made from cardboard and elastic. Ball and socket joints can be obtained from the butcher.

2. FOOD AND DIGESTION (TAKEN IN CONJUNCTION WITH WORK IN DOMESTIC SCIENCE)

Types of food and why they are required.
Food tests for starch, glucose, protein, fat.
Teeth, including care of teeth.
Why digestion is necessary.
The alimentary canal.
Digestion and absorption (simply). Ptyalin and pepsin action can be demonstrated.
Diet.

31

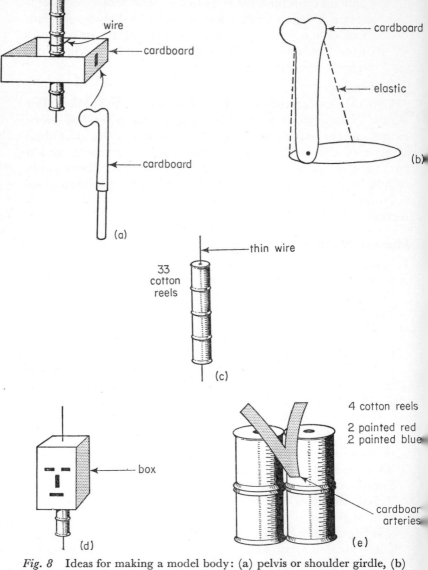

Fig. 8 Ideas for making a model body: (a) pelvis or shoulder girdle, (b) arm, (c) backbone, (d) head, (e) heart.

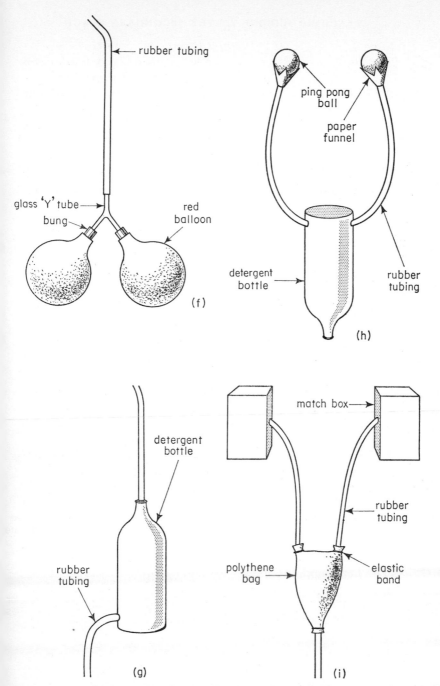

Fig. 8 cont. Ideas for making a model body: (f) respiratory system, (g) digestive system, (h) reproductive system, (i) renal system

Practical Work

(1) Charts of foods can be made, or boxes and bottles collected and put into groups: proteins, vitamins, etc.
(2) Some pupils enjoy making plasticine models of the alimentary canal.
(3) Simple enzyme action can be demonstrated by the action of saliva on starch. (Use Fehling's test before and after allowing to stand for half an hour for a good result.)
(4) The alimentary canal of other animals can be examined. A good selection of cine films is available from Unilever, Heinz, etc.

3. RESPIRATION

The purpose of respiration (ref. to chemistry of oxygen).
The structure of the chest cavity.
The mechanism of respiration (ref. to air pressure).
The spread of respiratory diseases.

Practical Work

(1) Make a model chest using bell jar, balloons, etc.
(2) Measure the approximate capacity of the lungs, breathing through a tube into a bell jar or gas jars inverted in a trough of water.
(3) Measure the size of the chest expanded and collapsed. Prove that carbon dioxide is breathed out.
(4) Prove that not only carbon dioxide is breathed out, but that the last air exhaled contains most carbon dioxide.
(5) Measure the rate of breathing before and after exercise.
(6) Lungs of a sheep can be examined. (Artificial respiration can be taught.)

4. CIRCULATION

The heart and circulatory system.
Blood under a microscope, both stained and unstained (fresh).
Transporting functions of the blood.
Pulse.
Pressure points.
The ability to form clots.

Practical Work

(1) Examine blood under a microscope.
(2) Examine a model heart or sheep's heart. (Preserve good specimens.)
(3) Make and use a model stethoscope. (Y-tube and rubber tubing.)
(4) Count the pulse.
Count the pulse rate after exercise.
(The more able pupils will be able to study blood groups and the Blood Transfusion Service. It is possible to borrow posters about this service.)

5. EXCRETION

The function of the kidneys. (Simply.)
The skin, its structure and functions. (There is a good Unilever film.) Perspiration and temperature control.

Practical Work

(1) A kidney can be examined.
(2) A piece of bladder can be examined under the microscope.
(3) A microscope slide of skin can be examined.
(4) Cooling effect can be demonstrated using an easily vaporised liquid.

6. THE NERVOUS SYSTEM

The eye, the ear, the tongue, the nerves in the skin.
The senses of sight, hearing, taste, smell, touch.
Co-ordination, the brain and the nerves.
Reflex actions.

Practical Work

(1) *The eye* A cow's or pig's eye can be dissected.
(2) *The blind spot* Use a paper with a cross on it and a spot drawn about three inches away from the cross. The spot is viewed with one eye, then it is possible to move the paper till the cross disappears.
(3) *The working of the iris* If the eyes are closed for a few minutes and opened while looking towards a window the action of the iris can be seen. (Have the pupils working in pairs or using mirrors.)

(4) *Binocular vision* Two pupils each with one eye closed each hold a pencil at arm's length, then move the pencils towards each other trying to make the points touch. Repeat the process with both eyes open.

(5) *Width of vision* Move a page of writing to right and left and up and down in front of the eye and discover the field of vision.

(6) Using one eye, observe a word in the centre of a printed page. Unless the eye is moved only a very few other words can be seen clearly.

This work can be done in conjunction with light experiments in physics and with lessons on the camera.

(7) *The ear* Most practical work on the ear will be covered in sound experiments in physics.

(8) *The ear as an organ of balance* Spin until dizzy.

7. DUCTLESS GLANDS, REPRODUCTION

The position of the ductless glands and the effects of their hormones.

The structure of the sex organs.

The process of reproduction.

Care of the young, the part played by both parents and also that played by the community.

Inheritance. A simple explanation of the process.

N.B. (1) Inheritance experiments can be carried out by breeding mice though the results in just one generation may be rather unexpected.

(2) It is helpful in the teaching of reproduction if the pupils have been brought up in their school life to care for and breed animals. (Mice and hamsters can be easily kept in classrooms. Stick insects are useful for comparisons as they exhibit parthenogenesis.)
(See also VOLRATH, J.P., *Animals in Schools* [U.F.A.W. and Murray].)

(3) It is sometimes possible to link up some of these lessons with work studied in R.E. lessons, where moral codes and behaviour are discussed.

8. PREVENTION OF DISEASE

Diseases of the respiratory system.

Diseases of the digestive system.
Diseases spread by insect bites, etc.
How the body reacts to germs.
Immunity.
Artificial immunity, vaccination, etc.
How to kill germs, using drugs, anti-biotics, etc.

This section can be taught by a series of biographical lessons:
Pasteur, Jenner, Lister, Ehrlich, Fleming, etc.

Bacteria

Practical Work

1. CULTURE

(1) Bacteria may be grown in nutrient jelly. The jelly can
be made in petri-dishes or half-pound jam jars with
plastic covers.

Preparation of jelly

A. *Agar jelly* Weigh 2 gm of agar, cover with water
and allow to soak overnight. Put the soaked agar in a
beaker with 100 ml of water and bring to the boil. Boil
for about half an hour. Then pour into sterilised dishes
or jars; i.e. dishes that have been boiled for half an hour
in a closed saucepan or boiler about one-third full of
water. Cover the jelly immediately and leave to set.

B. *Nutrient jelly* Heat with constant stirring 50 gm
powdered gelatine, ½ 'Oxo' cube (or ½ teaspoonful 'Bovril'
or 1 teaspoonful peptone) and 500 ml water. Boil until
the gelatine has dissolved. The mixture will be acid.
Testing with red litmus paper add small quantities of
powdered washing soda or 1 per cent caustic soda
solution, until the litmus paper turns blue. Filter and
pour into the sterilised jars and cover at once. Leave to
set.

Different microbe bearing material can be transferred
to the jelly using a needle first sterilised in a Bunsen
burner flame. The first dish should be the control, the
needle being first dipped into boiled water and then
streaked across the jelly. For other dishes needles can be
dipped in dust, scraped on the teeth or dipped into a
mixture of soil and water. The jelly can be sneezed on

or a housefly can be allowed to walk on it. The jars should be kept in a warm place. Colonies of microbes will germinate in a few days.

The importance of refrigeration can be noted if the experiment is repeated using material which gave a positive result but now putting the dish into a refrigerator. Similarly if an antiseptic is introduced into the jelly when it is made, bacteria will not germinate.

(2) Bacteria and other micro-organisms will germinate if hay, horse dung or minced meat is allowed to rot in water. The water should be examined under the high power of the microscope.

2. Useful Bacteria

(1) Examine washed roots of leguminous plants using a hand lens to examine root nodules. A nodule can be cut off and crushed. A small amount of crushed material should be placed on a clean microscope slide with a spot of diluted Indian ink. Then cover with a cover slip and examine under the high power of a microscope. The bacteria all being of a similar shape will show up against the dark background.

(2) Visit a sewage works and study the method of disposal. In the 'percolating filter' method aerobic bacteria act on the sewage in the filter.

In the 'activated sludge' method aerobic bacteria act on the sewage in the aeration tank and anaerobic bacteria act on it in the sludge digestion tank.

Some local sewage committees of the local councils have booklets available giving details of the method used and the quantity of sewage treated.

(3) Bacteria are useful in the preparation of various types of cheese. The easiest cheese to prepare in the school is plain milk cheese. Sour milk should be kept for a few days until it is solid. The clotted milk should be strained through butter muslin, then tied in the muslin and left to drain for about 24 hours. The cheese can then be put into a dish and salt and pepper or other spices added to taste.

Field Study

Due to school organisation it is often only possible to undertake field study in groups of twenty or more. It is essential therefore that this work should be thoroughly planned and every pupil given work which will keep them fully occupied.

1. The teacher should be familiar with the habitat, making visits to the place before even considering taking the pupils.

2. It is often helpful to make a booklet for the guidance of the pupils. A duplicated set of papers is quite easy to produce.

3. The work can be divided into sections and given to different groups of pupils; one group might study flowers, another trees, etc.

4. They can be given sets of questions to answer while actually on the site, or they may be able to do some sketching.

5. Specimens taken back to school should be discussed, then labelled and made into an exhibition.

6. City schools may find field study more difficult, though it may be possible to hire a coach for a day or half-day to visit a nature reserve. It is also often possible to combine with the geography department and hire a coach for the combined party.

7. A field study club can be formed as an out-of-school activity. Here numbers can be small and more advanced work can be tackled. Hostelling trips can be arranged.

See also *Science Teaching Techniques*, Nos. III, IV, IX, XI.

Bibliography

BIBBY, CYRIL. *Simple Experiments in Biology* (Heinemann).

BROCKLEHURST, K. G. and WARD, H. *General School Biology* (E.U.P.).

KNOWLES, FRANCIS. *Man and Other Living Things* (Harrap).

MARCHANT, D. H. J. *General Science Biology* (Bell).

CHEMISTRY

The S.M.A.'s memorandum, *Science and Education*, emphasised that the general intermediate course in science should be complete in itself, as about 75 per cent of the school population leaves at fifteen to sixteen years of age, many of this number never again to study science. Very few girls attend further education classes in the sciences. In view of the impact of science on society, the chemistry in the school syllabus should provide sufficient background knowledge for the non-specialist to have some understanding of modern applied chemistry. From the beginning at eleven-plus chemistry should mean something more to a pupil than a game with test-tubes and Bunsen burners played in a special room called a laboratory. All too often this is all that elementary chemistry signifies and, not for a moment, is there any link in the child's mind between the product of his work in the laboratory and the wide and fascinating field of applied chemistry.

The content of the G.C.E. syllabus is far too detailed and specialised for the non-specialist pupil, although, of course, some basic knowledge is necessary for an understanding of the applied field. A course must be prepared which introduces the pupil to both the principles and practice of much of the scientific phenomena with which he is surrounded in the modern world. An elementary knowledge of organic chemistry is fundamental to the pursuit of most fields of applied chemistry but this does not mean an 'A' level approach. All that is required is that the pupil should be introduced to a new branch of chemistry and know something of the nature of some of its compounds. This work can then be followed by study in a variety of chemical fields selected according to the age, sex, ability, aptitude, environment and interests of the class and the time available.

Some may argue that this approach to chemistry is too vocational and technical and out of place in a school where a liberal education is the aim. A. N. Whitehead wrote: 'The antithesis between a technical and liberal education is fallacious. There can be no adequate technical education which is not liberal and no liberal education which is not technical.'

Programme A. Basic Course (Two Years)

INTRODUCTION TO CHEMISTRY

A different approach is needed which enables the pupil to know something of the part chemistry plays in daily life and the width of its application.

A First Lesson

Arrange an attractive display of materials widely used in everyday life and all chemically derived, e.g. water, household ammonia, hydrogen peroxide, paint, a dye, polishes, perm lotion, aspirin, a medicine, detergent, food, cosmetics, coins, an alloy, bleach, a plastic, nylon, etc. Let pupils investigate and identify, or arrange a quiz. Hence, what is chemistry? What is a chemist? Derivation of science and knowledge, term natural philosophy replaced by natural science. Differentiate between a chemist and a pharmacist. Conclude with the realisation that one cannot know much about these rather complicated compounds (one formula on the blackboard) unless one knows some basic facts and principles of chemistry, i.e. the origin and nature of simple chemicals, how one substance reacts with another, conditions under which reactions will take place.

The further order of treatment might be:

(1) Burning, breathing and rusting—usual experiments plus the heating of a ball of steel wool.
(2) Physical and chemical changes—simple experiments including ammonium dichromate, iodine, coal, sugar.
(3) Elements, mixtures and compounds—iron and sulphur experiments.
(4) Air and constituent gases—usual experiments, oxygen from hydrogen peroxide and manganese dioxide, mention of the rare gases and use in illuminations.
(5) Water—general properties, composition, distillation.
(6) Action of metals on water—simple study of hydrogen, test-tube preparation only.
(7) Solution, solvent, solute. Types of solutions. Solubility, saturated solution—simple experiments to illustrate.
(8) Crystals—making and growing crystals.
(9) Acids—common acids, properties.

Testing acid drops, using universal indicator measure

41

the pH number, i.e. the acidity and alkalinity of a number of solutions, e.g. lemon juice, tartaric acid, vinegar, baking powder, sulphuric acid, toothpaste, cleansing milk, bicarbonate of soda, 'Domestos', liver salts (definition of pH not needed).

Draw a column graph of the results.

(10) Bases and alkalis—common examples, properties contrasted with those of acids.

(11) Salts—derivation from acid and base. Simple methods of preparation—neutralisation to form common salt—the five usual methods outlined in most textbooks.

(12) Types of water— hard and soft water. Estimation of hardness by using soap flakes ('Lux' or 'Kudos'). Methods of softening.

(13) Simple experiments demonstrating chemical change, solution, decomposition, combination, displacement, double decomposition, oxidation, reduction, catalysis, enzyme action.

(14) Ammonia (test-tube preparation), ammonium hydroxide —household ammonia, special properties of ammonium chloride. Use of the carbonate and sulphate.

(15) Simple study of coal gas—preparation of impure gas on test-tube scale. Reference to by-products and derivatives of coal gas.

(16) Atoms, molecules—simple ideas on electronic structure.

(17) Simple formulae, e.g. sodium chloride and water molecules; combination of elements; valence.

(18) The making of a chemical equation.

(19) Carbon—its different forms and uses (mention sulphur similarity—allotropes). This leads to a simple introduction to organic chemistry. The majority of elementary textbooks include all the practical work recommended for this basic course. There are now available a few books written specially for practical work, and others with a less formal layout, designed for junior forms only. Some books of American origin outline new simple experiments for familiar topics, together with many interesting everyday applications. The routine experiments are refreshingly presented as 'problems to solve'.

INTRODUCTION TO ORGANIC CHEMISTRY

(1) What is organic chemistry? A brief outline finishing with the definition: the chemistry of the carbon compounds other than the oxides of carbon.

(2) Hydrocarbons and petroleum products—demonstration of fractional distillation.

(3) Carbohydrates.

(4) Other elements combined in organic compounds, e.g. nitrogen, sulphur, phosphorus.

(5) This section may be concluded by showing and discussing the formulae of a few substances in common use, e.g. sugar, aspirin, a dye, D.D.T. This elementary knowledge of the organic field enables the pupils to begin to understand something of the composition of such complicated substances.

Some Fields of Applied Chemistry

There are many fields of applied chemistry which might be explored during the last 2–3 years of a science course. It would be impossible for one group to attempt all of these and the selection of the fields of study must naturally depend on various factors such as the ability, sex, interest and environment of the group.

The following subjects can all be the basis of a very interesting school course:

> food, textiles, dyes, laundrywork, detergents,
> metallurgy, industrial processes, plastics,
> cosmetics, hairdressing,
> paints, retail distribution.

Work in these fields will not only widen and stimulate the pupil's interest in the world around him but his knowledge of science generally will be considerably increased. In many cases too, such a background will be of inestimable value in the first years of many further education courses.

At first sight the content of such a course seems far too comprehensive and much too advanced for the average pupil. However, with careful selection of material and a thoughtful approach to teaching, a most interesting, stimulating and satisfying course for both boys and girls could be compiled.

Such a course would provide boundless opportunities for making observations, using a variety of practical skills, recording experiments and wide reading. At the end they should leave school having some appreciation of the function of chemistry as a science and of its impact on modern society.

SUGGESTIONS FOR COURSE WORK

(1) *Food* Experiments with carbohydrates, sugars, starch, flour, fats, proteins, vitamins.

Raising agents: comparison of the effect of sodium bicarbonate, sodium bicarbonate plus tartaric acid, baking powder.

Yeast action in bread making.

Experiments with milk, cheese making.

Preservation of food—simple study, but including modern methods, e.g. quick freeze drying.

(2) *Textiles* Natural and 'man-made'.

Examination of fibres with a microscope, thread counting with counting glasses.

Effects of burning, acids and alkalis, water, temperature.

Identification of fibres with Shirlastain 'A' (see the practical course in 'Textile Fibres', p. 194).

(3) *Dyes* Nature of a dye, making a dye, mordanting (organic theory not included).

(4) *Chromatography* Single paper chromatography—experiments with inks and Watman's No 4. Chromatographic Paper.

(5) *Chemistry related to rural studies* Experiments with slate, lime and vinegar, soil analysis, souring of soil showing progressive pH change.

(6) *Laundrywork* The links between science and laundrywork have been fully outlined in a section of *Science Teaching Techniques 12*.

(7) *Detergents* The chemistry of detergents is difficult and the content should be confined to (*a*) the elementary definition of detergent, i.e. 'a cleanser', (*b*) the differences between soap and soapless detergents, and (*c*) simple experiments as outlined in the article 'Science and Laundrywork' in *Science Teaching Techniques 12*.

44

(8) *Metallurgy* A study of selected metals and alloys. Practical work and applications as suggested in chapter 8 under the heading 'Craft Science'.

(9) *Industrial processes* Some processes may be included as a result of the work with metals. Local industry may influence this section too, otherwise the course may follow the pupils' interests. Industrial firms are always very generous with scientific literature, and a great variety of information sheets, charts, films and filmstrips is available.

(10) *Plastics* Some understanding of the term polymer and high polymer; nature of a plastic; outline of the development of plastics; thermoplastics and thermosetting plastics, examples.

Introduction to some common plastics, e.g. polythene, P.V.C., perspex, bakelite, melamine, terylene, orlon, etc.

(11) *Paints* The three essential ingredients of a paint: the vehicle (liquid medium), the body (base), lithopone (pigment). Some common pigments, preparation and properties of typical inorganic pigments.

Different types of paints—undercoats, finishing coats, emulsion paints, thixiotropic (non-drip) paints.

(12) *Cosmetics* History of cosmetics.

Preparation of selected cosmetics—good products made to recipes vetted by top-grade firms.

The nature and function of the ingredients. Relating the use of a 'safe' face preparation to the health of the skin.

(13) *Hairdressing* A study of the chemicals, chemical terms and processes encountered in hairdressing, e.g. alkali, spirit, detergent, antiseptic, solvent, solute, solution, emulsion, oxidation, bleaching, 'perm' lotion, shampoo, dyeing, wig cleaning, etc., softening water.

A number of suitable experiments are outlined in the book KILGOUR, O. F. G. and MCGARRY, M. *Introduction to Science and Hygiene for Hairdressers* (Heinemann).

(14) *Retail distribution* Chemistry concerned with textiles, dyeing, laundering, food, cosmetics, hairdressing. (See the special syllabus for this course.)

SUPPLIERS OF COSMETIC MATERIALS

Cosmetic	Quantity	Suppliers
Abracol	1 lb	A. Boake Roberts & Co. Ltd., Carpenters Road, Stratford, London E.15.
Acetoglycerides L/C, S/C, S/C/2	500 ml samples (or 1 lb)	A. Boake Roberts (*see above*).
Acetone	500 ml	Griffin & George Ltd., Ealing Road, Alperton, Wembley, Middlesex.
Borax	500 g	Griffin & George (*see above*).
Butylated hydroxyanisole	1 g	Griffin & George (*see above*).
castor oil (good quality)	W.qt	Griffin & George (*see above*).
Chalk pptd. (calcium carbonate)	500 g	Griffin & George (*see above*).
Cetyl alcohol (*see* empicol, i.e. Laurex 16)	1 lb sample	Marchon Products Ltd., 140 Park Lane, London W.1.
Collones. Samples of Texofors A.6, A.10, D.60	1 lb or 4 oz	Glovers (Chemicals) Ltd., Wortley Low Mills, Whitehall Road, Leeds 12.
Dyes (*see* lakes)		
Empicol L.Q. (*see* cetyl alcohol)	1 lb	Marchon Products (*see above*).
Emulsene	1 lb	A. Boake Roberts (*see above*).
Eosin	250 g	Griffin & George (*see above*).
Ethyl acetate	500 ml	Griffin & George (*see above*).
Ethylene glycol monomyristate (propylene G.M. can be used instead)	500 ml sample given	A. Boake Roberts (*see above*).

Cosmetic	Quantity	Suppliers
Glycerol	250 ml	Griffin & George (*see above*).
Isopropyl myristate	500 ml	A. Boake Roberts (*see above*).
Kaolin	1 lb	Griffin & George (*see above*).
Lakes: 1102 yellow 1117 fine red 1532 eosin 1658 pink 1898 pink 1901 orange 1903 red	1 lb, $\frac{1}{2}$ lb or $\frac{1}{4}$ lb	D. F. Anstead Ltd., Victoria Road, Romford, Essex.
Lanolin	500 g	Croda Ltd., Cowick Hall, Snaith, Goole, Yorkshire. *or* Griffin & George (*see above*).
Liquid paraffin (cosmetic quality)	W.qt	A. Boake Roberts (*see above*). *or* Boots.
Magnesium stearate	500 g	Griffin & George (*see above*). *or* B.D.U.
Magnesium carbonate	500 g	Griffin & George (*see above*).
Methyl ethyl ketone	500 ml	Griffin & George (*see above*).
Nipasol (methyl propyl butex)	10 g	Nipa Laboratories Ltd., Treforest Industrial Estate, Pontypridd, Glamorgan.

Cosmetic	Quantity	Suppliers
Perfumes	samples	A. Boake Roberts (*see above*). *or* International Flavors & Fragrances, I.F.F. (Great Britain) Ltd., Crown Road, Southbury Road, Enfield, Middlesex.
Potassium hydroxide	500 g	Griffin & George (*see above*).
Propyl gallate	50 g sample	W. J. Bush & Co. Ltd., West Bank Works, Widnes, Lancashire.
Propylene glycol	250 ml sample	Shell Chemicals Co. Ltd., Marlborough House, 15–17 Great Marlborough Street, London W.1.
Propylene glycol monomyristate (*see* ethylene G.M.)		
Sodium alginate (manucol SS/LU)	sample	Alginate Industries Ltd., Walter House, Bedford Street, London W.C.2
Sodium carbonate monohydrate	3 kg	Griffin & George (*see above*).
Sodium sesqui-carbonate	3 kg	Griffin & George (*see above*).
Sodium hydroxide (pellets)	250 g	Griffin & George (*see above*).
Stearic acid	500 g	Griffin & George (*see above*).
Talc (French chalk)	1 kg	Griffin & George (*see above*).
Titanium dioxide	500 g	Griffin & George (*see above*).

Cosmetic	Quantity	Suppliers
Triethanolamine	500 ml or ½ lb sample	Griffin & George (*see above*). *or* Shell Chemicals (*see above*).
Waxes: beeswax candelilla carnauba ceresine czokerite spermaceti	2 lbs of each or less	Griffin & George (*see above*). *or* Poth Hille & Co. Ltd., High Street, Stratford, London E.15.
Witch Hazel	250 ml approx.	Boots.
Zinc oxide	250 g	Griffin & George (*see above*).
Lipstick press	6 or 12 cavities 12-cavity costs about £18)	H. B. Arden & Co. (Instruments) Ltd., 15 Crescent Street, Sittingbourne, Kent.

Metal beakers
Long spatulas
Glass plates
Lipstick cases
Small screw-top jars or
  similar containers
Pill boxes

Programme B

This basis for a syllabus is offered as an alternative. It is designed to give the pupils simple but interesting experiments to illustrate chemical changes. It will be apparent that the teacher can fit in the more usual topics such as oxygen, carbon dioxide, hydrogen, etc., into the appropriate sections.

Class experiments involving small-scale techniques should be used wherever possible and teacher demonstration confined to such items as are not safe for a whole class to perform, or which can be clearly seen, understood, and appreciated by a class.

Industrial processes of particular interest, topics such as suggested in the previous syllabus or any particular chemical study can be added to this skeleton when and where it is found to be suitable for the class and the teacher.

Some teachers will probably find that they can add more theory to reinforce this experimental approach. For example some understanding of chemical bonding and simple atomic structure can be given without overloading the syllabus.

Chemistry is concerned with finding out what things are made of and with the making of new materials from those already known. Pupils are not expected to learn only dull facts about materials but to experiment, to observe, and to understand some of the methods the chemist may use and the rules which control the behaviour of the materials that he uses.

1. How to Start a Chemical Change

(1) Hold a penny or a strip of copper foil in the flame of a Bunsen burner. Examine the oxide film formed on contact with the air.

(2) Heat a small piece of magnesium ribbon in air. Protect the eyes from the dangerous ultra-violet radiation. Note the change produced.

(3) Heat a little starch in a small dry test-tube. Look for signs of a chemical change.

(4) Connect a low voltage D.C. supply via tungsten or platinum electrodes to a solution of potassium iodide.

(5) Make a solution of silver nitrate in distilled or pure water. Add a few drops of common salt solution. Leave for several hours in bright sunlight.

(6) Mix together half a teaspoonful of dry powdered tartaric acid and a teaspoonful of bicarbonate of soda. Add water.

2. Recognising a Chemical Change

(1) Put a little solid ammonium dichromate in a clean dry test-tube. Gently warm in a Bunsen burner flame and, as soon as the reaction starts, remove the test-tube from the flame. Note evidence of new materials and heat being produced. Try to dissolve the chemical before and after heating.

(2) Heat about 30 cm of magnesium ribbon in a weighed crucible and lid. Note any change in weight due to the chemical change. Mention can be made that a chemical change is not so easily reversed as a physical change.

(3) Using a mixture of 7 parts by weight of iron filings and 4 parts of sulphur investigate the properties of a mixture by examination through a lens, by separation by magnetism and by dissolving the sulphur in carbon disulphide. Heat the mixture, observe the signs of a chemical change and then investigate the properties of the resultant compound.

3. THE SUBSTANCES THAT TAKE PART IN CHEMICAL CHANGE, ELEMENTS, COMPOUNDS, METALS, NON-METALS, LIQUIDS AND GASES

(1) Examine a wide variety of these substances. Many of them could form part of an exhibition which should be regularly changed to give the pupils some acquaintance with the look, feel, smell and the more obvious properties of the materials which are safe for such investigation.

4. SOLUTIONS

(1) Dissolve rock salt in pure water, filter and evaporate the filtrate.

(2) Carefully evaporate tap water in a watch glass under an infra-red lamp. Check for dissolved solids.

(3) Prepare crystals of copper sulphate, potassium nitrate, magnesium sulphate, sodium sulphate, alum. Useful hints on growing large crystals can be found in *Crystals and Crystal Growing* by Alan Holden and Phyllis Singer, (Heinemann 'Science Study Series').

(4) Use of other solvents, benzene, carbon tetrachloride (care with toxic fumes needed), trichlorethylene, and amyl acetate.

(5) Extract the dyes from green leaves or grass by covering with methyl alcohol warmed by a water bath. Simple chromatic separation can be effected by dipping strips of filter paper in a test-tube containing a little of the chlorophyll solution and noting the separated bands obtained.

51

5. DECOMPOSITION

(1) Heat mercuric oxide. Identify the two elements produced.
(2) Heat sawdust and coal dust in small test-tubes.
(3) Heat copper carbonate. Test gas evolved by extracting it with a teat pipette and bubbling it into a small test-tube of limewater.
(4) Heat potassium permanganate.
(5) Heat ammonium dichromate.
(6) Electrolyse sodium chloride, copper sulphate and copper chloride solutions.

6. COMBINATION

(1) Heat iron filings and sulphur.
(2) Grind mercury and iodine together in a mortar.
(3) Heat zinc in air.
(4) Heat copper in air.

7. DISPLACEMENT

(1) Action of lithium, sodium, calcium, magnesium on water.
(2) Action of dilute sulphuric acid on zinc.
(3) Action of dilute sulphuric acid on iron—possibly razor blades.
(4) Action of copper sulphate with an iron nail or iron filings.

8. DOUBLE DECOMPOSITION

(1) *Precipitation of insoluble substances*
    (a) Add potassium iodide solution to lead acetate solution.
    (b) Add potassium chromate to lead acetate solution.
    (c) Add calcium chloride solution, say, to sodium carbonate solution, leading on to precipitation of calcium stearate when soap is added to hard water.
(2) *Salt formation*
    Action of concentrated sulphuric acid on chlorides, e.g. sodium chloride giving hydrogen chloride, and on nitrates giving nitric acid.
(3) *Neutralisation reactions*
    Neutralisation of hydrochloric acid by an alkali such as sodium hydroxide, by an oxide such as copper oxide or by a carbonate such as copper carbonate.

52

(4) *Hydrolysis*

Boil fat with caustic soda to obtain soap.

Boil sucrose or starch with hydrochloric acid and test with Fehling's or Benedict's solution to show the formation of glucose.

9. OXIDATION

(1) Heat copper foil red hot and then expose to air.

(2) Burn magnesium ribbon, taking care to protect eyes from ultra-violet light.

(3) Shake up fresh blood (obtained from an abattoir) with (*a*) oxygen or air, (*b*) carbon dioxide.

(4) Heat together in a test-tube a mixture of iron filings and sulphur. Remove from the flame as soon as the action starts. The iron is oxidised to iron sulphide (oxidation is not necessarily combination with oxygen).

10. REDUCTION

(1) Put the blackened copper foil with its oxide film back into the centre of the flame and note the change back to shiny copper.

(2) Hydrogen or coal gas may be passed over heated copper oxide if a more formal demonstration is needed.

(3) Heat lead oxide mixed with fusion mixture (sodium and potassium carbonates) on a piece of charcoal or a charcoal block.

(4) A piece of zinc is placed in copper sulphate solution. The zinc reduces the copper ions in the solution to copper atoms, which form a layer of deposited copper.

Reduction is always accompanied by oxidation, hence the term *redox* reaction. Batteries and accumulators operate by 'redox' reactions.

11. CATALYSIS

(1) Decompose hydrogen peroxide using manganese dioxide. Discuss oxygen, its properties and uses.

(2) Accelerate the production of hydrogen from zinc and dilute sulphuric acid by the addition of a few drops of copper sulphate solution.

E   53

(3) *Enzyme action* as a special case of catalysis.

Fermentation of sugar to form alcohol (use fractional distillation of this weak alcohol to illustrate an important process used in chemistry).

Digest starch with saliva in a test-tube. Add pepsin solution to a colloidal solution of egg white in water at body temperature (the cloudy solution is seen to go clear).

PHYSICS

Magnetism and Electricity

1. PERMANENT MAGNETS

Points of Approach and Applications
The magnetic compass, toys and games depending on the use of magnets, need for non-magnetic watches.
Magnetic job holders, magnetic letters for display boards.

Practical Work
(1) Class finds what they can 'pick up' with a magnet. (Some materials can be provided, but pockets and bags form an excellent and varied source.)
(2) Class finds through which substances a magnet will attract. (Sheets of glass and plastic are a help and the bases of lab stands provide a screening action. Iron filings or pins can be used to test.)
(3) Class finds where the power of a magnet lies using iron filings or tacks.
(4) Class suspends magnets in paper slings and find the direction in which they will settle.
(5) Using a second magnet the class finds the effect of poles on each other.
(6) Class makes a piece of clock spring into a magnet by stroking it.
(7) Class finds the polarity of the new magnet by bowing it slightly so that it spins on the bench.
(8) Class breaks the spring and dips the two ends into iron filings.
(9) Class finds the polarity of the two halves.
(10) Class makes one of the halves red hot and then tests with iron filings.

Formal Syllabus
Magnetism is thought to have first been noticed by the early Chinese in the ore magnetite.
Modern magnets are made from steel and alloys.
Magnets affect mainly iron and steel.

55

The power of a magnet lies mainly in its ends which are called *poles*.

The effects of magnetism will pass through most materials.

A freely suspended magnet will come to rest pointing roughly N–S.

Like poles repel, unlike poles attract.

A steel bar may be magnetised by stroking it with a magnet.

Breaking a bar magnet will form two complete new magnets.

Heating will destroy the magnetic effects in a steel bar.

Molecular (or Domain) theory of magnetisation.

2. Magnetic Fields and the Earth's Field

Points of Approach and Applications

Pocket compasses, magnetic toys, non-magnetic watches, mine detectors, degaussing of ships, mariner's compass.

Electrical effects, moving coil speaker, tape recorder.

Practical Works

(1) Class experiments with magnets, filings, compass needles, etc., to find through what distance a magnet exerts an effect. (The fact that the effects are three dimensional should be emphasised.)

(2) The direction of the 'lines of force' round a magnet may be shown using a long magnetised sewing needle supported by a small disc of cork and floating upright in a large bowl of water. The north pole of the needle should be just above the water surface and the magnet should be supported at water level. (This experiment shows that lines of force have direction.)

(3) Magnetic fields can be plotted using both iron filings and plotting compasses. A soft iron ring will show the effects of magnetic shielding.

(4) Electrical effects can be shown using a search coil and a very sensitive galvanometer (1–0–1 mA).

(5) The direction of the lines of force near the earth's surface can be shown using a compass needle and a dip needle.

(6) A mild steel bar can be magnetised using the earth's field. If it is placed in the magnetic meridian at the angle of dip and beaten hard with a piece of wood it will be found that the down pointing end will repel the north pole of a compass needle.

(7) A large coil of wire (3 ft square) connected in series with a sensitive galvanometer will cause deflections when turned so as to cut the lines of force of the earth's field.

Formal Syllabus

The space around a magnet in which its influence can be detected is called its *field of force*.

The field is conventionally shown as a series of *lines of force*. A *line of force* is the path followed by a north pole free to move near the magnet.

The field of force of a magnet has electrical effects.

The earth's field, declination and inclination, changes in declination.

3. Electricity—A Source of Energy

Points of Approach and Applications

Domestic heating appliances.

The effects of short circuits.

Fuses.

The development of electric lighting from the carbon arc to the fluorescent tube.

Uses of electro-magnets in industry. Magnetic cranes.

Electric bells, chime and trembler. The Morse buzzer.

The telephone receiver. Magnetic indicators. The relay.

Electrolysis and electro-plating.

Electric motors, simple treatment, common uses.

Practical Work

(1) Gradually increase the current through a short length of enamelled wire wound around the bulb of a simple test-tube thermoscope and observe the rise in temperature.

(2) Find by trial the length of 26-gauge 'Nichrome' wire which will get red hot when joined to a 12-volt L.T. supply. Wind it into an open coil, support it suitably and add a curved piece of tin plate to make a model electric radiator.

(3) Pass current from a 12-volt L.T. supply through short lengths of copper, eureka, iron and 'Nichrome' wire supported from two terminals. By means of a rheostat gradually increase the current in each case until the

wire melts or burns. Notice the amount of brightness achieved. It is worthwhile doing this also with a short piece of coiled tungsten filament from a burnt-out projector lamp.

(4) Demonstrate a model carbon arc lamp by using current from a 12-volt or preferably a 24-volt L.T. supply through two dry cell carbons, or, on a smaller scale, use a 4-volt supply and two lead pencils. (View through blue glass or blue gelatine.) Note that the starting current is rather heavy.

(5) Demonstrate the principle of the electric discharge lamp by passing H.T. from a spark coil or E.H.T. power pack through air at low pressure. This can be done by fitting a 30-cm length of 25-mm glass tube with a one-holed rubber stopper at one end and a two-holed stopper at the other. Insert a short piece of metal rod at each end to act as an electrode and a glass tube in the remaining hole to connect to the vacuum pump. If the water pressure is strong enough a good filter pump may be adequate.

If a sufficiently good vacuum cannot be obtained in any other way, the method used by Cavendish in 1750 may be adopted. Fill an equal armed U-tube at least 30 in long with mercury. Remove air bubbles, close the ends and invert into two small troughs of mercury. A double barometer is formed having a common vacuum. The mercury columns are then used as conductors of the H.T. supply to the vacuum.

(6) Demonstrate other discharge tubes as available, e.g. neon, mercury vapour. Try also burnt-out filament bulbs and old fluorescent tubes.

(7) Repeat Oersted's experiment using one accumulator, a key, a magnetic needle and a straight conductor held over the needle in line with it. The current may be limited by including a torch bulb in the circuit.

(8) To show the magnetic field due to a straight conductor insert a length of brass rod through the middle of a sheet of 'Perspex' or hardboard and connect to a 12-volt supply, a rheostat and a key. Sprinkle iron filings on the sheet. Depress the key and tap the board. Alternatively, use plotting compasses.

(9) To show the magnetic field of a solenoid wind one layer of 26-gauge copper wire on a 6–8 in length of 3-in diameter postal tube. In one side of a 12-in square of hardboard or three-ply make two parallel saw cuts to accommodate the coil centrally, afterwards filling up the slots with plastic wood, etc. Paint white or cover with white paper. Pass current from a 2–4 volt supply through the coil and sprinkle with iron filings.

(10) Given a supply of small solenoids of a few hundred turns, centre tapped, and soft iron and steel cores, the class may perform a variety of experiments on electro-magnetism. Such coils may be used to set up temporary models of trafficators, chime and trembler bells, etc.

(11) Join about 18 in of thin aluminium tape to a key and a source of 2 or 4 volts d.c., letting it rest between the poles of a strong U-shaped magnet. Note the movement

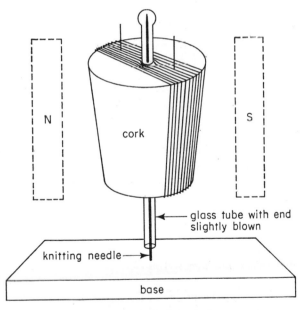

Fig. 9 Simple cork motor

Magnets are supported in position shown.
Leads from battery are held against ends of coil which
are shown sticking upright.

of the tape when the key is closed. Repeat with reversed current.

(12) Class makes simple two-pole 'cork' motors (see Fig. 9).

(13) The need for the reversal of the current at the appropriate moment may be shown by setting up a 5- or 6-in magnetic needle between two solenoids connected so as to obtain opposite poles facing. These are joined in series with a reversing key and a suitable source. If the current is reversed at the right time the needle will rotate.

(14) Using simple apparatus electrolyse water, copper sulphate solution etc., to show that some kind of chemical change takes place. Carbon electrodes may be used or, it has been suggested, old electric light bulbs provide a useful pair of electrodes in the nickel lead-in wires. If possible, demonstrate the electrolysis of acidulated water using platinum electrodes to show the proper ratio of hydrogen and oxygen.

(15) Electroplate a carbon rod or plate using a copper plate for the anode and copper sulphate solution as the electrolyte.

Formal Syllabus

Heat and light When an electric current is passed through a conductor, heat is produced and the temperature of the conductor rises. The conductor then radiates heat energy and, when hot enough, light energy as well. The limit is reached when the wire melts or oxidises.

Light energy is produced in a carbon arc. It is also produced when electricity flows through a gas at low pressure.

Magnetism When a current flows through a wire a magnetic field is produced. This is multiplied by winding the wire into a coil. The strength of an electromagnet depends on the number of turns, the current flowing and the nature of the core.

Mechanical The interaction of a current and a magnetic field will tend to cause motion in the conductor in which the current flows.

Chemical When a current is passed through a conducting liquid (not mercury!) chemical changes are produced.

4. USING ELECTRICITY

Points of Approach and Applications

The electric hand torch. Simple circuitry.

The importance of insulation in all electric apparatus.

Parallel circuits in domestic installations.

Commonly used units. Reading the meter. The principle of
earthing.

Practical Work

(1) Class uses various substances to fill a gap in a simple
circuit containing a torch bulb. The teacher may also
demonstrate the effect of using mains current and tap
water.

(2) Class makes series and parallel circuits with torch bulbs
using 1, 2 and 3 bulbs. The type of bulb used must
depend on the L.T. supply available. Circuits can be
laid out tidily on pegboard.

(3) Use a circuit board (see Fig. 11) to demonstrate voltages
and current used in these circuits. For this purpose
6- or 12-volt bulbs are preferable.

(4) Use a circuit board to show the layout of a two-way
circuit.

(5) The current used by various domestic appliances may
be measured by putting them in series with an a.c.
ammeter.[1] (Care with possible exposed terminals may
be necessary.) Calculate also the power of the appliance.

(6) Put a measured volume of water in an electric kettle
and record the time it takes to boil. Calculate the power
used and the cost.

(7) Connect various pieces of apparatus to a surplus household
electric meter[1] and check the energy used.

(8) Measure the current passing through yard lengths of
copper, eureka and 'Nichrome' wire of the same gauge
when joined to a 2-volt accumulator.

(9) Measure the current passing through similar lengths of
one of the above wires using several different gauges.

(10) Find the effect of shortening the length of one of the
wires.

[1]N.B. Apparatus involving the use of mains current should be handled only by
the teacher.

(11) The importance of earthing metal apparatus can be shown in the following way. Place an old electric iron on a piece of hardboard resting on a metal plate (earth). Connect the live and neutral plug terminals to a 6-volt accumulator with a 5-amp fuse and a switch in the live lead (see Fig. 10). Solder a wire from the live terminal of the iron socket to the case of the iron internally to simulate a fault, and connect a wire from the negative terminal of the battery to the metal plate. Leave the earth wire from the iron unconnected. Close the switch and, by means of a test bulb, show that the case is live. Open the switch and connect the green wire to earth (the metal plate). Close the switch. The fuse melts. Use the test bulb to show that the case is now safe. (It should be pointed out that this is a demonstration only, since a pressure of 6 volts will not force a large enough current through a person to affect him.)

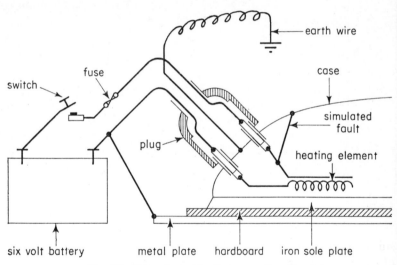

Fig. 10   Experiment to show use of earth wire

Circuit Boards

An electric circuit board can be built up on a hardboard or a pegboard base (see Fig. 11, p. 63). Conductors of 20 S.W.G. aluminium strip, ⅜ in wide are bolted to the base. A vertical 4 mm socket is mounted at the end of each conductor and a

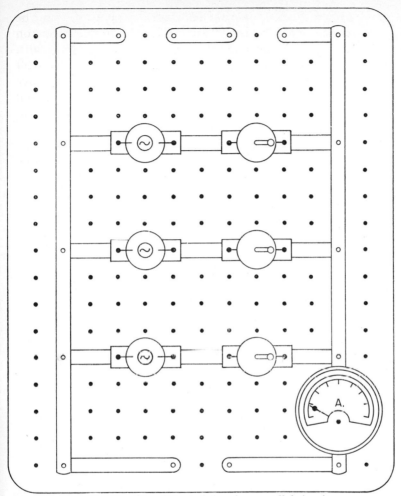

Fig. 11   Circuit board showing parallel circuit

suitable gap is left between the ends of the strips. The length of the gap can be 2 in on hardboard but on pegboard it must depend on the spacing of the holes. Components are mounted on wood or hardboard bases with 4-mm plugs beneath, suitably spaced.

Mounted components may comprise: lampholders, both S.B.C. and M.E.S.; switches; ammeters; voltmeters; solenoids; resistors (fixed and variable), etc.

Formal Syllabus

The simple electric circuit and its essential parts: (*a*) the energy source, (*b*) the energy path, (*c*) the appliance using energy, (*d*) the control.

Conductors and insulators. Circuits without wires—the hand torch.

The use of light bulbs with current and voltage measurement to show the characteristics of series and parallel circuits.

The supply of electricity to the home: general layout, safety precautions, correct wiring of plugs, etc.

Electric units The use of the water or coal train analogy to convey ideas of pressure, current, resistance and power. Effects of resistance: voltage drop. The relationships

$$\text{volts} \times \text{amps} = \text{watts};$$
$$\text{volts} \div \text{amps} = \text{ohms}.$$

The 'Board of Trade unit' and the cost of using energy.

5. Sources of Electrical Energy

Points of Approach and Applications

The 'dry' cell, including the power pack type.

The accumulator.

The cycle dynamo.

Transformers.

Electric guitars, tape recorders and record players.

Thermo-couple thermometers.

Photo-electric cells—exposure meters and other uses of P-E cells.

Induction furnaces, induction welding, etc.

The 'grid' system.

The induction coil.

Practical Work

(1) Take about 15 in each of copper and iron or eureka wire and twist together one end of each. Join the free ends to a milliammeter and heat the twisted ends in a Bunsen flame.

(2) Connect a selenium-selenium oxide photo-electric cell to a milliammeter (0–1 mA) and notice the effect of varying the amount of light falling on the cell. A photo-transistor (Mullard OCP 71) may also be used for this experiment. (A more sensitive meter may be needed.)

64

(3) Place plates of copper (or carbon) and zinc in a beaker of common salt solution or dilute sulphuric acid and join to a suitable ammeter. Notice the probable falling away of the output and investigate. (Try a 2·5-volt torch bulb in series.)

(4) Examine wet and dry Leclanché cells, including the layer type cells (power pack) and, if possible, Mallory mercury cells, to show their constituent parts.

(5) Place two lead plates in a beaker of dilute sulphuric acid and test with a torch bulb. Join the plates to a convenient source of electricity (4–6 volts, d.c.) and leave for one or two minutes. Disconnect and again test with the torch bulb. Observe the appearance of the plates before and after the treatment.

(6) Using a strong bar magnet, a suitable coil (500 turns tapped every 100) and a centre-zero milliammeter (2–0–2) investigate the production of induced currents. With a sufficiently strong U-shaped magnet (Magnetron) results can be obtained with a single conductor.

(7) Take a cycle dynamo to pieces and identify the parts. Reassemble and turn very slowly while the leads are joined to a centre-zero milliammeter. Notice the alternations of the current.

(8) Fix a cycle dynamo to a wooden base and drive it from an electric motor whose speed can be controlled. Investigate the variation of output voltage with speed and the change of speed when a load is applied.

(9) Swing a lighted neon bulb in a vertical circle of about two feet in diameter, anchoring the lampholder securely to the hand by means of a length of cord. The separated images of the glow show that the current is not continuous. This is best done in a darkened room.

(10) Make a simple strobe disc by drawing a number of radii on a circle of card. Attach this to the spindle of an electric motor and rotate it rapidly, viewing it by the light of one or two neon bulbs in a dark room. Vary the motor speed until the radii appear to advance, recede or remain stationary.

(11) Take two similar coils (the solenoids suggested in section III, expt. 10 would serve) and place them end to end.

Fitz Memorial Library
Endicott Jun or College
Beverly, Massachusetts 01915

29096

Join one to a 2-volt battery and a key and the other to a centre-zero galvanometer, shunted if necessary. Close the key and notice the slight movement of the needle at make and break of the current. Repeat with a soft iron rod linking the coils.

(12) Hang a small aluminium ring about 1 in in diameter by means of a bifilar cotton suspension from a clamp stand. Push one pole of a strong magnet towards the opening of the ring. Notice the slight repulsion. Withdraw and repeat rhythmically in step with the oscillations. Do this also with a wooden rod to show that the movement is not caused by air currents.

(13) Mount a 4- to 5-inch copper or aluminium disc between punch dot bearings so that it can spin freely. Spin it in a strong magnetic field and notice the reduced time of rotation.

(14) A transformer with detachable yoke and interchangeable coils can be used to perform many striking experiments demonstrating the basic principles of the static transformer.

(15) A model demonstrating the principle of the grid system can be set up with two of the above transformers. For the transmission line use thin wire of such resistance that a torch bulb fed from a 2-volt cell will light up only dimly. When 2 volts a.c. is fed into the first transformer, stepped up and transmitted, the stepped-down voltage at the second transformer should be sufficient to light the bulb reasonably.

Formal Syllabus

Electricity is generated when:

(a) a junction of dissimilar metals is heated,

(b) light falls on a certain type of metallic surface,

(c) two different conducting materials are placed in a conducting liquid,

(d) a moving conductor cuts magnetic lines of force or vice versa.

The value of an induced electromotive force depends on the speed of motion, the strength of the magnetic field and the number of conductors.

The direction of an induced electromotive force is such as to oppose the force producing it.

An electromotive force can be stepped up or down by a device known as a transformer.

6. SIMPLE RADIO

Points of Approach and Applications
The radio set and its uses for communication.

Practical Work
Most of this work needs careful adjustment to obtain good results. It is advisable to demonstrate first before the pupils try out ideas for themselves.

(1) A magnetised tuning fork is sounded near a coil of wire. The audio frequency a.c. is fed into the gramophone input of a radio or some other suitable amplifier. The whole class will be able to hear the note of the fork. The effect can be explained in terms of a moving magnet near a coil. The effect of the amplifier can be explained as simply 'increasing' the current.

The effect will be found to fall off rapidly with increase of the distance between the fork and the coil.

(2) A very simple spark transmitter can be made using an induction coil with about a half-inch spark. One side of the spark gap is earthed while the other is attached to about 6 ft of wire. (Don't let the children touch the wire!) This will have a range of about 150 yd and it broadcasts on all bands!

This can be picked up on the radio but not on the simple coil attached to the amplifier.

A simple explanation can be given of the rapid surge of electrons up and down the aerial at each 'make' and each 'break'. These movements form currents which in turn produce a 'vibrating magnetic field' but its frequency is too great for the speaker diaphragm on the amplifier to respond to it.

(3) The effect of a simple crystal diode can be demonstrated using a milliammeter.

With the diode in the circuit with the original coil

67

and amplifier, the spark transmitter can be clearly heard. The cutting out of surges in one direction needs explanation.

(4) A simple crystal receiver can be made using a diode and about 150 turns of 28-gauge wire on a 1½-in former. With a good aerial this will allow the Home Service to be heard on headphones. Fed into the amplifier it will entertain the whole class.

Similar sets can be constructed by the children but a good aerial at home is essential to avoid disappointment.

Transistor amplifiers can be added but explanation is difficult at this stage.

Fundamental Theory

In simple terms, radio transmission depends on the fact that a series of electromagnetic waves is generated by the transmitting station and these set up high-frequency currents in the receiving aerial.

Heat

1. HEAT AND EXPANSION, TEMPERATURE

Points of Approach and Applications

Spaces round hot plates on cookers, cracking of thick glass dishes, bimetal strips, thermostats, fire alarms, winking lights, expansion of pistons and cylinders.

Thermometers, use of temperature measurements in cooking and horticulture, body temperatures.

Explosions, blasting, firearms, internal combustion and jet engines.

Practical Work

(1) Class uses gauges and bars, rod and pointer apparatus, etc., to convince themselves of the expansion of solids.

(2) Demonstration of the force of expansion and contraction using 'breaking bar' apparatus.

(3) Class shatters glass rods or tubes by heating and plunging them into water. (Explain.)

(4) A similar experiment to No. 3 using a silica rod will show no effect due to the small coefficient of expansion.

(5) Demonstration of a bi-metal strip. (Arrange it to switch on and off an electric lamp.)

(6) Class experiment with a test-tube full of water and a long glass tube in a cork to form a rough thermometer. (Heat only gently.)

(7) Demonstration of a model thermometer using a flask and tube. (Class should be able to observe the first apparent contraction.) The effect is very marked if a plastic bottle is used instead of a glass flask.

(8) Class to examine and *use* thermometers to measure temperatures of various substances including a freezing mixture and hot oil or brine above the boiling point of water.

(9) Class plots a conversion graph of Centigrade and Fahrenheit temperatures by slowly warming water in a beaker and taking its temperature on two thermometers. The Bunsen should be removed and the temperatures allowed to steady before taking each reading.

(10) Class demonstration of maximum and minimum thermometers.

(11) Class experiments using empty test-tubes with the ends under water. The test-tubes are warmed in the hand to show the expansion of air. Plastic bottles may be used instead of test-tubes.

(12) Demonstration of the explosion of an air-gas mixture in a syrup tin. (The tin should have a small hole in its base and be placed upside down on a tripod with its lid *loosely* in place. Fire the mixture with a Bunsen flame.)

Formal Syllabus

Expansion of solids, liquids and gases treated qualitatively. Thermometers and scales should be introduced, however.

2. QUANTITY OF HEAT AND HEAT CAPACITY

Points of Approach and Applications

It takes longer to raise a full kettle of water to boiling point than a half-full one. A definite amount of fuel needs to be burnt or electrical energy used to produce a given amount of heat.

Food oxidises in our bodies as a fuel to give us heat and energy. Foods have calorific values (fats 7,000 to 8,000 calories per gramme, starches 2,000 to 3,000 calories per gramme). An average adult needs between 2,000 and 3,000 kilocalories a day.

On a sunny day the beach becomes hotter than the sea while by night the reverse is the case.

A person sun bathing will not become as hot as the stones on the beach.

Low water content animals such as beetles keep out of the direct sunlight.

The large heat capacity of water makes it a useful medium for heat transfer as in hot water heating systems, car cooling systems, the blood system, etc.

Practical Work

(1) Class heats a beaker full of water over a Bunsen for 2 minutes and notes the *rise* in temperature. Without altering the Bunsen adjustment the same beaker half-full of water is heated for the same time and the new temperature rise noted.

(2) Class heats a measured quantity of water for 2 or 3 minutes over a Bunsen flame and note the temperature rise. From this can be calculated the amount of heat given per minute by the flame.

(3) The amount of heat yield by measured amounts of methylated spirits, paraffin or solid meta fuel can be measured in the same way.

    If a small gas meter can be obtained the heat yield per cubic foot of gas burned can be calculated.

(4) An electric kettle and an electric kwh meter can be used to find the heat yield per kwh.

(5) Class heats $\frac{1}{2}$ lb or 1 lb of water over a fairly low Bunsen flame for $\frac{1}{2}$ minute. They can judge its temperature by dipping their fingers in it. With the Bunsen on the same adjustment a $\frac{1}{2}$ lb or 1 lb iron weight is heated for the same time and *cautiously touched*.

(6) Demonstration. *Equal weights* of water and turpentine are heated in a beaker for the same time over the same Bunsen and the temperature rise noted.

(7) Class warms 200 gm of water to about 50° C in a beaker. The exact temperature is noted. This water

is added to 100 gm of water at room temperature (exact temperature noted). The final temperature is noted. The heat lost by the hot water and the heat gained by the cold water can be calculated. They should agree within about 10 per cent. (Class can suggest possible errors.)

(8) The class can estimate the approximate temperature of a red-hot bolt as follows:

An iron bolt (about 25 gm) is heated in boiling water to 100° C. and dropped into about 50 gm of water. The temperature rise is noted. The same bolt is raised to red heat and dropped into the same amount of water. The new temperature rise is taken.

The temperature rise produced in the water is proportional to the heat given out by the bolt in cooling. We can assume that the bolt cooled by about 80 degrees in the first case and hence find by how much it cooled in the second.

This experiment bristles with errors but they tend to cancel out and give a result of between 1,000 and 1,400 degrees. The class will enjoy spotting the errors.

(9) Reasonable results for the specific heats of iron and lead can be obtained by heating 25 to 50 gm of the metal in boiling water and transferring to about 30 gm of water in a beaker. For such experiments weighing of water is not needed, graduated cylinders are sufficiently accurate. The use of insulated calorimeters forms a useful exercise in the pursuit of experimental accuracy.

Formal Syllabus

A gas flame; burning coal; a current passing through an electric wire all give off heat.

This heat can pass into water and make it hotter. The rise in temperature produced by a given amount of heat depends on the quantity of water being heated.

Amount of heat absorbed by the water = weight of water × temperature rise.

The *units of heat* in general use are:

(a) The *British thermal unit* which is the amount of heat needed to warm one pound of water by 1 Fahrenheit degree.

71

(b) The *therm* which is 100,000 Btu's and will heat about 60 gallons of water from room temperature to boiling.

(c) The *calorie* which is the amount of heat needed to warm one gramme of water by 1 Centigrade degree.

(d) The *great calorie* which is 1,000 calories and is used in the calorific values of foodstuffs and fuels.

The different heat capacities of different materials.

The effects of the very large heat capacity of water.

3. MELTING AND BOILING

Points of Approach and Applications

Ice melts and water boils at a definite temperature under normal circumstances. Different temperatures are needed to melt different materials.

It is said to be difficult to get very hot water at the top of a high mountain.

Pressure cookers cook food quickly because the water is at a higher temperature than normal boiling point.

Under low pressures foods can be dried or condensed at comparatively low temperatures.

Steam turbine boilers produce steam at pressures of up to 900 pounds per sq. in and temperatures of 900° F.

Separation of liquids of different boiling points is the basis of petroleum distillation. Reduced pressures are used to keep the temperatures low.

Water pipes burst in severe weather.

The formation of snowballs, the ease of movement of a skater and the movement of glaciers form examples of the effect of pressure on the melting point of ice.

Practical Work

(1) Class to watch a beaker of water come slowly to the boil and note temperature changes. (Air bubbles rise to the surface; evaporation may be 'seen' at the surface; steam bubbles form in the water, rise and finally burst at the surface.) Class to note that temperature does not rise after this stage.

(2) Water can be boiled at a reduced pressure in a round bottomed flask.

(a) Water is boiled in the flask, the source of heat removed and a tight cork placed in the neck of the flask. If the flask is now put under the cold tap the steam in it condenses, the pressure is reduced and the hot water boils violently.

(b) The flask may be exhausted by means of a filter pump and the pressure in it measured by means of a mercury manometer. (Care must be taken that the manometer holds sufficient mercury to prevent any risk of it being forced into the flask.)

A thermometer in the flask will allow the boiling point to be measured for different pressures.

(3) Demonstration of fractional distillation. Solution is made from 2 parts water and 1 part methylated spirits. It will not burn. Using a water bath or a large beaker a boiling tube of this solution is heated to about 75° C. The meths. will boil and the vapour can be passed into a condenser. The meths. collected will burn easily.

(4) Lead or 'Tinman's' solder show a definite melting point when heated in a ladle.

(5) Melting ice must be warmed in a beaker with a very small flame indeed if it is wished to demonstrate that the temperature stays at 0° C. until all the ice is melted.

(6) Castings can be made in lead using a small quantity of moulding sand. This should be demonstrated (molten lead is dangerous). Good results depend on moisture content of the sand.

(7) Demonstration. A small aspirin bottle is filled with water and the lid screwed on. It is placed in a freezing mixture (3 parts crushed ice, 1 part salt). The expansion of the water on freezing will burst the bottle.

(8) Class to join two pieces of ice by pressing them together,

(9) An ice cube can be 'cut' by a fine copper wire with a weight hung on it. (The freezing point is lowered by the pressure of the wire. The water flows round the wire and freezes again above it.)

Formal Syllabus

Boiling in a liquid takes place at a definite temperature. This depends on the air pressure above the liquid.

The melting or freezing of a substance takes place at a definite temperature. The effect of pressure in this case is much less marked.

The expansion of water on freezing and the effect of pressure.

4. LATENT HEAT

Points of Approach and Applications

When a kettle of water is boiling on a stove its temperature remains steady although heat is still being supplied.

If we stand about in wet clothes or a wet bathing costume our body becomes chilled as the water evaporates.

Simple butter or milk coolers make use of evaporation from porous material.

Refrigerators. Wet and Dry bulb thermometers.

Water is efficient as a fire fighter. (The high specific heat and latent heat quickly enables the water to cool the burning material below its flash point.)

The fall of temperature in the atmosphere by night is checked at the dew point due to the release of latent heat. This reduces the risk of frost in moist conditions.

Practical Work

(1) Class allows water to come to the boil and note that when the boiling point is reached the water does not become any hotter although heat from the Bunsen is still being absorbed by the water.

(2) Class measures the time needed to boil about 100 gm of water in a can and then notes the time needed to evaporate half the water. A rough value of the latent heat of evaporation can be calculated.

(3) Class puts 300 gm of water in a beaker and takes its temperature. Steam is then allowed to bubble into the water from a boiling flask with a bent delivery tube until the temperature is about 70° C. The amount of steam condensed can be found with a measuring cylinder (about 30 ml). The latent heat can be calculated.

(4) A more accurate value of the latent heat of steam can be found using an electric kettle and a kilowatt-hour meter. The kettle should be well lagged and about a pound of water should be boiled away.

(5) Class drops about 50 gm of ice which has been wiped dry into 500 gm of water which is a few degrees above room temperature. When all the ice has melted the final temperature is taken. The weight of ice used can be found by weighing or by measuring the volume increase. The latent heat of ice may be calculated.

(6) Class to find the effect of wetting their fingers with water and then with methylated spirits.

(7) Class to place aluminium milk tops containing ether on a few drops of water on the bench. The water will freeze when air is blown on the ether using a straw. (WARNING: Ether vapour is very inflammable. *All Bunsens, etc., in the laboratory should be turned out.*)

(8) A very effective demonstration can be performed using ether in a beaker and blowing air through it by means of a pump. Temperatures of $-20°$ C. can be obtained and the whole beaker coated in frost.

Formal Syllabus

In order to change the state of a substance from a solid to a liquid or a liquid to a gas we have to supply heat. This heat does not raise the temperature of the material. The heat used in this way is called *latent heat*. This heat is released again when the substance solidifies or condenses.

The value of the *latent heat* of a material is usually stated as *the amount of heat needed, in calories or British thermal units, to change the state of 1 gm or 1 lb of the material.*

The statement that

the latent heat of steam $=$ 536 calories per gramme

means that it takes 536 calories of heat to change 1 gm of water at 100° C into steam at 100° C.

Latent heat effects are used considerably in refrigeration.

5. How Heat Travels

Points of Approach and Applications

Soldering irons, cooking vessels. Table mats, knobs and handles, lagging of pipes, etc.

Hot water systems.

Convector heaters—ventilation and draughts.

The vacuum flask, gas and electric radiators.

The cooling of car engines. The car safety lamp. Light and dark soils.

Practical Work

(1) Heat equal rods of different metals, the unheated ends being waxed.

(2) Heat water and mercury at their surfaces in hard glass test-tubes and note in any convenient way the rate of rise of temperature of the bottom of the liquids.

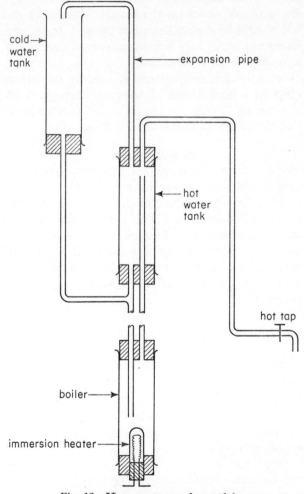

Fig. 12 Hot water supply model

(3) Heat with a small flame a beaker of water containing fine aluminium powder (add detergent to wet it).

(4) Set up a suitable glass tubing model of a hot-water heating and/or supply system and demonstrate its working (see Fig. 12).

(5) Demonstrate the differing densities of hot and cold fluids.

(6) Compare the transfer of heat from a Bunsen burner by convection and radiation by holding the hand above and to the side of the flame.

(7) Compare the absorption and reflection of radiant energy by dull black and shiny surfaces respectively.

(8) Compare the radiation of thermal energy from dull black and shiny surfaces respectively using any suitable type of differential radiator, e.g. Leslie's cube—or an electric lamp bulb painted longitudinally half black and half silver (see Fig. 13).

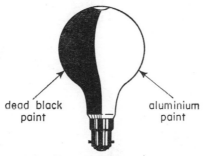

dead black   aluminium
paint   paint

Fig. 13 Differential radiator (a useful substitute for Leslie's cube)

(9) Compare the heat insulating properties of a proper vacuum flask, one with a broken seal, and an ordinary, but insulated, flask by putting the same volume of boiling water in each and noting the rates of cooling.

(10) Set up and demonstrate any convenient model designed to give general ideas of molecular motion.

See also *Science Teaching Techniques X* (John Murray) for further experiments in this section.

Formal Syllabus

Heat may travel by *conduction* in solids, by *convection* in fluids, and by *radiation* through space. Good and bad heat conductors.

77

Fluids, except mercury, are poor conductors of heat. The mechanics of convection. The sun is the principal source of thermal radiation with no apparent medium needed. The absorption, reflection and emission of radiant energy. The idea of heat as the movement of molecules.

6. Turning Heat into Mechanical Energy

Points of Approach and Applications

Model steam and internal combustion engines, car and motor cycle engines, steam engines and steam turbines, jet and turbo-jet engines.

Practical Work

Some of the working models listed below may be demonstrated, some may be worked and examined by individuals or small groups, some may be made at home or in the school workshop by interested individuals.

(1) *Hero's Steam Turbine* (see Fig. 14).

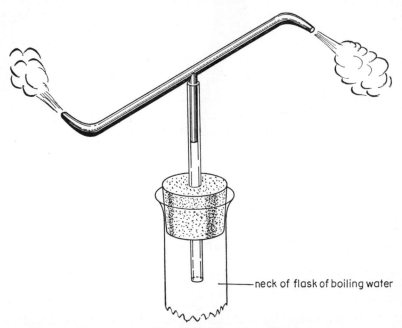

neck of flask of boiling water

Fig. 14 Working model to show principle of Hero's steam turbine

78

(2) *Hero's Machine for Opening Temple Doors* (see Fig. 15). In Hero's time slave labour was cheap and abundant and it was not fashionable for intellectuals to be interested in manual labour. This probably accounts for the fact that these principles were not put to practical use. Steam as a source of energy was not developed until the end of the seventeenth century.

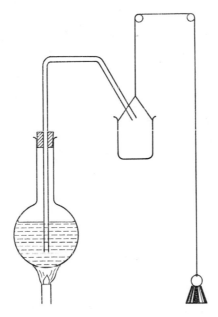

Fig. 15 Hero's engine for opening temple doors

(3) *Savery's Mine Pump* (see Fig. 16). This was developed at the end of the seventeenth century when an increasing demand for minerals was met by the sinking of deeper mine shafts. This, together with the increasing cost of labour, required more efficient pumping methods.

1. Open A and C.
2. Open D and B. Close A and C (wait until cylinder fills with water).
3. Close B. Open A and C. Close D (when water has been forced out, repeat from 2).

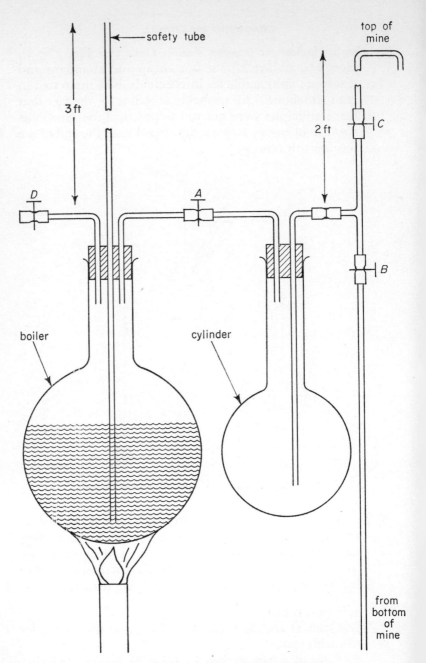

Fig. 16 Model of Savery's mine pump

(4) *Atmospheric Beam Engine* (see Fig. 17).

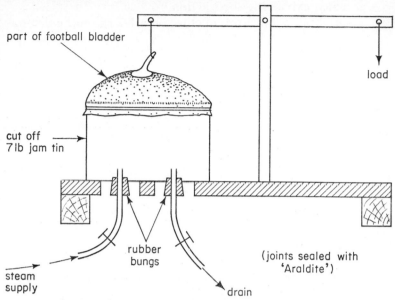

part of football bladder

load

cut off
7 lb jam tin

rubber
bungs

(joints sealed with
'Araldite')

steam
supply

drain

Fig. 17 Demonstration model of atmospheric beam engine

(5) *Pressure Steam Engines* These developed as materials for boilers and cylinders became more reliable.

The 'toy' steam engine and the slide valve engine are examples (see Figs. 18*a* and *b*) and models will

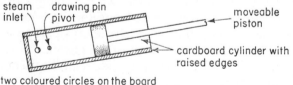

steam   drawing pin
inlet \   / pivot

moveable
piston

cardboard cylinder with
raised edges

two coloured circles on the board
placed to indicate steam inlet and exhaust

Fig. 18a Board model to demonstrate a toy steam engine

probably be obtainable from the class. The blackboard demonstration material illustrated will help to explain their action.

(6) *The Internal Combustion Engine* Several films provide excellent diagrams of the working of the various types of this engine.

81

The following demonstrations will be found useful when explaining their action.

(a) Spill a few drops of ether on a board on the demonstration bench. *Replace the stopper and remove the bottle to a safe distance.*

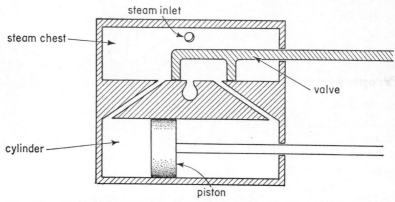

Fig. *18b*   Cardboard model to demonstrate double acting steam engine

Strike a match and put it near the bench surface. The ether vapour will explode with a sheet of flame.

This emphasises the fact that it is the vapour and not the liquid which burns.

(b) The model 'cylinder' helps the class to understand the action of a reciprocating type of engine.

(7) *Steam Turbine*   This can be shown in principle by a simple model. It can be pointed out that the low efficiency of the reciprocating engine is due in part to the wasteful back and fro movement of the piston.

(8) *Jet and Turbo-Jet*   The principle can be demonstrated using a paraffin blow lamp.

The lamp should be emptied and then 'pumped up'. The jet of air can be shown to have little thrust.

The construction of the lamp can be shown and the arrangement for preheating the fuel pointed out.

If the lamp is now lit the reaction is sufficient to drive a small metal propeller.

Fundamental Theory

The idea may be suggested that Western Civilisation and the

82

comforts of living which we enjoy are only possible because of the replacement of wind and water power by heat engines.

The individual models will create interest but emphasis should be laid on the following points:

(*a*) Development occurred when social or economic conditions demanded it.

(*b*) Development was directed towards increased efficiency.

(*c*) Development depended on the availability of materials to actually construct the engines.

Properties of Fluids

1. WATER VAPOUR IN THE ATMOSPHERE

This work overlaps the geography syllabus and co-operation is necessary between the two departments. It is suggested that climatology, weather recording, synoptic charts, frontal systems, etc., belong to the domain of geography.

Points of Approach and Applications

Clothes will dry on a washing line and water will evaporate from a saucer. This water must move into the air.

Water drops form on an ice-cream carton and on a cold window pane. This water must have come from the air.

The formation of dew, fog, cloud and rain are extensions of these ideas. At lower temperatures frost and snow are produced.

High humidity reduces the excretion of moisture by the lungs and causes us to feel lethargic.

Humidity conditions are important in industry particularly in textile factories. Air conditioning can control both temperature and humidity.

Practical Work

(1) Class observes the formation of water droplets on the outside of beakers containing ice cubes.

(2) Class cools water in test-tubes by adding small amounts of ice. An approximate value for the dew point can be obtained by noting the temperature at which the test-tube mists over.

(3) The effect of a decrease of pressure can be shown by letting the class blow hard into flasks provided with tight-fitting corks, rubber tubes and clips. The clips

are then closed and the flasks allowed a few minutes to cool. When the clips are opened the decrease in pressure will cool the air sufficiently to produce condensation.

(4) A demonstration of the same effect can be done with a bell jar on a vacuum plate. Mist can be produced as the air pressure is reduced. On a very dry day the air can be moistened by putting a piece of wet filter paper in the jar. A trace of smoke will show the effect of condensation nucleii.

(5) Changes of pressure with height can be shown using a large earthenware cider jar. A piece of capillary tube is bent at right angles and sealed in the neck so that part of the tube is horizontal. A mercury pellet in the tube will show the expansion of the air as the jar is raised only a few feet.

A large vacuum flask can be used to show the same effect.

(6) The principle of a wet bulb thermometer can be shown if the bulb of a thermometer is moistened with water slightly warmer than the air in the laboratory. The reading will soon drop below the temperature of the air.

(7) Other types of hygrometers using natural fibres can be shown.

Formal Syllabus

Evidence that there is water vapour in the atmosphere and that the amount that can be held invisibly depends only on the temperature.

The different methods by which air can be cooled and the conditions which lead to the formation of cloud, mist, dew, frost, etc.

2. THE SURFACE SKIN OF LIQUIDS

Points of Approach and Applications

Use of the surface film by pond creatures.

Treatment of stagnant water. The behaviour of rain on umbrellas, tents and porous raincoats.

Raindrops and dewdrops. The use of detergents—wetting agents. Water repellents—silicones.

The removal of oil or grease stains.

The use of absorbent materials—wicks, towels, etc.

Drip-dry materials, pleated skirts.

Practical Work

(1) Carefully place a needle, razor blade, a cover slip or a half-inch square of wire gauze on the surface of water.

(2) Float a small waxed wire gauze sieve and add a small load. With care such a sieve can also be made to hold water.

(3) Gently spray a jet of water on to a piece of smoked paper.

(4) Carefully drop a small quantity of any thick oil from a dropping funnel into a mixture of water and industrial methylated spirits of the same density as the oil. This can be effectively projected.

(5) Float two matches one inch apart and parallel and touch the water between them with a pointed piece of soap, a glass rod dipped in meths. or a hot wire.

(6) Adjust the water supply to a tap so that the water falls slowly in drops. Observe the effect of allowing alcohol to run down the outside of the tap.

(7) Stir a little soot or sulphur in water. Observe the effect of adding a few drops of detergent solution.

(8) Add a little olive oil to a test-tube half filled with water and shake well. After observing the separation add a drop of detergent and shake again.

(9) Fill the bottom of a shallow dish with coloured water and add a few drops of meths. to the middle of the water surface.

(10) Draw out a number of capillary tubes of different diameters and dip in ink.

(11) Obtain several grades of sand by sifting through a nest of sieves. Fill a 2-ft length of 1-in glass tube with each grade of sand, having plugged the bottom of each tube with cotton wool and stand in a shallow trough of water.

(12) Stuff some gabardine into the bowl of a thistle funnel and add water. It holds. Now add a little detergent and note the effect.

(13) Use a silicone spray on a square of blotting paper and compare its absorptive properties with those of an untreated square.

Note: Some detergents are made to lower tension at solid-liquid surfaces but not at air-liquid surfaces hence experimental results may be better with some detergents than with others.

Formal Syllabus

The existence of surface tension. The strength of surface tension. Drop formation. Reducing surface tension. The surface tension of liquids other than water. Capillarity. The emulsification of grease by detergents.

3. AIR PRESSURE

Points of Approach and Applications

The pressure of the wind and the damage that it can do indicates that the air has 'weight'. Other effects are:

Working of vacuum cleaners, suction dredgers, milking machines, etc., drinking of milk through a straw, suction pads on toy arrows, difficulty in breathing at great heights, a baby's first breath, the use of aneroid barometers as altimeters, vacuum assisted brakes, breathing using an aqualung, the use of the 'iron lung'.

Practical Work

(1) Let class feel the pressure from a powerful fan. (If air can push things it must have weight.)

(2) As a demonstration exhaust a flask with steam and weigh empty and then full. Estimate the number of flasks which could be stacked in the laboratory and hence the weight of the air in the laboratory.

(3) Demonstrate the crushing can experiment using, if possible, a large square 'Tate and Lyle' syrup tin.

(4) Demonstrate difficulty of removing a bell jar from a vacuum plate.

(5) Prepare test-tubes with tight corks and about 8 inches of glass tube. Using a small quantity of water let children exhaust the tubes by boiling them and then dipping the ends under the surface of water in a beaker. Discuss why water is forced in.

(6) Seal the top of a milk bottle with a cork containing a glass tube and let a child try to suck out the milk.

(7) Fill a tall jar with water and cover with a sheet of paper or glass. Invert the jar. How high a water column will the pressure support?

(8) Demonstrate the principle of the mercury barometer.

(9) Show the working of an aneroid barometer and an altimeter.

Formal Syllabus

The air is a real substance and has weight. We live at the bottom of an ocean of air and under a very great pressure. We do not notice this pressure because our bodies have adapted themselves to it.

This pressure can be measured by a barometer, mercury or aneroid.

The pressure is normally 14-15 lbs on a square inch at sea level.

4. PRESSURE IN FLUIDS

Points of Approach and Applications

Leaking containers and pipes. Water flows uphill in pipes.
Fountains, water towers and stand pipes.
Traps in sinks, drains and toilets. Canal locks.
Hydraulic brakes, jacks, car lifts and presses.
Atomisers. The lifting effect of an air stream on an aerofoil.
Streamlining

Practical Work

(1) Place a hand in a plastic bag and immerse in water.

(2) Cover a thistle funnel head with thin rubber and tie tightly (see Fig. 19). Connect to a suitable pressure gauge. Immerse the funnel head in a large vessel of water to different depths and also point it in different directions at the same depth.

(3) Repeat the above experiment with similar beakers of water, alcohol and mercury, immersing the funnel head to the same depth in each.

(4) Repeat also with vessels of different shapes and sizes containing water to the same level. Compare the pressure at the bottom of each.

(5) Drill a $\frac{1}{16}$-in hole in the centre of the base of a syrup tin.

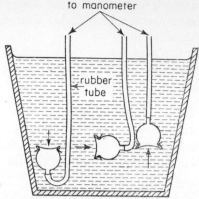

Fig. 19 Pressure in a fluid is the same in all directions at the same depth

Drill four similar holes in the side of the tin at opposite ends of two diameters at right angles and as near the base as possible. Support the tin over five beakers and fill it with water. The height of water in all the beakers should be approximately equal.

(6) Join two burettes or suitable lengths of glass tubing with a length of flexible tubing. Support them in an upright position and pour in water. Notice the levels. Raise and lower one of the tubes and observe the effect on the levels. Replace one tube by a large funnel or an inverted bell jar and repeat.

(7) Set up a simple model water works by joining a yard or so of flexible tubing to an aspirator supported about 3 ft above the bench level. Connect a glass tap or a glass jet and a spring clip to the other end of the tubing. Show the effect of height on the water pressure at the tap. If the jet is pointed upward the height of the resulting fountain can be observed. For greater reality use a small electrically driven water pump and pump water from the sink (well) to the aspirator (water tower).

(8) Set up a Cartesian diver using a small test-tube in a large bottle or jar. For individual construction a smaller floater may be used such as a rubber or plastic teat suitably weighted or a small glass bulb with a short stem. In this case a medicine bottle makes a convenient container. Place enough water in the 'diver' to make it

88

just buoyant, invert it and carefully place it in the bottle of water. Some dexterity may be needed here. Insert a cork, or in the case of a wide mouthed jar, tie a piece of sheet rubber on the end. Pressure on the cork or rubber will cause the diver to sink. With careful adjustment the diver in a medicine bottle can be actuated by pressure on the flat sides of the bottle.

(9) Construct a model hydraulic press or lift by securely joining about 6 ft of flexible tubing to a football bladder or rubber hot water bottle. Connect a funnel to the other end of the tubing. Place a piece of board on the bladder or bottle. Place some weights or heavy objects on the board. Pour water down the funnel, allowing air bubbles to escape, until the water level can be seen. Note the effect of raising the funnel.

On a larger scale a motor car inner tube with the valve removed could be used, a pupil standing on a drawing board on the tube serving as the weight.

(10) Fill a medicine bottle with water. Carefully insert a cork, leaving as small an air bubble as possible. Hold the bottle over a sink, grasping the neck firmly in a duster and strike the cork a sharp blow with the fist. The result is not always certain but the bottle usually breaks or at least cracks with the transmitted pressure.

(11) Suspend two ping pong balls 2 or 3 in apart by threads about a yard long. Blow steadily between the balls.

(12) The working of an atomiser can be shown thus. Support a 6-in glass tube upright in a beaker of water. Hold a similar tube at right angles to the first so that its end

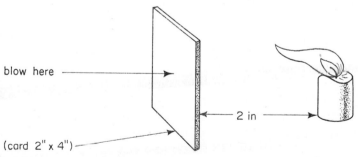

Fig. 20a Pressure in fluids, experiment 13

89

butts against the edge of the upright tube. Blow through the horizontal tube adjusting its height until the water rises in the vertical tube.

(13) Hold a piece of card upright in front of a lighted candle (Fig. 20a). Blow hard against the card. The flame is drawn back towards the card by the turbulence of the air stream. Replace the card by a cylindrical bottle and repeat. (Fig 20b). The flame moves away from the bottle. This is due to the streamlining effect of the bottle.

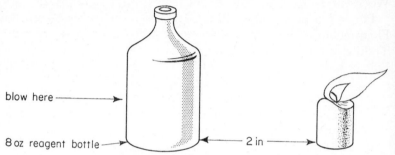

blow here ⟶

8 oz reagent bottle ⟶   ⟵ 2 in ⟶

Fig. 20b   Pressure in fluids, experiment 13: the effect of streamlining

(14) Take a strip of paper about 8 in × 2 in. Form it into the shape of an aerofoil by gumming two short edges together. Support it by allowing the curved edge to rest over a pencil held horizontally. Blow a stream of air so that it impinges on the leading edge.

(15) The variation in fluid pressure can be demonstrated with a Bernouilli tube. This consists of a horizontal glass tube of a wide bore with a constriction near the centre and with a small side tube in each section for the attachment of manometer tubes. It can be used for either water or air streams.

Formal Syllabus

Fluids exert pressure.

The pressure on any point in a fluid:

(a) depends on the depth,

(b) is the same in all directions at the same depth,

(c) depends on the density of the fluid,

(d) is independent of the shape and size of the containing vessel.

Liquids always seek their own level.

Liquids are practically incompressible and therefore transmit pressure.

When a fluid is moving the pressure is less where the speed of the fluid is high and greater where the speed is low.

5. DENSITY AND FLOTATION

Points of Approach and Applications
What is meant by iron being 'heavier' than wood?

Wood floats in water, iron sinks, but an iron ship floats; the Plimsoll Line, submarines.

Floating of a human being and underwater swimming.

Testing of battery acid and of milk.

Balloons.

Practical Work
(1) The class can be provided with rectangular blocks of various woods (including balsa) and metals cut to 'easy' sizes. Using these and a lever balance the class can calculate the densities of the various materials.

(2) Similarly the densities of various liquids may be found using graduated cylinders and lever balances. The density of mercury can be measured by the teacher.

(3) Class floats thin test-tubes (empty cigar cases can be used instead of test-tubes) upright in water using sand or lead shot. The depth to which they sink can be marked using a strip of paper inside the tube. The tube can then be tried in brine and in methylated spirits.

(4) Demonstration. Float a bowl on the surface of water in a glass trough previously filled to the brim. Catch the overflow and weigh the water. Compare with the weight of the bowl.

(5) Demonstration. Repeat the previous experiment but in place of the bowl use a brick suspended from a spring balance and compare the loss of weight with the weight of the overflow.

(6) Class makes and floats a small Plasticine 'boat'. The same piece of Plasticine rolled into a ball will sink.

(7) Weighted sticks, 1 cm square, about 20 cm long and of known weight can be used as simple hydrometers. The

class should calculate the density of various liquids by measuring the depth to which the sticks sink (A commercial flotation hydrometer should also be shown.)

(8) The working of a Cartesian diver forms a useful discussion point at this stage (see section 4 experiment 8).

(9) The variation in the densities of gases may be demonstrated. A 400 ml beaker is placed on the pan of a chemical balance and weights added to obtain equilibrium. With the balance arm raised the air in the beaker is displaced by CO_2 prepared by adding vinegar to washing soda.

Formal Syllabus

The difference between weight and density.
Variation in density among different solids and liquids.
Flotation.
Simple hydrometers.
Variation in density of gases.

Force, Energy and Work

1. FORCES AND THEIR EFFECTS

Points of Approach and Applications

The use of spring balances for weighing and measuring force.
Other types of weighing machines—lever balance, etc.
Using friction—brakes, rubber tyres, driving belts, clutch linings.
Minimising friction—lubrication, ball and roller bearings.
The see-saw and other examples of levers.
Walking and cycling—the art of balancing, starting and stopping. Inertial effects.
Stability and design.

Practical Work

(1) Suspend a spiral spring from a clamp stand. If necessary, add a suitable weight to extend the coils of the spring; then, continue to load the spring, measuring the extension each time. Find the extension for unit load and show how the spring may be used as a force or weight measurer.

(2) Devise methods of finding if other kinds of springs behave in the same way.

(3) Allow a ½-in diameter ball bearing to run down a short ramp on to a smooth horizontal surface (side bench or floor). Time it on the flat over measured distances. Notice the tendency for the velocity to decrease as the run becomes longer.

Also, time a ball bearing down a suitable slope and find acceleration. By experiment, find a slope which will give a displacement of 1 foot in 1 second, 4 feet in 2 seconds, etc., thus making the arithmetic easier.

For the slope, use a length of angle iron or a grooved plank at least 9 ft long.

(4) Demonstrate the starting, stopping and changing of motion with a bicycle or small trolley.

(Low friction trolleys and ticker tape electric timers are now available for work covered by experiments 3 and 4.)

(5) By means of a spring balance pull a heavy box on the floor, on the bench top and along a sheet of glass, noting the force needed in each case. Repeat with the box supported on rollers (round pencils) or on a small trolley.

(6) Make a model ball race with two syrup tins and a number of marbles of uniform size. Place the marbles in the groove of the first tin which stands upright on the bench and invert the second tin on to the marbles.

(7) Use half-metre rules, drilled at the 5, 25, and 45 cm marks to investigate turning effects. Pivots can be made by pushing a 1½-in wire nail into a cork and cutting off the head. The cork can then be held in a clamp. For this experiment the rule is pivoted at the 25 cm hole. Weights can be hung on cotton loops.

(There is also some advantage in sometimes using a 6-ft moments bar, clearly marked, and larger weights.)

(8) Pivot the half-metre rule at the 5 cm hole and balance the rest of the rule by adding weights to the short arm. Work out the weight of the rule and verify by actual weighing.

(9) Find the centre of gravity of various cardboard or plywood

93

laminae by suspending freely from several points in turn and dropping a vertical by means of a plumb line.

(10) Investigate stability by fixing a plumb line at the centre of gravity of one face of a rectangular solid (wood or cardboard box), standing it on another face and tilting it. Measure the angle of tilt in each case.

(11) Set up various balancing tricks as described in many popular science books, etc.

Formal Syllabus

Pushes, pulls, the tension in a string, friction and gravity are examples of different kinds of forces.

Forces change the shape or size of an object—the extension of a spring is proportional to the force producing it (within limits) and can be used to measure force.

Forces start and keep an object moving, stop or change its motion (in speed or direction) or have a tendency to produce these effects. Inertia.

Forces balance each other to keep an object stationary. The centre of gravity as a balancing point. The stability of an object depends on the height of its centre of gravity and the size of its base. Forces may produce turning in an object whose general movement is limited. Moments.

2. MAKING WORK EASIER

Points of Approach and Applications

The lever, single and double levers as tools.

Pulleys in simple systems, block and tackle.

The bicycle, wringer, brace and bit, hand-drill gear and sprocket wheels.

The inclined plane, loading ramp, etc. The screw jack.

Practical Work

(1) Class lifts weights and calculate the work done. Actual weights may be used or they may lift themselves on to stools or walk upstairs.

(2) Class examines tools to find position of fulcrum, effort and load.

(3) Set up various pulley systems and find the mechanical advantage, velocity ratio and efficiency in each case.

A spring balance may be used to measure the effort. Brighter pupils could also find the efficiency for gradually increasing loads.

(4) Using an adjustable inclined plane and a small roller or trolley, work out the efficiency for various angles of tilt. Other kinds of machine may also be used as available.

(5) Gears from surplus stores or Meccano parts may be used to demonstrate the use of gears and sprocket wheels.

(6) Use a bicycle to study various aspects of machines.

(7) Measure the weight of several pupils and time them running up a flight of stairs in turn. Work out their rate of working in horse-power.

(8) Find the horse-power of a small electric motor by gearing it down, making it lift a suitable weight through a measured height and finding the time taken.

Formal Syllabus

Work is measured by the product of a force and the distance moved in the direction of the force.

Work may be done *by* forces—lifting weights, overcoming friction—or *against* forces—simple machines.

Machines may (*a*) multiply force, (*b*) multiply speed, (*c*) change the direction of a force or (*d*) transfer energy.

The *mechanical advantage* of a machine is the number of times it *actually* makes work easier: load/effort.

The *velocity ratio* of a machine is the number of times it *ought* to make work easier: effort distance/load distance.

The *efficiency* of a machine is the amount of work got out of it compared with that put in: work done on load/work done by effort.

Power is the rate of doing work: ft lbf per sec.

One *horse power* is a rate of 550 ft lbf/sec.

Mechanical energy—potential and kinetic.

3. Energy and its Transformations

In whatever way physics may be subdivided, it remains the study of energy and it is essential that our pupils be constantly reminded of this. They should be made aware of the different forms of energy and the extreme usefulness to man of the many transformations from one form to another. Every effort should

95

be made to illustrate experimentally the interchangeability of the various forms of energy. This may be done either by appropriate insertions in the various sections of the syllabus or, alternatively, in one series of connected lessons. Such a series of lessons could form a revision course of this important concept.

Many of the experiments described in this syllabus can be used as illustrations of energy transformations. Some typical examples are suggested briefly below.

Practical Work

(1) *Heat energy to kinetic energy*

Heat a large beaker of water containing fine aluminium powder and note the convection currents.

(2) *Heat energy to potential energy to kinetic energy*

Boil water in a flask fitted with a suitable outlet and allow the steam to impinge on the blades of a simple rotor.

(3) *Heat energy to light energy*

Strongly heat an iron nut, a piece of chalk or incandescent gas mantle in a roaring Bunsen flame.

(4) *Heat energy to electrical energy*

Heat a simple thermocouple connected to a milliammeter.

(5) *Light energy to electrical energy*

Allow light to fall on a photo-electric cell joined to a suitable milliammeter.

(6) *Electrical energy to heat energy and light energy*

Pass an electric current through a length of resistance wire so that it becomes red hot.

(7) *Electrical energy to kinetic energy*

Supply current to an electromagnet and let it affect a compass needle. By breaking the circuit at the appropriate moment the needle may be made to spin. It is, perhaps, more realistic to supply current to a small electric motor and to use the kinetic energy thus made available to drive a model.

(8) *Electrical energy to sound energy*

Supply a suitable current to an electric bell or a low-voltage a.c. to a loudspeaker.

(9) *Potential energy to kinetic energy*

Let a ball bearing run down a length of curtain rail containing an 8-in circular loop.

Discuss the simple pendulum.

(10) *Potential energy to kinetic energy to electrical energy*

Drive a small electric generator by means of a water wheel driven from the cold water tap.

(11) *Radiant energy to kinetic energy*

Observe the effect of light on a Crooke's radiometer.

(12) *Chemical energy to electrical energy*

Set up any simple voltaic cell.

(13) *Electrical energy to chemical energy*

This may be shown by any of the usual electrolysis or electro-plating experiments.

(14) The previous two examples may be combined in the simple lead plate accumulator experiment.

(15) *Chemical energy to light energy*

Dissolve a pinch of 'Luminol' in a litre of water, add a few ml of sodium hydroxide and of hydrogen peroxide. Add to this 100 ml of a filtered extract of bleaching powder (sodium hypochlorite). A brilliant luminescence is seen. ('Luminol' is ortho-amino-phthalic cyclic hydrazide and is obtainable from B.D.H.)

(16) *A multiple transformation*

Taking suitable precautions, fire a pellet from an air gun into a block of balsa wood suspended as shown (see Fig. 21).

The chemical energy stored in our muscles is turned into potential energy in the spring of the gun. This is transformed into kinetic energy in the slug. Some of this appears as heat energy scorching the wood but most is transferred to the block first as kinetic and finally as potential energy as the block reaches the top of its swing. The amount of this energy can be estimated by measuring the height to which the block rises.

Many more examples will doubtless suggest themselves to the reader and it will soon be evident that energy permeates all our science and not only the physics section.

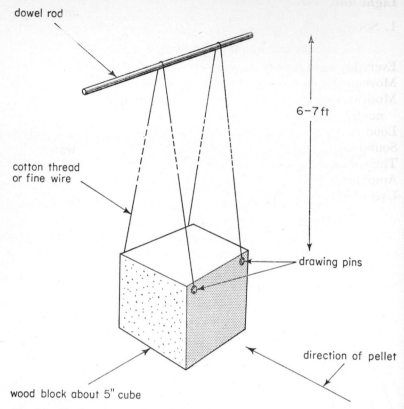

dowel rod

6-7 ft

cotton thread
or fine wire

drawing pins

direction of pellet

wood block about 5" cube

Fig. 21   To show suspension of the balsa wood block in the energy conversion experiment

In our chemistry we must look out for the thermal energy (and sometimes light also) that results from exothermal chemical reactions and also the mechanical energy that results from explosions.

In biology we must constantly stress the importance of the energy that all animals derive from their food and the fact that the chemical energy in the food has reached the earth as radiant energy from the sun and been stored by the process of photosynthesis in plant leaves. This stored chemical energy is also used as a source of heat in the form of coal and oil.

Light and Sound

1. SOUND

Points of Approach and Applications

Everyday sounds, their origin—movement.
Movement takes time to travel—thunder, echoes.
Musical instruments and their sounds. High notes and low notes.
Loud notes and soft notes.
Sound ranging. Echo sounding.
The control of reverberation in rooms. Lessening noise.
Amplification of sounds by resonators.
Uses of ultrasonic vibrations.

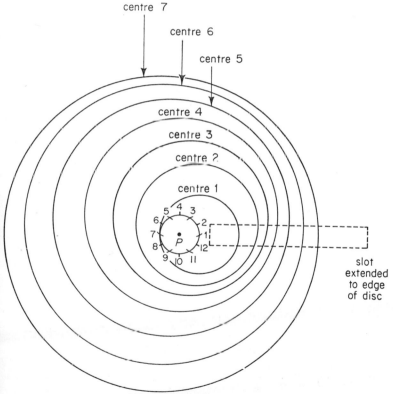

Fig. 22 Crova's disc (incomplete) showing construction

99

Practical Work

(1) Investigate the production and behaviour of waves in a simple type of ripple tank. Pupils could do this in a limited way by using a trough of water.

(2) Show progressive and stationary waves by means of a length of rope (15–20 ft) fastened at one end and waggled at the other.

(3) A clearer idea of the motion of the layers of air during the propagation of sound waves may be obtained by constructing Crova's disc (see Fig. 22). Draw a circle

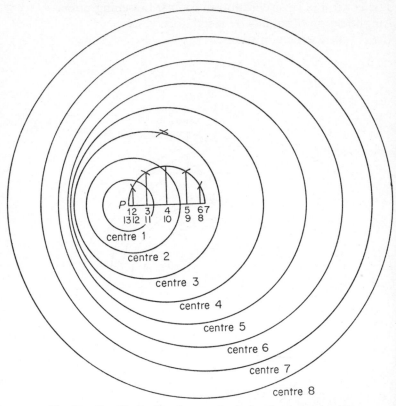

Fig. 23 Cheshire's disc (incomplete) showing construction

of 5 mm radius in the middle of a large sheet of card about 12 in square. Mark off twelve equidistant points on the circumference of this circle and from these points,

100

taken as centres in regular succession, draw circles with radii increasing successively by, say, 5 mm. The card may be cut out around the final circle. Spin the card and view as a whole or, preferably, through a narrow slot in a fixed card placed in front to render more evident the significant parts of the motion.

Cheshire's disc (Fig. 23) illustrates standing waves and can be constructed as follows. Draw a semicircle on a 2-cm diameter and divide it into six or eight equal parts. Drop perpendiculars from the dividing points to the diameter thus dividing the latter unequally. Taking the dividing points of the diameter as centres in succession, and starting with a radius of 5 mm, describe circles increasing the radius by 6 or 7 mm each time. The centres travel backwards and forwards across the diameter until the diagram is big enough. Cut out the card and view as Crova's disc.

(4) Place four pennies touching each other on the bench top. Hold down the first three with the first three fingers respectively. Sharply slide a fifth coin against the first penny and note the movement of the fourth.

(5) Clamp a half-metre rule at one end, set it vibrating and listen to the note by putting an ear to the bench. Repeat with a shorter length vibrating.

(6) Touch a watch, lying on the bench, with a length of dowel rod and listen at the other end to the tick. Try also gripping the free end of the rod with the teeth.

(7) Touch the surface of water or a glass vessel with the vibrating end of a tuning fork.

(8) If a good vacuum pump is available show that the sound of an electric bell inside a bell jar dies away when the jar is exhausted of air.

(9) Sound a simple whistle then attach to a rubber tube from the gas point and sound it again by gas pressure. Notice the difference in pitch.

(10) The speed of sound in air can be determined by using a starting pistol and a stop-watch and timing the sound over a large measured distance in both directions. If a suitable pistol is not available use two large white boards clapped together.

(11) Obtain two umbrellas and wet the outsides of both with a watering can. Stand them with open sides facing, some distance apart on the bench. Suspend a watch at the focus of one umbrella and place the ear at the focus of the other one. The ticking of the watch should be heard.

(12) A model stethoscope can be constructed from glass and rubber tubing, a glass or metal Y-piece and a thistle funnel head.

(13) Connect two funnels by a long length of rubber or plastic tubing and use as a speaking tube.

(14) Make a string or wire telephone using cocoa or syrup tins.

(15) Allow a piece of card to touch a toothed wheel as it revolves at different speeds.

(16) Make various 'musical' instruments:

    (a) Stick pins in a board to different depths for a dulcimer.

    (b) Add water to medicine bottles to different heights. Either blow across the top of the bottles or hang them up and tap with a rod.

    (c) Make a milk straw reed pipe by flattening one end of a straw for about half an inch, cut off the corners, place the whole end of the straw in the mouth and blow. Cut pieces off the straw to raise the pitch of the note.

A tape recorder and an oscilloscope, if available, are very useful adjuncts to the teaching of this topic.

Formal Syllabus

Vibrating objects produce waves in the air around them. Sound results from our response to these waves.

The nature of the vibrations reaching us enables us to identify sounds as to their loudness, pitch and quality.

Vibrations can travel through solids and liquids as well as gases, but they cannot travel through a vacuum. The speed of vibrations through air is affected by various factors.

Vibrations can be reflected causing echoes.

Irregular vibrations produce noise: regular vibrations, such as those produced by musical instruments, give rise to pleasing sounds.

Pitch depends on frequency of vibrations. Resonance. The human ear responds to a limited range of frequencies. Ultrasonic vibrations.

2. LIGHT AND SHADOWS, BI-FOCAL VISION

Points of Approach and Applications

Pupils will be familiar with the shadows cast by objects in sunlight and artificial light. They will have some knowledge of eclipses.

Shadows are often used for effect in stage productions and on television.

Shadowless lighting is used in factories and on roads to help avoid accidents.

A single eye is used in rifle shooting and when threading a needle.

Three-dimensional viewers use two eyes in order to get the effect of depth.

A small baby has very poor judgement of distance mainly due to the lack of eye control.

Predatory animals and birds usually have bi-focal vision.

Range finders usually have some form of double image mechanism.

Practical Work

(1) Shadows from large and small light sources can be demonstrated. The source can be a clear 'mains' bulb or a car headlamp bulb. The filament can form the small source and a tissue paper cover on the bulb will form the large source. Blackout is necessary for good effect.

(2) A film strip projector, a tennis ball, and a golf ball can be used to show eclipses and phases of the moon. (On this scale the sun is a ball 25 ft in diameter and about half a mile away.)

(3) If light from a powerful source is allowed to fall on a sheet of white paper diffuse reflection from its surface can be shown.

(4) The need for bi-focal vision to estimate short distances can be shown by using first two eyes and then one to
(a) put a compass point in a milk straw in a direction *at right angles to the line of sight,*

(*b*) knock a cork off the end of a ruler using the same idea as above,

(*c*) touch a retort stand by bringing a finger across from the right or the left.

(5) A clear electric lamp bulb is placed in a shoe box and stout brown paper put over the top. The bulb is lit and, in a blacked-out laboratory, holes are punctured in the paper using a compass point. Each hole throws an image of the filament on the ceiling.

(6) Simple pin-hole cameras can be made by the class using a hole in a book cover and a bright window as an object.

Formal Syllabus

Shadows from large and from small sources, eclipses, phases of the moon. The application of these ideas to room, street and factory lighting.

We see things because they reflect light, and this light enters our eyes.

We are able to judge the direction of an object because the light from it travels to our eye in a straight line.

We estimate the distance of an object using *bi-focal vision*.

3. REFLECTION FROM MIRRORS

Points of Approach and Applications

Domestic mirrors for personal use. Driving mirrors both plane and convex. Mirrors used at road junctions.

Simple periscopes.

Reflectors in electric torches and in car headlamps.

Make-up mirrors and shaving mirrors.

Large mirrors for concentrating the sun's heat.

Use of mirrors in large telescopes.

Practical Work

(1) Using ray boxes the class can note the difference in the reflection from white paper and from a mirror. Angles of incidence and reflection can be measured.

(2) Demonstration. A long mirror is placed on its long edge, on the bench facing the class. A retort stand is put about 18 in in front of the mirror so that its image can be seen by all the class. A second stand is moved behind the

mirror until the part of it seen over the mirror appears in line with the image of the first stand seen in the mirror, for all positions in the room. This can be done by instructing the class to raise their hands when they see it in line and to drop them when it is moved out.

(3) A similar experiment can be done with a candle or a miniature bulb in front of a sheet of polished glass. An unlit candle or bulb is put behind the glass and moved until it is coincident with the image seen in the glass. If the direct light of the candle or bulb is shielded from the class the room does not need to be blacked out.

(4) Class can find the position of the image of a pin by direct sighting using small mirrors and rulers.

(5) Class to experiment with multiple images using two small mirrors and a small bead as an object.

(6) Class to examine the effect of curved mirrors on a beam of light using ray boxes.

(7) Class to examine the images formed by curved mirrors.

Formal Syllabus

Regular reflection and the fact that the angle of incidence equals the angle of reflection.

The formation and position of the image formed in a flat mirror.

Simple ideas on the multiple images formed by two mirrors.

Effect of curved mirrors.

Scale drawing for the position and size of images in curved mirrors.

4. Refraction of Light and Total Internal Reflection

Points of Approach and Applications

Distortion seen through window glass, shimmering effects seen over a fire or a hot road, apparent bending of a spoon handle in water, the effect of a 'burning' glass.

The glitter of dewdrops and of diamonds or cut glass beads, the white appearance of foam, mirages over the desert or a hot road, form examples of internal reflection.

Practical Work

(1) Class works in pairs putting metal discs in the bottom of

105

evaporating dishes. One partner holds the dish under a tap, the other moves until he just loses sight of the disc below the edge of the bowl. As water is run in the disc again appears.

(2) Demonstration. A deep bowl with a lamp in the bottom is placed in the middle of the blacked out laboratory. The shadow of the edge of the bowl can be seen on the walls. As water is run into the bowl the edge of the shadow can be seen to move downwards.

(3) Using ray boxes (or demonstrating with a narrow beam of light from a film strip projector) the bending of a beam of light may be shown
  (a) through a glass block,
  (b) through water in a rectangular tank (the water should be tinted with ink or milk).

(4) By using glass blocks and ray boxes the geometrical relationship

$$\frac{\sin I}{\sin R}$$

can be obtained by construction.

(5) Using ray boxes the class can examine the track of a beam of light through a right-angled prism. (Total internal reflection is sure to occur in some cases.)

(6) Total internal reflection can be seen at the under surface of the water in a beaker held above eye level. A pencil put through the surface helps to show the effect.

(7) Total internal reflection can be demonstrated in a rectangular tank with tinted water. A mirror on the end of a stick is held in the water. A vertical beam of light is passed into the water and the reflected beam from the mirror allowed to strike the under surface of the water.

(8) The class can examine the appearance of an empty test-tube when partly under water.

(9) The use of two 45° prisms to form a periscope can be demonstrated.

(10) The effect of air at different densities may be shown using a lighted Bunsen burner to throw a shadow on a screen from a point source of light (car headlamp bulb).

The convection currents are easily seen. Blackout is an advantage.

(11) An artificial 'mirage' can be arranged in the laboratory as shown in the diagram (Fig. 24).

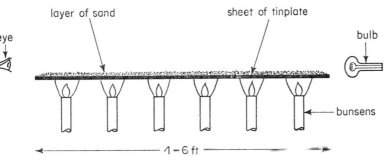

Fig. 24   Apparatus to show mirage effect in a laboratory

(12) A jet of water, a bent glass rod or a clear plastic coat hanger can be used to show 'ducting' of light.

Formal Syllabus

A beam of light changes direction as it crosses the boundary surface between two transparent media of differing densities.

The track of the light through a glass block and through a prism.

Total internal reflection.

The geometrical laws relating to refraction.

5. LENSES

Points of Approach and Applications

Magnifying glasses and burning glasses, the use of spectacles to correct eye defects.

The camera, the eye, the projector, the telescope and the microscope. Types of binoculars and their characteristics.

Practical Work

(1) The class should examine and handle convex and concave lenses.

(2) The class should use convex lenses to throw real images on a screen. The object can be a piece of Bunsen gauze illuminated from behind by a miniature bulb. A movable screen is an advantage. An optical bench is not essential

at this stage. The lenses can be held in the grip of a retort stand. The ideas of magnification, focusing, etc. should come by experience. Further experiments with lenses may be found in the specimen lessons.

(3) The track of light through a lens can be shown by a ray box and board.

(4) Scale drawing can be used to find the position of an image. The cause of virtual images will become apparent.

(5) The simple optical principles of the camera can be demonstrated and compared with the eye.

(6) In connection with the eye the following experiments can be done by the class:

    (*a*) *Focusing* Using *one* eye each pupil can look at his own finger held up at a distance of about ten inches. Distant objects seen beyond the finger will appear blurred. If the distant objects are now 'looked at' the finger will appear blurred.

    (*b*) *Use of spectacles* A short focus lens can be adjusted to throw a clear image of a lamp filament on a screen. The lamp is then moved until its image is blurred. The image can be made sharp again by placing a long focus convex or concave lens in front of the original lens.

    (*c*) *Adjustment to light intensity* The variation in the size of the pupil of the eye can be shown if the eyes are closed for a short period and then opened near a bright window.

    (Experiments to show blind spot, yellow spot, field of vision, etc., will be found in biology section.)

(7) The working of a filmstrip projector can be demonstrated showing the reflector, the condenser, the heat filter and the projection lens.

(8) The simple astronomical telescope can be demonstrated using two convex lenses of very different focal length.

(9) The magnifying glass and the compound microscope allow simple explanation. (Ray diagrams need not be attempted.)

(10) The meaning of 8×30, etc., can be demonstrated using a telescope with a series of cards to control the aperture.

(11) The process of photography can be demonstrated. A piece

of cardboard with a cut-out design covered in tissue paper is illuminated from behind. A box camera is used to photograph this using contact paper instead of film. (On a sunny day the view from the laboratory window can form a more interesting subject.)

This can be processed in a partly lit laboratory. The resulting negative can be used to prepare a positive print using another contact paper and a bright exposure lamp.

Formal Syllabus

Concave and convex (diverging and converging) lenses and their effects. Real and virtual images. Magnification.

The 'focus' of a lens. The use of scale drawing to find the position of an image.

6. Light and Colour

Points of Approach and Applications

The rainbow.

Effects of coloured street lighting.

The matching of colours in artificial light.

Varied stage lighting effects.

Colour photography and colour printing.

Dawn and sunset colours.

Practical Work

(1) Form a spectrum on a screen. This can be done by pupils using ray boxes and students' quality prisms. A wider, brighter spectrum can be demonstrated by using as a light source either a strip projector with a 'slit' in the slider carrier, or a line filament car bulb, of as high a power as possible, the filament of which is brought to a focus on a screen by a 10-cm convex lens mounted on a sliding carrier. The prism should be of dense flint glass (refractive index: 1·65). If available, a second similar prism can be used to widen the spectrum or to recombine the colours to white.

(2) If the spectrum is formed on a screen containing a narrow slit, the colours can be allowed to pass through the slit in turn and to fall on a second prism to show that no new colours are produced.

109

(3) Paint the spectrum colours in sectors on a cardboard or wooden disc 6 or 8 in in diameter. Attach it to a spindle and spin it rapidly. It should appear near white, the nearness depending on the purity and proportion of the colours.

(4) Place various colour filters in the spectrum beam and establish primary and secondary colours. Allowance may have to be made for the impurity of theatre grade filters.

(5) Examine various coloured surfaces—books, posters etc.—in red and green light respectively. Make up the appropriate slides to fit the slider carrier of a projector.

(6) Make up three slides of coloured gelatine, in the primary colours, mounted between $3\frac{1}{4}$-in square lantern slide glasses. Place one in each of three similar light boxes fitted with 12-volt, 24-watt car bulbs and place them about 2 feet from, and facing, a white screen. Switch on the lights (*a*) singly (*b*) in pairs and (*c*) all together, and observe the appearance of the screen.

Note: (1) The rather dark blue filter can, with advantage, take a more powerful bulb.

(2) It is convenient to be able to control the brightness of the bulbs by means of a rheostat placed in each circuit.

If larger scale apparatus is preferred, use biscuit tins and mains bulbs.

It is also interesting if not necessary to place an obstacle between the light boxes and the screen and to discuss the various shadow effects.

(7) Mix the secondary colours by subtraction. Overlap in pairs the three secondary filters and hold them up to the light. Discuss the reason for the primary colours seen in the overlapping portions.

(8) *Tyndall's experiment* Into a tall cylindrical jar (12 inches or longer) place a solution of sodium thiosulphate (5 gm to a litre of water). Stand the jar over a hole in the top of a box or tin containing an electric light bulb. Add 15 ml of hydrochloric acid containing about $\frac{1}{2}$ ml of concentrated acid. The colour of the 'sun' is observed by viewing downwards through the solution while the

scattering effect of the sulphur particles formed is seen by viewing horizontally (see Fig. 25).

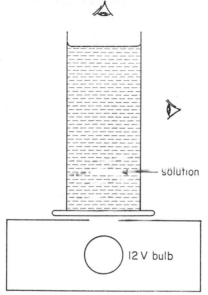

Fig. 25   Apparatus for Tyndall's experiment

(9) To demonstrate the formation of a rainbow, paint a 12- or 15-in square of hardboard with dead black paint. When tacky, sprinkle on it minute polystyrene beads (obtainable for the purpose from the leading laboratory suppliers). Support the screen in an upright position and fix a small torch bulb a few inches away from the middle of the screen. Shield the lighted bulb from the eyes and view from the front.

The filters used in these experiments are cut from 'Cinemoid' obtainable from The Strand Electric Company Ltd., 29 King Street, London, W.C.2.

Those usually recommended are: No. 1 yellow, No. 14 ruby, No. 24 dark green, No. 15 peacock blue, No. 13 magenta and No. 20 primary blue. No. 15 can be replaced by No. 16 blue green, and No. 13 by No. 12 deep rose.

It will doubtless be realised that all these experiments except Nos. 3 and 7 must be done in a darkened room.

Formal Syllabus

White light is the name we give to the effect on the eye of all the colours of the spectrum reaching it together.

A triangular glass prism bends the different colours by different amounts to produce a spectrum.

A *primary filter* allows light of only one colour to pass, all the other colours being absorbed.

A *secondary filter* allows two colours to pass, all the others being absorbed.

A *primary coloured dye or pigment* absorbs all colours but its own, which it reflects.

Primary colours can be added to produce secondaries.

Secondary colours can be subtracted to produce primaries.

7. RADIATIONS BEYOND THE VISIBLE SPECTRUM

Points of Approach and Applications

The knowledge that we can feel invisible heat on our skin, the existence of X-rays and 'radiations' from atomic explosions; fluorescent paints: infra-red photographs.

The connection with radar, wireless and with very short wavelengths can only be explained; direct demonstration is not possible.

Practical Work

(1) It can be shown that a burning glass concentrates not only the light but also the heat given out by the sun or any other hot source.

(2) An intense spectrum can be thrown on a screen using a narrow beam of light from a filmstrip projector. An extra dense flint glass or a carbon bisulphide prism should be used. The spectrum will not be very pure but it can be used to show

(a) heat radiations beyond the red using either a thermopile or a phototransistor. The heat filter must be removed from the projector. Connect the transistor, e.g. Mullard OCP71, in series with a 1·5-volt cell, a 1·5-kilohm resistor and a 0–1 mA meter. The positive lead should be joined to the emitter and the negative lead to the collector. The base connection

112

is not used. For convenience in use the transistor should be mounted in a suitable holder.

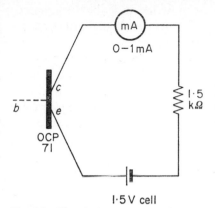

The leads to the transistor should be long and flexible to allow it to be moved about through the spectrum.

Fig. 26 Circuit for phototransistor used as detector of infra-red radiation

   (*b*) ultra violet radiations using either a fluorescent paint or a luminous zinc sulphide screen.

(3) The effects of various parts of the spectrum on fluorescent paints may be demonstrated.

(4) Materials may be examined in ultra-violet light (SCREEN DIRECT LIGHT FROM THE CLASS). Modern washing powders form interesting material as do any shirt cuffs which have been washed in them ('whiter than white').

    (Ultra violet lamps, some 12-volt 60-watts which work directly off 12-volt supply a.c. or d.c. are available at ex-Govt stores.)

Fundamental Theory

A very hot source emits radiations other than those which can be detected by the eye. These radiations have practical applications.

Using other types of source it is possible to produce an even greater range of wave lengths with applications in the fields of medicine and communications.

The Earth's Crust (Geology)

The approach to this subject in school should at all times be practical and not formal. In the initial stages the immediate environment should be the basis of the study, using its scenery, its minerals or its fossils as starting points. It is unlikely that a school will be so situated that no practical approach is possible. Later the framework may be broadened, in stages, until an overall but not too detailed picture of the geology of the whole country is arrived at.

The wider environments (or specimens of it) may be brought nearer the classroom as a result of school journeys and pupils' holidays: the local environment is always around us and can be visited at will. Co-ordination with the work of the geography department would greatly enhance the value of this work.

Points of Approach

The local environment. Scenery.
Building materials. Common minerals.

Practical Work

(1) Make collections of rocks and minerals.
(2) Study individual rocks for structure, hardness, reaction to acid, etc.
(3) Visit and study a quarry, rock exposures or a mine if possible.
(4) Make collections of fossils from various sources—examine lumps of coal at home.
(5) Make leaf or twig casts in plaster of paris to show how fossils are formed. Try also various shells.
(6) Various experiments may be performed on soils to show porosity, water holding properties, erosion, etc.
(7) Cool a piece of heated glass tube with water to show the effect of uneven contraction illustrating the breaking up of rock into soil.
(8) Various chemical experiments can also be done on rocks and minerals illustrating their economic uses, e.g. the calcium carbonate, oxide, hydroxide series.

Formal Syllabus

The nature of 'rock' and its implications in terms of man's existence.

The identification of common minerals and rocks and their overall classification into sedimentary, igneous and metamorphic types.

The broad classification of fossils.

Some simple study of the bedding of rocks and their ageing.

Measurements of thickness of strata, direction and amount of dip using simple apparatus only (home-made clinometer, etc.).

The following of junctions between beds by exposures, soil differences, etc.

Folding, faulting and weathering leading to differences in scenery.

Some idea of the relative dating of rocks by use of fossils and, more accurately, by radioactive mineral decay, leading to broad grouping into geological systems.

Throughout the course stress should be laid on the economic uses of rocks and minerals, and on the practical aspect of this study.

Towards the Infinitely Large (The Universe)

Much of the work suggested below will doubtless be found in the geography and mathematics syllabuses and will not need to be duplicated. How much can be covered in the science course will depend on the interest and enthusiasm of the individual teacher. The present interest in space and space travel should be utilised and a sound background knowledge inculcated in order to combat the often uninformed fantasy of space-science fiction.

Points of Approach

Day and night. The heavens by day and by night.
The moon's phases. Probing into space—space satellites.

Practical Work

A. *With a telescope*

For those schools fortunate enough to possess or to have access to a suitable telescope (6 in reflector?) the practical work possible is fairly obvious though it will have to be done mainly after school hours, perhaps through the medium of a school club. Direct observations should be made of the moon, sun (sun spots), planets, star clusters, double stars and nebulae.

B. *Without a telescope*

(1) Show the rotation of the earth by means of a Foucault pendulum. This can be done successfully with a pendulum 8 to 10 ft long using a suitable suspension (see Fig. 27).

115

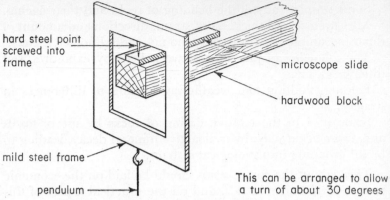

hard steel point
screwed into
frame

microscope slide

hardwood block

mild steel frame

pendulum

This can be arranged to allow
a turn of about 30 degrees

Fig. 27 Possible support for Foucault's pendulum

(2) Make a simple theodolite (astrolabe) for finding latitude or bearing of a star from the N–S meridian.

(3) With a rubber ball and an electric lamp demonstrate the cause of the seasons.

(4) With the same apparatus demonstrate the cause of difference in length of night and day in some places.

(5) Project light down a cardboard tube of about 1 in by 1 in cross-section inclined at different angles to a horizontal surface to show the effects of the angle of the sun's rays on the amount of heat and light received by the earth. Alternatively, use a focusing torch.

(6) Set up a shadow stick and measure the length of the sun's shadow several times a day at different seasons of the year.

(7) Observe and make drawings of the moon over the period of a lunar month.

(8) Using a rubber ball and an electric lamp demonstrate the cause of the phases of the moon.

(9) Demonstrate how an eclipse of the moon occurs using a large ball, a small ball and an electric lamp.

(10) Make a model to illustrate how an eclipse of the sun occurs.

(11) Make a simple model of the solar system using different scales for size and distance. Emphasise the great difference between the scales. This could be done by making

also a model to the same scale of size and distance. If this is impracticable, work out the positions of the planets in the environment of the school based on a sun in the laboratory.

(12) Observe the main constellations around the Pole Star and make a simple star map.

(13) On a clear moonless night set up a camera pointing to the Pole Star and make a 4–6 hour exposure.

(14) Set up a simple constellation projector. This consists of a box with one end removed. An electric lamp is placed in the box and the open end is closed with a slide of cardboard in which small holes are punched to represent the stars of a given constellation.

(15) Make a simple transit telescope (sighting hole and cross wires) and use it to observe the difference between the time taken by a star to encircle the Pole Star and our 24-hour day.

Formal Syllabus

The earth, its motions and their effects.

The moon and its phases. Eclipses. Tides.

The sun and the solar system. Size, distance and orbital times of the planets. Meteors, meteorites and comets.

Some ideas of the work of Eratosthenes, Aristarchus, Ptolemy, Copernicus, Brahe, Kepler and Newton.

The stellar system—galaxies, constellations.

Colour, distance and size of stars. Light years.

Cosmic rays and radio astronomy.

Space and its attributes, absence of air, heat, gravity and the consequences. Man's efforts to overcome the attendant difficulties—physical and biological.

Problems of space exploration. From satellite to space ship.

Jet propulsion and rockets—escape velocity.

Space stations, space suits. Reaching the moon or further.

Towards the Infinitely Small (Within the Atom)

Points of Approach and Applications

The existence of the atom.

The atomic bomb.

The atomic power station.

I   117

Practical Work

(1) Make models of the simpler atoms using wire orbits and cork balls, clay or Plasticine for particles.

(2) Perform the usual electrostatic experiments showing attraction by a charged rod (plastics) of pieces of paper, etc., attraction and repulsion of unlike and like charges respectively. Use inflated balloons on silk or nylon threads or bundles of polythene and acetate strips, respectively.

(3) Make a simple electroscope and/or electrometer for detecting and/or measuring charges.

(4) Hold a strong magnet near a TV screen and observe that moving electrons can be attracted and repelled.

(5) Produce electron beams by passing H.T. from an induction coil, or preferably an E.H.T. power supply unit, through a glass tube exhausted of air to the required degree (streamer stage). Show the effect of a magnetic field on their movement. Try also a burnt-out lamp bulb.

(6) Show radioactivity by a luminous watch or clock dial, placing face downward in the dark on a photographic film or plate in a light proof container and left for a week or longer. (The self-luminous type of dial must of course be used.)

(7) Do the same with pieces of gas mantle, interposing a flat opaque object between them and the film. A rather longer exposure will produce a shadow photograph of the object.

(8) Use a spinthariscope to observe the scintillations when certain substances are hit by particles or gamma rays from a radioactive source.

(9) Observe the luminous part of a radium watch dial through a low power microscope in the dark.

(10) Make a model to show the nature of a chain reaction.

Note: The attention of the teacher is drawn to the fact that unwanted, harmful radiation may be emitted from apparatus such as that used in Experiment 5. The Ministry of Education *Administrative Memorandum No. 1/65* should be consulted.

Formal Syllabus

The atom, made up of electrons, protons and neutrons. Isotopes.

Electric charges as displacements of electrons; their identification, detection and measurement.

Electric currents as electron flow.

The movement of electrons in gas at low pressure—cathode rays.

Simple descriptive treatment of X-rays.

Natural radioactivity, its nature and occurrence. Its hazards.

Cosmic rays.

Splitting the atom—fission and fusion—artificial radioactivity—radioisotopes and their uses. Nuclear power.

4. BUILDING THE SYLLABUS

Two elements must be present in the minds of those planning a campaign; first, the objective and second, the means of attaining that objective. Like the campaigner, the teacher must have his objective as outlined in his syllabus, and his means of attaining it in his method of presentation.

In the hands of a 'live' teacher no syllabus can or should stagnate. Those of us who have taught for a while remember how each cherished syllabus was improved and developed and gave rise to a better, so that now it might be thought, with all this pooled experience, the committee could produce the ideal scheme. No such 'ideal' is possible, there are too many variables. They include:

(1) The 'aims' of the course.
(2) The qualities of the pupils.
(3) The qualities of the teacher.
(4) The circumstances and/or the environment of the school.
(5) The time available.

In no two schools are such factors likely to be identical, neither are they likely to remain constant in any one school. It therefore behoves every teacher critically to examine his scheme of work, and, in the light of his changing circumstances, to modify it from time to time. The school's terminal or annual examinations can often provide data enabling teaching success or failure in a particular field to be diagnosed. When the diagnosis is 'failure' in teaching a particular topic it may well be that the approach has been uninteresting or has had insufficient introduction and, therefore, has not been understood by the pupils. In either case the teacher should change his methods or omit the topic.

'Success in teaching science is not guaranteed by any syllabus.' Unfortunately, where external examinations are concerned, unless the syllabus is carefully covered, success for the pupil at the end of the course can be jeopardised. It has been this measuring of science teaching by examination results that has led to the syllabus acquiring such an important status. In the secondary school the syllabus of the first three years should be wide and determined by the needs of the pupils, the environmental conditions of the school, and the ability and interests of the teacher.

A teacher who has been well trained as a teacher and a scientist but who has gaps in his scientific background should be quite able by systematic private study and experiment (if suitable courses are not available under the L.E.A.) to acquire the necessary knowledge to cover the whole field of the work. Probably the hardest gap to fill is that caused by lack of biological studies. These difficulties can be overcome, and sometimes this late study of a subject makes the teacher more aware of the difficulties of comprehension by the pupil. This 'filling in' of the gaps in the teacher's own education in science should be considered a priority and it is a confession of failure to use these gaps as an excuse for omitting sections of the work.

Young teachers should be careful not to regard these sample syllabuses as ideals towards which every science teacher should strive.

Choice of Material

Since the original report, *Secondary Modern Science Teaching*, was published in 1953 there has been considerable development and broadening in the outlook of these schools which has led in many areas to the dropping of the term 'modern'. Today an ever-increasing number of these schools are developing courses enabling some of their pupils to take external examinations successfully. The content of the syllabus such pupils will follow after their third year will be laid down by their examining body, but the order and the method of presentation remains the concern of the teacher.

Here we are concerned with those pupils not aiming at an external examination other than C.S.E., and even with the C.S.E. it is possible for the school to submit and examine its own syllabuses. In deciding what to include and what to leave out the committee have born in mind three criteria:

(a) The topics chosen should be those that are the concern of the pupil as a future citizen of the modern world; as far as possible they should relate to the things he notices about him and to the discoveries, inventions and achievements about which he reads and hears (television in

121

particular has greatly widened his horizons of recent years).

(*b*) The topics chosen should lead to and exemplify the principles and the generalisations that weld the phenomena into an intelligible whole. The learning of a mass of disconnected fragments is not education. It is essential that the inter-relationships of the biological sciences with physics and chemistry should be made evident, wherever possible, at all stages of the course.

(*c*) The course should illustrate the scientific method of collecting facts before theorising, and of basing conclusions on observations. The emphasis is therefore upon experiment and individual observations.

Class Experimental Work

In chapter 3 will be found much of the data required for experimental work. The topics and concepts studied are not set down in any particular order either of priorities or timing (see introduction to the chapter). While it is true that some topics in a syllabus cannot be dealt with practically in a laboratory, nevertheless wherever possible some practical activity on the part of the pupils should be encouraged, e.g. in discussing disease prevention or the history of diphtheria immunisation, the pupils might be given the task of examining local statistics and possibly investigating what has taken place in their own immediate family circle (i.e. grandparents, parents, aunts, uncles, cousins, etc.).

If the syllabus is considered to be the 'skeleton' support of the work in science, then chapter 3 provides the flesh and muscle with which to 'clothe' this skeleton to make it a real live study. No experimental work has been included which has not been tried out by one or more members of the committee and found to be satisfactory. Care has been taken to keep the apparatus required as direct and simple as possible.

.   .   .   .

The two suggested syllabuses that follow were written separately by two members of the committee and it will be noted, that there is considerable overlap in their approach and pre-

sentation. The Committee as a whole has 'vetted' these specimen efforts and amended and amplified the original manuscripts
where it has been deemed necessary.

Planning a Scheme of Work in General Science for a Country Secondary School

The majority of young teachers, on leaving college, will serve
in departments under men and women of experience. Others,
particularly those going to rural areas, may find themselves
faced with the formidable task of producing and using a scheme
of work in science before they have had adequate practical
experience in teaching the subject. It is to help such that the
following guiding lines are put forward, but let it be clearly
understood that they can be no more than 'guiding lines'. The
finished scheme will be influenced by such factors as the
qualities of the pupils and of the teacher, the position and
circumstances of the school, the time allotted to the subject; and
these factors are not likely to remain constant for long in any
one school. Under these circumstances it is not possible to
devise a universal syllabus. A scheme of work should be a living
organism, which in the light of experience and changing
conditions develops, grows, and suffers modification continu-
ously—it evolves.

In deciding what to include and what to leave out the teacher
should have the three criteria in mind that are to be found
more fully described under 'choice of material' in the introduction to this chapter, namely:

(a) The topics chosen should be those which are the concern
   of the pupil as a future citizen of the modern world.
(b) The topics chosen should exemplify and lead to the
   principles and generalisations that weld phenomena into
   an intelligible whole.
(c) The course should illustrate the scientific method of
   collecting facts before theorising and of basing conclusions
   on observations. The emphasis is therefore upon experiment and individual observation.

Having decided what material should be included in his science
course the planner has to arrange an order of presentation.

An error to be avoided is, so to overload the ground to be covered that only by taking the shortest and quickest route, omitting all deviations, red herrings and much practical work, can the teacher hope to cover the vast field of material selected. An order broadly based on that of historical discovery is capable of giving the subject a very attractive romantic background. Some knowledge of the men and women behind the great advances in our understanding of nature can have a very humanising effect upon what might otherwise be a somewhat arid study. It is difficult to improve on a study beginning with air and leading on to water and living things; from such a study every aspect of science seems to radiate.

The scheme for a country school need differ from that of an urban school only in emphasis and in the illustrations used to demonstrate a scientific principle. The principles themselves are universal and cannot vary from school to school though some may be omitted. Fortunately the basic principles involved are fewer than might be supposed because of a tendency to state and restate a single principle from a number of viewpoints.

The Scheme

The scheme for a country school might begin by examining experimentally the simple physical properties of air, showing that air is material and has weight, giving meaning to 'pressure' (see chapter 3). Doubtless every teacher will soon acquire a a fund of favourite experiments and will wish to add to or substitute for some of those in chapter 3. In this connection the *Science Masters' Books*, containing descriptions of experiments selected from the *School Science Review* over the years, and *Science Teaching Techniques* are invaluable (see bibliography at end of this chapter).

Water in the air, simple hygrometers and washing days are still of interest to the countryman in spite of our spin-driers. The science behind the construction of a dew pond still has value in the remote chalk-hill farms; it serves admirably to illustrate the application of science to a farming problem.

This talk of wind and washing-days introduces the subject of 'the weather', a subject of immediate interest to countryfolk and one which might have greater emphasis in the country school scheme. Here are some of the topics: wind and convection currents; 'where shall we plant the orchard?' (beware of the valley with its late frosts); the cause and effect of wind rotation about a 'low' and a 'high'—cyclones and anti-cyclones; temperature changes in a cyclone; why the cold spell often breaks after a snowfall; clouds and cloud formation; the land and sea breezes on our coasts. At this point it may be convenient to say a little about ocean currents and their effect on climate.

Man's use of convection currents fits in naturally here, e.g. chimneys, draughts, the 'Baxi'-type fire, the hot-water system, the coolant at the top of the refrigerator and the gas-flame at the bottom of the gas oven. Early railway engines had tall chimneys. As engines became larger and the chimney shorter the draught was created by directing exhaust steam through the smoke-box. On large ships the blast is created by increasing the air pressure in the stokehold by electric fans.

It is worth while at this stage to try and establish something of the physical structure of the air. It has been seen to be material yet very compressible and expansible. If gas leaks in one corner of the room it is quickly smelt on the far side. How did it get there in still air? To explain these and other facts about air and similar gases scientists have put forward the theory that air is not a continuous substance, but that it is made up of minute particles, called molecules, with empty spaces in between them. Further the theory suggests that these molecules are all bouncing about and bumping into each other even in still air, and the bouncing does not get less with time as it does with a bouncing ball. It is true that compression could be explained as a pushing together of the molecules, and the diffusion of the escaping gas from one side of the room to the other could be explained in terms of the bouncing molecules, but would it not also mean that a small piece of material ought to be knocked this way and that as molecules bump into it first on one side then on the other? Such a bumping about of small pieces of material was demonstrated visibly by an experimenter called Brown in the first half of the last century. Fortunately it is not difficult to demonstrate the Brownian Movement; the whole problem is first to find material particles small enough to show the movement, and second to render the movements visible. The particles in smoke from smouldering

125

hemp cord are probably the simplest to prepare, but a micro-scope giving ×70 magnification and the smoke cell illuminated from the side with a black background as in the ultra-micro-scope is necessary to see the effect. Brownian Movement can also be shown in daylight using a hand lens if a suspension of minute crystals of lead carbonate is used. Dissolve 1 gm of potassium carbonate in 100 ml of distilled water (solution A). Dissolve 1 gm of lead acetate in 100 ml of distilled water (solution B). These two stock solutions will keep. To use, add about 1 ml of solution A to about 250 ml of distilled water in a beaker. In a second beaker add about ½ ml of solution B to about 100 ml of distilled water. Mix the two dilute solutions together in a large beaker and stir. (If the mixture appears milky the con-centrations have been too high.) Stand the beaker on a dark ground and illuminate strongly from the side with a beam of light. View from above using a magnifying glass. The suspen-sion of lead carbonate crystals shows countless starlike particles which twinkle as they rotate in consequence of the bombard-ment they are experiencing (E. J. Wenham, *S.S.R.* 1960, 145, **41**, 496).

We can feel the wind, but what is it? The Greek philosopher, Aristotle (384–322 B.C.), taught that all things are made of one or more of four elements—earth, air, fire and water. When wood burns the fire can be seen coming out leaving ash, therefore, it was argued, wood is made of fire and earth. We still say on a stormy night, 'Listen to the elements.' Naturally the ash weighs less than the wood for it has lost the fire. Over 300 years ago Jean Rey, a Frenchman, burned tin and found the ash weighed more and not less than the tin. The explanation remained obscure until Lavoisier in the mid 1770's showed that burning is really 'joining with oxygen'. We can conduct experiments very similar to those which convinced Lavoisier of the nature of burning:

(1) Weigh a photographic flash bulb, fire it and weigh again. There is no loss or gain in weight.

(2) Make a small hole in a new flash bulb under water—gas escapes. Now make a hole in the used flash bulb under water—water goes in. In burning some of the 'air' has been absorbed into the magnesium ash.

An instructive series of experiments on the nature of wood is as follows:

(1) Heat some wood chips strongly in a closed crucible. Wood gas escapes and burns on meeting the air. When no more gas is evolved, cool and examine the charcoal.

(2) Reheat the crucible containing the charcoal with the lid off, very gently blowing across the crucible to make the hot charcoal glow. Continue until all the charcoal has burned away leaving a trace of ash, cool.

(3) Add three drips of distilled water to the trace of ash in the crucible and test with red litmus paper—it turns blue. Test the other end of the litmus paper with distilled water—no change.

Thus we learn that wood contains charcoal, it contains potash and from it can be driven an inflammable gas. Charcoal is now known to be made very largely of the element carbon. The number of elements is not, as Aristotle thought, just four but over one hundred. Who can now forget that potassium is an essential plant element? The potash came from the soil in which the plant grew. If the soil is lacking in potash the plant becomes sickly. Often other plant fertilisers will not yield up their plant food unless potash is present and it must therefore be added to the soil to replace that taken away in crops. Potash is particularly important to tomato growers. Sandy soils tend to be dificient in potash, a shortage which reveals itself in the scorched edges of the leaves on raspberry canes grown in this soil (see chapter 3).

The power of charcoal to remove smells and colours is worthy of note. Put in flower water or bulb fibre, it keeps things sweet. Eaten in the form of charcoal biscuits it relieves flatulence, the black dog-biscuits contain charcoal. Animal charcoal is used at the sugar factory to remove the trace of colour from the crude sugar. An instructive class experiment is to remove the colour from vinegar by boiling it for a few minutes with some animal charcoal and then filtering.

At this point we might turn to the simple chemistry of air to discover what air is.

Having come to the conclusion, after much experiment, that the main constituents of air are nitrogen, water vapour, oxygen and carbon-dioxide, and that burning and breathing tend to use up the oxygen and produce carbon-dioxide we might be tempted to wonder why all the oxygen had not been used up long ago.

We find the answer in growing plants by a study of the structure and function of leaves in sunshine and in darkness. We recall how, when burning in oxygen, carbon compounds become carbon-dioxide plus heat energy. Now in the reverse process we find that carbon-dioxide can only be converted into carbon compounds like sugar and starch when energy is available in the form of heat and light from the sun. This reverse process is therefore called photosynthesis. The green substance chlorophyll can be removed from the chloroplasts leaving the leaf white. Without chlorophyll a plant is unable to synthesise carbohydrates from carbon-dioxide and water. Nevertheless some plants have no chlorophyll, e.g. toadstools, moulds and yeasts. Such plants live as parasites, sometimes on a living plant and sometimes on food already made by green plants. All living things finally depend upon green plants for their food.

Some Dependent Living Things

The mould which grows on bread develops from fine black spores which are always floating in the air. The mould depends for its energy on that stored up by the wheat plant growing in the sunshine. In the air are dozens of living specks of dust which, when they meet the right conditions, give rise to living plants. When fruit falls to the ground in the garden it may ferment, it may develop a mildew, it may rot. In each case the result is due to the presence of living spores. The process is slowed down or even stopped by low temperatures. Decay in plant or animal substance is caused by yeasts, moulds or bacteria. One way of preventing decay is to kill the yeast, mould or bacterium by heat or chemicals and then prevent the entry of fresh ones.

Formaldehyde is a chemical capable of killing yeasts, moulds or bacteria and is often used for preserving specimens in museums, but it is not suitable for preserving foods. In general, chemicals which destroy bacteria are not likely to be suitable for foods.

Salt, sugar and vinegar are common substances used in the

effective preservation of food, e.g. the salting of beef, pork or bacon, runner beans, hedge nuts. Sugar is used in peel, jam, etc. Vinegar is used to preserve hardboiled eggs, onions or cabbage. It will be noted that sugar is not a protection against moulds. In each case the preservative creates conditions in which the yeasts, moulds and bacteria do not flourish. Some yeasts and moulds do not flourish unless a good deal of moisture is present, so fruits and vegetables may be preserved by drying, e.g. apple rings, dried peas and beans, dried mint and sage.

In canning or bottling fruit the purpose is to kill any moulds, yeasts and bacteria by heating and, while still hot, to seal to prevent access by fresh 'living dust'.

Among the many instructive experiments possible in this field of 'living dust' is wine making. A chopped-up stick of rhubarb is soaked in a pint of water for four days. The rhubarb is then taken out and a little sugar is added to the liquid. After a few more days, if the liquid is kept at about 20° or 25° C. fermentation will begin and bubbles of carbon-dioxide will be seen rising in the liquid. Boiling and sealing stop the fermentation, but on exposure fermentation will soon begin again if the liquid is warm enough. No yeast is added in this experiment, the air is full of yeast spores. In wine making steps are taken to kill and exclude unwanted yeasts. To make plum wine: Cut up 4 lb of plums and pour over them 1 gallon of boiling water. Allow to stand for four days, stirring each day. Strain through muslin and add 4 lb of granulated sugar to the juice. When the sugar has dissolved add $\frac{1}{4}$ oz or less of yeast (brewers' yeast will do but better wine-making yeasts are obtainable). Leave in a warm place undisturbed (between 20° and 30° C) for some weeks so that the layer of carbon-dioxide from the fermentation lies on the surface of the liquid and excludes air. This fermentation does not need oxygen, but if oxygen is not excluded certain bacteria in the air will oxidise the alcohol produced turning it into acetic acid and the final result will be vinegar and not wine. When the fermentation has ceased, leave a further two weeks and bottle within an inch of the cork. Any sediment will settle and the wine will be ready after six months. Decant carefully.

Many excellent experiments on the culture and detection of bacteria are to be found in the appropriate section of chapter 3.

So far the scheme has been worked out in some detail to show how the material of chapter 3 might be integrated into a continuous whole, avoiding distracting breaks and yet bringing in every branch of science. An attempt has been made to emphasise those aspects of science of particular relevance to country life. This is only the beginning of a scheme, the rest is indicated in outline only, but it is hoped that this chapter will help beginners build up useful schemes of their own.

The scheme might go on to: bread and doughcake making; ginger beer and other fermented drinks; soda water and fizzy lemonade; useful bacteria in the soil; vinegar making; cheese making (some kinds of cheese are ripened by certain moulds). The part played by harmful bacteria or viruses in disease, e.g. blood poisoning, influenza, colds. How diseases may be transmitted, e.g. by food, by contact, by droplets, by milk and by water, by flies and other insects (malaria and the mosquito —Anopheles, bubonic plague by rats' fleas). The importance of cleanliness in the fight against disease; the life history of flies and the protection of food; the life history and destruction of mosquitoes; the control of rats and mice.

Water and solution; the water cycle; our water supply; distilled water; hard and soft waters; limestone caves; springs; the water-table; drainage; sewage disposal; river pollution.

Ice, water and steam; volume changes from ice to steam (roughly 1 cu in of water gives 1 cu ft of steam at atmospheric pressure); burst pipes and autumn ploughing; specific heat; latent heat; conduction of heat; good and bad conductors and their uses; potato clamps; frost protection; haystack fires; thatch for comfort; corrugated iron for discomfort in both summer and winter; conductivity explained on kinetic theory; the nature of heat; absolute zero; cooling by evaporation explained on kinetic theory; refrigerators; heat a form of energy; radiation—a wave motion; other forms of energy; mechanical work.

Simple machines and pulley systems; pumps; the hydraulic jack; efficiency; friction and heat; rate of doing work; power; mechanical equivalent of heat; the steam engine; the internal combustion engine.

Electricity another form of energy; heating effects; electric light; chemical effects; magnetic effects; motors and their convenience as a source of power; sources of electricity and their applications, e.g. thermocouple in haystack to measure temperature rise; application of electromagnetic induction to electric fences; time switches for poultry houses; thermostatic control in incubators or glasshouses; primary and secondary cells and the connection of their action with corrosion, e.g. it is an error to keep damp coke in galvanised bins; an internal phone system.

The Making of Soil

Glacial action; water action; frost action; root action; animal action; the kinds of and structure of soil; raw materials for plant food: C, O, H, N, P, K, Fe, Mg and traces of many others; losses and replacements. Water in soil and soil temperatures; water used by crops; tillage; surface tension; water-table; drainage; swamp land; irrigation; living things in the soil; soil bacteria and their functions.

Soil and plants; roots as anchorage; roots and food transfer within the plant, e.g. starch made soluble by diastase; food storage by plants; assimilation (or how the plant uses stored food).

Food and Animals

Teeth, chewing, digestion; the heart and blood circulation; transport of food and its storage in the body; some functions of the blood; digestion and exercise; respiration (food and work); food and temperature; food and repair; food balance; food hygiene.

Reproduction in Plants and Animals

How yeast cells multiply; reproduction in spirogyra (pond scum); vegetative reproduction in the garden; flowers and seeds; pollination by wind or insect; compatible and incompatible varieties in fruit trees; self-compatibility; interplanting. For apples, diploid (34 chromosomes) is good pollen; triploid (51 chromosomes) is bad pollen. Diploids are much more effective pollinators than triploids. Blenheim Orange (triploid) interplanted with Grenadier (diploid), Blenheim would be well fertilised, Grenadier would not. A triploid needs at least two diploids to be interplanted with it. Bramley's Seedling is a well-known triploid. Most apples are diploid. The same sort of incompatibility occurs in sweet cherries and in pears. Victoria plums are self fertile but many varieties are not and should be interplanted. Overproduction in plants and the fight for life. Spawn, tadpoles and frogs; reproduction in birds; varieties in poultry; heredity and natural selection; artificial selection in plants and animals on the farm; reproduction in mammals.

SOME SPECIALISED ORGANS OF THE BODY

Light and the Eye
(This subject might conveniently have been inserted after Radiation' at the end of the section on heat). The nature of light (allied to radiated heat); reflection; refraction; lenses; the spectrum and colour; factors influencing colour seen: object, light, eye, surroundings; colour-blindness; the eye and its simple defects; spectacles; microscope; telescope; camera; the elementary principles of colour photography; the blue sky and red sunset (see chapter 3).

Sound and the Ear
(This subject might conveniently follow 'light'.) The nature of sound; noise and notes; basis of musical instruments; resonance; microphones and telephones; the limits of hearing; why two ears and two eyes? depth-sounding at sea; radar.

Bibliography
The following pamphlets and articles will be found useful:
Science Teaching Techniques (published by John Murray for A.S.E.),
> *No. II:* 'How I teach Meteorology'.
> *No. III:* 'Classroom Experiments with Soil', 'Some Suggestions for Field Work'.
> *No. VI:* 'Watercress as an Aid to Biology', 'Genetics on the Farm'.
> *No. VII:* 'The use of Animals in the Teaching of Genetics', 'Geology in the Science Course', 'Beekeeping in the Secondary School'.
> *No. VIII:* 'Safe Chemistry', 'Individual Plant Studies'.
> *No. XI:* 'The Use of Animals in Teaching', 'Simple Practical Human Physiology'.

(*Note:* Nos. I to VI are out of print but copies can be found in Institutes of Education and Education Authorities Libraries.)

Natural Science Leaflets (published by The School Natural Science Society),

No. 8: 'Water Animal Identification Sheets'.

No. 9: 'The School Aquarium'.

No. 10: 'Birds in the Open, and How to Distinguish Them'.

No. 11: 'The Keeping of Animals and Plants in School'.

No. 12: 'Identification Sheets. Insects and Other Land Arthropods'.

No. 15: 'Sea Shore Life'.

No. 16: 'Earthworms'.

No. 17: 'Simple Experiments with Leaves'.

No. 18: 'Study of Soil'.

No. 19A: 'The Natural History of a Piece of Wood'.

(*Note:* A full list of these publications can be obtained from M. J. Wootton, B.Sc., 19a Kings Gardens, Cranham, Upminster, Essex, to whom all orders for pamphlets should be sent. Postage is free.)

Planning a General Science Scheme for an Urban Secondary School

The field of scientific knowledge is so wide today that in preparing any syllabus the chief difficulty is not what topics shall be put in, but what topics can justifiably be left out because of the time factors involved. The teaching syllabus should be built up with the following principles in mind:

(1) The interests of the pupil which are, or can be, created or developed as a result of its environment.

(2) The training of the child in scientific thinking.

(3) The creation of a sense of wonder in the pupil's mind regarding scientific facts and development which have a natural or artificial origin.

(4) That as much of the work as possible should be experimental or practical in nature.

(5) That all the work attempted should be familiar to the teacher and that he or she should have the necessary technical knowledge and practical skill required to

carry out the experimental and practical side of the work satisfactorily.

(6) That while practical conditions may mean that work in physics, chemistry and biology may be attempted at separate times, the links between the branches of science are always brought out and where necessary emphasised.

(7) That in the later stages of the work, e.g. in the last year at school, the work can be given a vocational or environmental bias, so stimulating interest and encouraging effort.

It should be remembered that examination syllabuses are not teaching syllabuses. The order of study both of branches of science and concepts covered can be changed from that of the examination syllabus. A common syllabus for all in scope, if not in depth, should be the aim for the first two years at a minimum. In any case, no pupil should be regarded as a potential candidate for any examination until he has reached at least the third year in the secondary school.

The principles (1) to (7) above are but signposts pointing out the general directions along which we should travel. There are certain fundamental scientific facts and concepts which should be included in every syllabus. Briefly these are:

The Physics, Chemistry and Biology of the Atmosphere

Air pressure; the gases of the air; oxidation; fires and oxygen; animal and plant respiration.

Natural and Artificial Sources of Heat energy changes

Effects of Heat on Solids, Liquids and Gases

Expansion and contraction; change of state; temperature and temperature scales; conduction, convection, radiation; capacity for heat.

The Physics, Chemistry and Biology of Water

Water pressure; flotation; purification of water supplies, followed by solution, suspension and crystallisation (the extent to which these topics are developed will depend on the school's environment and the interest of pupils).

Composition by analysis and synthesis; water always a product of combustion of everyday fuels; importance of water to living organisms; problems posed by scarcity.

Light

Natural and artificial sources (history of lighting can be made a fascinating topic); propagation, reflection, refraction (how far these topics can be developed depends on the interests of both teacher and pupils).

The production of colour.

The eye, its structure, care and correction of defects: the camera, the cine camera, still and cine projectors, the microscope. (Since photography is such a common hobby nowadays this can prove a useful starting off point even if the complex chemistry of producing the photograph is not dealt with in detail.)

Sound

What is sound and how is it produced; how we hear; the human ear.

Simple practical experiments only, no theoretical arguments on wave motion; if the school has an orchestra use their instruments.

Electricity

Some ideas on this are a necessity for all of us. If there is no intention to develop the subject at all deeply then it could be tackled from the historical point of view round important figures like Gilbert, Franklin, Oersted, Faraday, Fleming and Marconi, for example. Safety precautions when using electricity should always be stressed. While the teacher may handle apparatus connected to the mains the children should NEVER experiment with a higher voltage than 25 volts.

Coal, Iron and Steel

The economic strength of our country depends on these substances to such a large extent that this topic should never be neglected. Our future prosperity will depend on the wise use of these natural resources.

Naturally how far the topic will be developed will depend on the locality of the school and, although the amount of experimental work that can be done is limited, there is a plethora of first-class visual aid material which used widely can counterbalance this. The by-products of coal are almost universal in their applications and play a great part in the well-being of

135

both the town and the country dweller, the industrialist and the farmer.

So far much of the work suggested has included little biology, but not from lack of desire but because when we enter this field of study it is almost impossible to set down a list of 'musts' as the field of study is so wide. However, it is suggested that there are three points which should receive attention in this work, i.e.,

The Interdependence of Animal and Plant Life
A well-balanced aquarium which does not need artificial aeration is a permanent example of this.

Simple Human Physiology
This could be dealt with from the 'hygiene' point of view if desired, but is often better linked with the study of the structure and function of some animal, preferably a mammal.

The Miracle of Evolution in both Plant and Animal Life
The one scientific topic which shows man in his proper perspective with the rest of the universe.

Assuming that the essential topics that have been enumerated have been studied in the first three years (although not necessarily to finality nor in the same detail for all groups) the question arises as to the direction in which the study or studies in the fourth and fifth years shall move. It is at this point that the teacher on the spot can be the best judge. Pupils at this stage are often stimulated by work which may have a bearing on their future occupation or hobbies. This is not only true of science but other subjects as well. For the less able pupil, interest can be even further stimulated if natural, not artificial, links with these subjects can be obtained. There may be work in science that can be linked with the local industries to which many of the pupils will go. If this is not possible then topics linked with their environment, the home or the use of their leisure, are often profitable; remembering always that there are still those who enjoy acquiring knowledge for its own sake and that these pupils are not necessarily always in the academic streams.

Whichever direction the science topics take, whether local industry, or hobbies, or mothercraft or local services (water, gas, electricity, sewage, etc.), the knowledge of phenomena outside the pupil's environmental area should not be forgotten. Biological studies should not be neglected and such studies can be given a practical bias if full use is made of the open spaces available. National and world health; local, national and world food supplies; the conservation of natural resources; these can and should be part and parcel of the science topics. To be put into the right perspective they require a more experienced and mature mind but under the guidance of the teacher, vital problems of the modern world can at least be partially understood by pupils of this age, although full understanding may have to wait till they have become adults.

Some suggested topics for study in the last years at school for an urban area follow below:

Sanitation services and sewage disposal.
Street lighting (reference to monochromatic lighting).
Production of electric power and its distribution, followed by the a.c. transformer, overhead H.V. cables, etc.
Home heating: central heating, storage heating, radiant and convector heaters, ventilation.
Electricity in the home: cables, switches, fuses, safety precautions, effects of overloading, circuits.
Corrosion of metals and its prevention.
Care of children; mothercraft, simple nursing.
History of preventive medicine, safe handling of food (boys should know much of this as well as girls—simple work on bacteriology always arouses interest).
Safety in the home.
Simple ideas on plastics: their types and uses, precautions in handling.
Fire and its prevention, fire-fighting methods.
The physics and chemistry of house building.
Care of household pets.
Food storage and preservation (modern methods).

How deeply and how many of these topics would be studied depends on pupils' and teacher's interests. The interest of both boys and girls can be aroused in any of these topics if the approach is correct and the timing of their introduction is right.

．　　　．　　　．　　　．

Two other points on the building of a syllabus remain:

(1) Its length. One can usually reckon on a maximum of 36 school weeks in a year. During each year or term the teacher should plan to cover the work that is the foundation for next year's or next term's work. Nothing puts a scheme of work out of gear so quickly as having to do in one term what should have been done in the last.

(2) The syllabus should be concentric. Each *topic* is developed to finality but not necessarily each *subject*. Let an example be quoted:

HEAT

First Year
Expansion and contraction of solids, liquids and gases.
Change of state: melting solids, casting, distillation of liquids.
Temperature, thermometers.

Second Year
Temperature revision, thermostatic controls.
Conduction of heat, convection of heat in liquids and gases, radiation of heat.
Heat and the vacuum.

By planning the syllabus in this way, some physics, some chemistry and some biology are tackled each year and the necessary skills and techniques in carrying out the planned individual work by the children are not forgotten so easily. The change of subject often has a livening effect on the children's interests.

Having read so far, many teachers will ask about 'mechanics', 'specific gravity', 'force of gravity', 'surface tension', etc. etc. Where do they come in? Go back to the principles quoted at the beginning of this syllabus. One cannot deal with air pressure without talking about air having weight and weight is due to the force of gravity—but how far one develops this question of what the force of gravity is, depends on the interests of both pupil and teacher. The same kind of argument can be put forward for many other topics which have not been enumerated—much will depend on how wide and how deep is to be

138

the study of the items already listed and to the teacher's own scientific knowledge of particular branches of science.

The sex of the pupils will also have a bearing on the syllabus, but it is incorrect to say that girls are interested only in the biological sciences and boys only in the physical sciences. The interest in a particular subject may need to be stimulated and the method of doing this will probably vary not only with the sex but also with the environment of the pupils being taught. Only the teacher on the spot can decide these points but much can be learnt from the techniques used by other teachers in similar surroundings. This is one of the reasons why books such as this and the pamphlets *Science Teaching Techniques* and the A.S.E. monographs are published. It is one valid reason for joining a science teachers' association and taking an active part in its meetings.

Assume that you have drawn up your syllabus, planned out your lessons and commenced work. All goes well at first but then, quite suddenly, interest begins to flag. Why is this? It may be that the ideas or concepts have been introduced too early before the pupil can realise their importance or their merits. Whatever the cause of this sudden change of attitude the teacher is well advised to cease work on this topic, to reconsider the position and to start something new, but in a manner which does not let the pupils realise that it is their lack of interest which has caused the new topic to be introduced. Such a situation, however, should give the teacher food for considerable thought and heart searching to see if it is the method of presentation rather than the subject matter which is causing this kind of problem to arise. With 'C' streams and those of even lower ability, it is often that the manner of treatment has not been simple enough, and that not enough repetitive work has been given to satisfy their delight in doing things that they know they can do and understand. Remember that what would probably bore you to tears to do over and over again is quite often very acceptable to some pupils. Again, *you* will have to make the decision on this.

5. SPECIMEN LESSONS

THESE specimen lessons are not printed in any particular order although grouped under traditional headings. As will be evident to the reader, they are the work of several experienced teachers. This has been done deliberately in order that the differences in layout, experimental techniques and method of approach are apparent.

The young or inexperienced teacher of science is well advised, in the beginning, to prepare his or her lessons along similar lines and with the same careful detail. As the teacher becomes more experienced in techniques and more practised in the construction of lessons and schemes of work it will probably not be found necessary to plan in such detail. Short terse notes or headings will be sufficient and the teacher will automatically clothe this skeleton with flesh once the lesson has begun. But even the most experienced teacher prepares his lessons, albeit years of practice enable this to be done in the mind instead of on paper.

Those teachers who are fortunate enough to have the services of a laboratory assistant or technician will find that it is in everyone's interest to plan ahead so that the necessary apparatus and materials are ready for the lesson before it begins. If such planning is written down on cards these can be kept and used for future lessons, but leave space for additions and changes to be made in the light of further experience.

Biology Lesson 1

Object
To teach structure of a dicotyledonous seed and the conditions necessary for germination of seeds.

Previous Knowledge
Biology: parts of a plant.
Chemistry: air dissolved in water can be removed by boiling the water.

Apparatus (for each pair of pupils)
A number of dry broad bean seeds

Broad bean seeds soaked in water overnight
6 gas jars lined with blotting paper (or jam jars)
Air free water
Oil
Mounted needle or scissors
Iodine solution.

Method
(1) Pupils are instructed to examine a dry and a soaked seed
    and look for differences. The soaked seed will have a
    softer testa. The soaked seed can be broken open care-
    fully and the testa removed, using a mounted needle
    or small scissors. Care should be taken in removing the
    testa above the radicle; it is easier to leave this part till
    last.

      The cotyledons will separate easily and the embryo
    plant (plumule and radicle) can be seen. On the inside
    of the testa the pocket for the plumule can be found.

      At this point in the lesson the pupils should be able
    to draw diagrams of their seeds and then discuss the
    functions of the cotyledons. Pupils with knowledge of
    starchy foods can then test the cotyledons for starch with
    iodine.

(2) Having established that the seed is an embryo plant and
    a food store, conditions necessary for germination can
    be discussed. Heat, light, air and water are generally
    suggested. If this is the first biology experiment the
    pupils have done, the need for a control experiment
    may have to be explained.

      Given gas jars (jam jars), blotting paper, bean seeds,
    boiled water and oil, the average pupils can set up their
    own experiments with the minimum of help.

      The sample without heat can go into the refrigerator
    (by arrangement with the domestic science teacher or
    the cook, or even taken home); the ones without light
    can go into a cupboard; the ones without water using
    dry blotting paper; the ones without air having the jar
    filled with boiled water and topped up with oil; and
    the control experiment with light, warmth, water and
    air.

Further experiments will follow to show the true effect of light. *Note:* refrigerators are dark places. The experiments are best left for 10 to 14 days, then the results can be recorded.

Biology Lesson 2

Object
To teach the parts of a typical flower leading to further study of the functions of the parts and pollination.

Previous Knowledge
Parts of a typical flowering plant and their functions.

Apparatus
Plenty of buttercups, including buds and fruits
Other regular flowers: hawthorn, rose, etc.
Hand lens
Scalpel
Gripfix or other paste glue.
Note: Pupils should have at least 3 flowers each.

Method
(1) Pupils should examine the flower using a hand lens if necessary to determine how many parts there are.
(2) One flower can be taken to pieces and the parts stuck on to a piece of paper, either in rows: sepals, petals, stamens, seed box; or arranged in concentric circles with sepals on the outside.

    The names of the parts can be given and the functions discussed. The function of the sepals can be seen on the flower buds. The nectary and colour gives the clue to the function of the petals. Seed boxes can be opened using a scalpel to reveal the ovule. (Pollen grains can be examined under a microscope.)
(3) The more able pupils can cut a flower in half longitudinally, from the stem upwards, and using a hand lens if necessary, study the half flower and make a diagram of it.
(4) The procedures (1) and (2) can be repeated with other regular flowers as time permits.

142

Biology Lesson 3

Subject: Introduction to Photosynthesis

Third Year. Summer Term (about May). Age of pupils: thirteen-plus

Previous Knowledge

FIRST YEAR: food chains, pyramid of numbers (see note below), differences between animals and plants.

SECOND YEAR: foods, food tests, digestion in a mammal.

THIRD YEAR: some idea of an element, of a molecule; chemical change involving energy take up and release.

Aim of Lesson

(1) To establish by discussion and demonstration experiment the idea that all food in the world is obtained from plants.

(2) To establish the idea that plants make their own food from simple raw materials using an energy source— concentrating first on sugars and then carbohydrates in general.

(3) To make a list of possible sources of these raw materials.

Subsequent Lessons

(1) Design of experiments to test ideas above.

(2) Importance of chlorophyll—plants without chlorophyll, e.g. fungi.

(3) Waste gas of photosynthesis—importance of balance of O_2 and CO_2.

(4) Source of protein food, importance of nitrogen, rotation of crops, leguminous plants.

(5) Agriculture, world food supply, etc.

Lesson

1. INTRODUCTION (10 minutes)

Revise the idea of food. Establish:

(*a*) large molecule,

(*b*) made of different elements,

(*c*) held together by energy.

Use of food:

(*a*) new body material,

(*b*) broken down to release energy.

143

Source of all foods—refer to work done previously on food chains.

All food chains end in plants.

2. QUESTIONS FOR LESSON (5 minutes)

Where do plants obtain this food?

Possible answers from class:

   (a) soil,

   (b) air,

   (c) make the food themselves (unlikely the class will suggest this).

How can we find out the correct answer?

   (a) Test leaves for a reducing sugar.

   (b) Test soil for a reducing sugar.

If leaves contain a reducing sugar and soil does too, answer is clear.

If leaves contain a reducing sugar but soil does not, further questions must be answered.

3. PRACTICAL (demonstration 10 minutes, or class practical 20 minutes)

   (a) Tradescantia cuttings grown in full culture solutions for about 6 weeks previously.

   (b) Grind up leaves in mortar and pestle, allow to settle or centifruge out debris.

   (c) Decant liquid.

   (d) Test with Benedict's solution.

   (e) Repeat Benedict's test on culture solution.

4. This should establish that

'Plants make sugar themselves.'

NEXT QUESTION: How?

The best way to find out is to attempt to discover the constitution of sugar.

5. PRACTICAL (10 minutes)

Better as a quick demonstration.

Burn some sucrose (ignore the fact that this is not a reducing sugar) on a deflagrating spoon. Hope that class will notice:

   (a) water vapour—condense on test-tube of cold water.

   (b) carbon.

   (c) burns vigorously, i.e. 'energy'.

6. CONCLUSION (5 minutes)
Plant needs following elements for sugar manufacture:
  carbon, hydrogen, oxygen.
Possible sources:
  water from soil = hydrogen and oxygen.
  Carbon from CO_2 of air,
    from carbonates of soil.
Also a source of energy: light.

7. NEXT LESSON
Start to design experiments to test above ideas.

8. HOMEWORK
Record experiments done in this lesson. (*Editor's Note:* This
  lesson is framed for pupils who will take C.S.E.)

Note: 'Pyramid of numbers', e.g.

ONE hawk
A FEW small birds
A LOT OF grasshoppers
MILLIONS OF blades of grass

Idea of a large number of something at the base of a food chain
  concentrating to a large single carnivore at the top.
Numbers decrease towards top end of food chain.

Chemistry Lesson 1

Physical and Chemical Change

Each pupil should have three test-tubes containing naphthalene crystals. VERY SMALL QUANTITIES OF THE NAPHTHALENE
CRYSTALS SHOULD BE USED.

The pupils should already know about states of matter and
changes of state. The first part of the lesson will revise this subject for them. It would be good technique to combine the
initial teaching of states of matter, etc. with a first introduction
to physical and chemical change.

The naphthalene in the first test-tube is heated until it is just
melted and then allowed to cool. The nature of the changes
which have taken place and how they were brought about is
discussed. The conglomerate of naphthalene crystals now in the
test-tube is taken out, crushed, felt and smelled in order to
establish that it is indeed naphthalene.

145

The effect of further heating of the liquid naphthalene is discussed and then this is done with the second test-tube. A discussion follows on

(1) the condensation seen to take place,
(2) the effect of the condensation on the test-tube walls; the test-tube is allowed to cool. This time crystals more like the original naphthalene will be seen on the cooled test-tube walls.

Discussion follows on what would happen if the boiling naphthalene was heated still further. This is then done with the third test-tube and when naphthalene vapour is seen issuing from the test-tube mouth it is allowed to ignite at the Bunsen flame.

All of this work can be summarised on the board as each stage is done, as shown in diagram form in Fig. 28, and this summary is used in the following discussion.

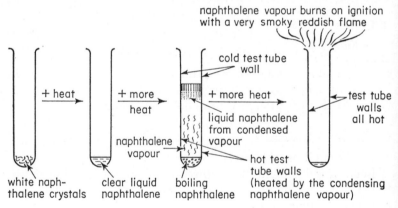

Fig. 28 Blackboard drawing to accompany chemistry lesson on chemical and physical change

In the discussion, using ideas on what chemistry and physics are (which should have been discussed earlier in the pupils' science studies) the pupils can be led to definitions of physical and chemical changes and a realisation of the differences between them.

They should then carry out a series of experiments illustrating physical and chemical changes which can be obtained from any practical textbook. They should write down what they observe and discuss with evidence whether a chemical change or a physical change took place. An excellent first chemical change is to heat a single largish crystal of ammonium dichromate.

This piece of work should not be hurried and can easily take two double periods. It lends itself to many revision points and embellishments but one should be careful not to submerge the main point of the lesson.

For the lesson immediately following this work, an examination of the changes involved in the burning of a candle is a useful way to reinforce the work on physical and chemical change. This lesson can be used to extend and test the pupils' deductive powers. Since many quite able pupils think that it is the wick burning which produces all the light and heat, it is also a good test of the teacher's ingenuity to lead them to a deduction of what is really happening and what is the true function of the burnt wick.

Chemistry Lesson 2

The Rusting of Iron

Put out on the bench:
  (1) a large beaker of cold water from a cold tap which has been left running into the beaker to increase the dissolved air content,
  (2) fused calcium chloride in a glass dish or some other drying agent (e.g. silica gel). Some of the drying agent should be on view in a closed glass container.

Discuss with the pupils:

$$\text{Iron} \underline{\quad\quad\frac{\text{left in}}{\text{the open}}\quad\quad} > \text{What happens?}$$

Examine rusty iron, scrape off and examine some of the rust. Lead pupils to the conclusion that iron rust is a different substance from iron, therefore a chemical change has taken place.
BUT (1) What kind of substance is iron?
  (2) Therefore what kind of chemical change must have taken place?
  (3) But for an element to take part in a chemical combination what must happen?
  (4) What substances can come into contact with the iron in the open?

147

(5) Is the air alone or the water alone enough to rust iron or does it need both?

Lead pupils to see that this last question cannot be answered by deduction and that an experiment must be designed and carried out in order to answer. Most pupils can suggest the kinds of experiment which must be done.

Choose a good suggestion for the experiment to see if air alone is able to cause iron to rust and subject it to critical analysis. With the aid of the exposed, now moist, calcium chloride lead the pupils to see how the experiment must be carried out.

Do the same with a good suggestion for the experiment to see if water alone is necessary for the rusting of iron. Use the example of the air which has come out of solution from the water in the large beaker to illustrate how the experiment must be carried out and the need for precautions to prevent air redissolving in the boiled, air-free water.

The set-up for the third experiment will now be clear and all three experiments can be set up by the pupils and left until the next lesson.

This next lesson lends itself well to the same method of attack,

(1) What is necessary for the rusting of iron?
(2) What is air?
(3) Are all the gases in air necessary for the rusting of iron? etc. etc.

Chemistry Lesson 3

Starting a Chemical Change

Investigation of methods of starting a chemical change as an introduction to further experiments to assist recognition of such changes.

Apparatus

Tongs, copper foil, magnesium ribbon, starch, cycle lamp batteries or low-voltage d.c. supply connected to a broken mains electric light bulb with glass bulb and filament removed thus leaving the filament supports as electrodes (the connections to the electrical supply are made through the normal cord-grip lamp-holder), silver nitrate solution, sodium chloride.

Note: Experiment 4 can be set up at perhaps four stations and be used by individual pupils during the period.

Method

EXPERIMENT 1.

Hold a piece of copper foil in the flame of a Bunsen burner by means of tongs. When it is red hot let it cool in air. Still holding the copper, watch for any change that takes place as the metal cools. Scrape off some of the oxide film.

EXPERIMENT 2.

Hold about $\frac{1}{2}$ in of magnesium ribbon with tongs in a flame. Protect the eyes with a piece of smoked or dark glass (or turn away) to avoid the danger of damage to the eyes by ultra violet radiations when the ribbon catches fire. Notice what happens before the metal burns. Note the change in appearance after this action.

EXPERIMENT 3.

Heat a little starch in a dry test-tube. Note signs of chemical change which take place. Is the residue left in the tube a different substance?

These experiments have shown chemical changes brought about by heat energy. Will other forms of energy produce chemical changes?

EXPERIMENT 4.

Place the filament supports of the lamp in a small beaker of potassium iodide solution. Switch on the low-voltage d.c. supply. The supports act as convenient electrodes. Notice signs of a chemical change near the electrodes in the solution.

EXPERIMENT 5.

Bringing substances together by solution in water.

Mix together half a teaspoonful of dry powdered tartaric acid and a teaspoonful of bicarbonate of soda. Look for any sign of a chemical reaction. Now add water to the mixture.

EXPERIMENT 6.

Make a solution of silver nitrate in distilled water. Add to this clear solution a few drops of common salt solution. What evidence is there of a new substance being produced?

Now leave half of this in the light and half in the dark. Note any change produced by the effect of light upon this new substance. This reaction is slower, but similar to that used in

L

film emulsions in photography. (This experiment can be further developed to show the part played by silver salts in photography.)

Physics Lesson 1

Object
To introduce the subject of *magnetism*.

Previous Knowledge
That magnets attract iron.
That a compass consists of a freely suspended magnet.

Apparatus Required by Each Pupil
A watchglass or similar vessel.
A disc of cork from the cap of a 'lemonade' bottle.
A 4-in length of straight florists' iron wire.
Two 4-in lengths of 'dead hard' unmagnetised steel piano wire, 24 or 26 s.w.g.
Some iron filings in the middle of a sheet of paper.
A 3-in compass needle freely mounted on a stand.

After completing the first two experiments each pupil will require: a good, straight, unmarked anilco (or similar) magnet.

If the class is an 'A' form, a sheet of instructions, on the following lines, may be given to each pupil. A less able form should perform the same experiments on receiving each individual instruction from the teacher. In either case the class should be warned to take care as the soft iron wire is very easily bent and the steel wire is very brittle and easily broken. The experiments *must* be performed in the order given.

Experiments
   (1) Test the soft iron wire and the hard steel wire separately for magnetism by seeing if either will pick up any of the iron filings.
   (2) Test each wire in turn to see if either will attract the pivoted compass needle.
   (3) By magnetic attraction stick one end of the soft iron wire across the end of the steel magnet (with which you have just been provided) as shown. While still stuck together test the other end of the wire for magnetism by dipping it into the iron filings. Estimate the strength of the magnetism by the size of bunch of filings lifted.
   (4) Carefully detach the magnet from the wire to see whether

the wire remains fully magnetised. Using finger and thumb, wipe the filings from the wire and, after dropping the wire on to the floor and picking it up, test it again for magnetism with the filings. Is it still magnetised? Record results.

(5) Repeat experiment 3 using one of the steel wires.

(6) Repeat experiment 4 using the same steel wire as in experiment 5.

(7) Mark one end of the magnet and one end of the *second and unused* steel wire with chalk for identification purposes. Starting with the two chalked ends in contact, draw the steel wire once across the chalked end of the magnet. With filings test the steel wire alone for magnetism. Will it pick up filings equally all along the wire?

(8) Using the mounted compass needle bring the chalked end of the magnet towards the North-seeking end of the compass needle and note the effect. Now try bringing the same end of the magnet towards the South-seeking end of the compass needle.

Repeat the experiment using the chalked end of the steel wire which was magnetised in experiment 7. Does this make the compass needle behave in the same way or in the opposite way as the chalked end of the magnet? What conclusions can you come to concerning the magnetism of the chalked ends of the magnet and the wire?

(9) Float the disc of cork on the watch glass full of water and balance the magnetised wire on the disc so that it can rotate freely. Is the chalked end a North- or a South-seeking pole? (The rough direction of North can be discovered by remembering that 'the golden Sun sinks in the West'). Can you now, without further experiment, mark the North-seeking pole on your magnet?

(10) It has now become clear that the two ends of a magnet are not identical. Try to separate the two ends by breaking the wire magnet in the middle after identifying the nature of the original ends with the compass needle. Test each half for magnetism (*a*) with iron filings and (*b*) with the compass needle. Record your conclusions on the nature of the magnetism in each half and on your success in separating the N from the S-poles.

(11) Using your floating cork disc find out whether similar poles attract or repel each other.

(12) See if you can break off a piece of your magnetised steel wire so short that it is magnetised only at one end. Test with iron filings. (It is not difficult to break off a length of ⅛ in or less with the thumbnail.)

(13) Bring the end of the powerful magnet *very* close to the end of the compass needle it repels. It now attracts it. How can this be explained?

Discussion following the experiments

Experiment 12 suggests, if carried to its logical conclusion, that a single steel molecule is a magnet.

DEMONSTRATION

Show that a ½ × 6 in test-tube full of steel filings can be magnetised by stroking it from end to end with the end of the powerful magnet. Freely suspended in a paper sling by a fine nylon thread it acts as a compass needle and reacts to an approaching magnet as the compass needle did. If now the tube of filings is shaken the magnetism is no longer apparent and may well offer an explanation of experiment 4; the individual magnetised steel filings would tend to stick N to S and form rings each N-pole neutralising its attached S-pole.

Now let the form consider each experiment in turn starting with number 3 and let them suggest an explanation verbally.

The results of experiments 2 and 13 might be taken together at the end giving a satisfactory meaning to 'magnetic induction'.

With a good class and a little guidance the whole of the above experiments and discussion have been completed in a double period of 80 minutes.

This subject is one which lends itself to show the heuristic method as an effective system of teaching because the experiments applicable are many and time required for each is short. Many more experiments using this simple apparatus are possible, e.g. the effect of heat on a magnet, consequent poles, etc.

To prepare the hard steel wire take a length of 26 s.w.g. piano wire and apply sufficient force to pull it out straight. Run along the stretched wire with a Bunsen making it just red hot; when cold it will remain straight and can be cut into 4-in lengths.

Close one end of a 6-in length of steel conduit tube with an iron plug. Pack the tube loosely with the 4-in lengths of wire. Heat the whole to a bright red heat in a fire and pour the wires into a large gas jar of cold water. The wires are then ready for use. It is most difficult to keep such wires from one year to the next without their picking up some magnetism, but if they must be stored, keep them at right angles to the magnetic meridian and well away from all magnetic material.

Physics Lesson 2

Lens Images

Object
To see how a lens forms a real image.

Previous Knowledge
How a pin-hole camera image is formed.
Refraction at a plane surface (not quantitatively).
The simple prism as a bender of rays, but little or nothing of chromatic effects.
Experience of obtaining a real image with convex (converging) lens.

Apparatus Required by Each Pair of Pupils
A convex lens of between 10 and 30 cm focal length.
A V-filament car headlamp bulb, with means of lighting it.
Three plain white cards, each large enough to cover the lens.
A lens stand and suitable supports for object and screen (plasticine).

Method
Pupils are instructed to make two holes of about 1 mm diameter separated by a distance of about 1 cm less than the diameter of the lens in one card, and to set up the lamp, the holed card and a second card (as a screen) so that two pin-hole images of the filament appear inverted on the screen. If the holed card is now removed the images are lost and the screen appears uniformly illuminated.

Instead of removing the holed card, more holes might be made in it, each extra hole producing an extra image. Finally the card would be all holes and no card and the effect would be the same as removing it. Thus the uniform illumination of the screen by the lamp might be regarded as made up of an infinite number of overlapping pin-hole images of the filament.

So too the illumination within a room by the light coming through the window might be regarded as due to an infinite number of overlapping images of the scene outside. Given a lawn and a clear sky outside, consideration of the disposition of these images leads one to expect a greenish tinge on the ceiling, or on a white card held high, compared with the tone on it when held low down.

Remembering how a prism bends a ray of light, the pupils replace the holed card and again get two pin-hole images on the screen. Now they place their lens against the holed card so that both beams pass through the lens near opposite edges. The prism effect of the glass makes the two beams converge. As the screen is moved nearer or farther from the lens a point can be found at which the two images are superimposed and form a single bright image. The removal of the holed card will give rise to a single, very bright, image of the filament. The experiment is now repeated with four or five holes distributed over the holed card.

At this point it should be pointed out to the class that the lens does not magnify the images. At any distance from the lens each separate pin-hole image obeys the same rule as any other pin-hole image, namely:

$$\frac{\text{size of image}}{\text{size of object}} = \frac{\text{distance of image*}}{\text{distance of object}}$$

This rule may therefore be applied to the size of an image produced by a lens, imagining the pin-hole to be at the centre of the lens since the lens does not bend those rays.

The lens might thus be regarded as a series of annular prisms, the angle of the prisms increasing from zero at the centre to a maximum at the rim. Since the amount of bending a ray receives depends upon the angle of the prism and not upon the thickness of glass traversed, a great deal of the glass found in a normal lens could be missed out by building the lens of a series of annular prisms. For lightness such lenses are used in lighthouses.

*Distance being from pin-hole.

154

Mathematicians have shown that if lens surfaces are ground and polished to form parts of spheres the annular prisms so generated are very nearly the correct shape to superimpose all the pin-hole images from every part of the lens, giving a single brilliant image of the object at one particular distance from the lens. The image of the object is then said to be 'in focus'. Most lens surfaces are ground to the spherical form.

In focusing a projector it is helpful to cover the lens with an opaque cap which has a hole cut in it at each end of a diameter. The lens is then adjusted until the double image on the screen merges into a single one. This device is particularly useful when focusing an enlarger in the darkroom.

Returning to the original experiment in this lesson, take the third card and make three holes in it forming an equilateral triangle just inside the rim of the lens. Set up the apparatus so that the screen is nearer the lens than is the focal point. The three images formed will make a triangular pattern the *same* way up as the pattern of the holes in the card.

The experiment can be adapted to show that the image focused on the retina of the eye is inverted. Let the pupils make three fine pin-holes forming an equilateral triangle of $\frac{1}{16}$-in side, in the middle of a piece of paper about 1-in square. In the centre of a second 1-in square of paper a single pin-hole is pierced. Holding the three pin-holes almost in contact with the eye, so that all three can be seen through at once, the pupils look at the single hole in the other paper held towards the light and about 4 or 5 in away from the eye. A pattern of three images of the single hole will fall upon the retina the *same* way up as the pattern on the paper held close to the eye (this has been learned from the experiment above). The pattern will seem to be inverted, showing that the brain inverts it in interpreting the pattern on the retina. Thus the cow in the field is seen to be upright because on the retina the cow's four feet point upwards.

From the lens experiment it will be clear that success in the above eye experiment depends on the single holed paper being held nearer to the eye than its near point, for otherwise the eye would adjust the single hole into focus and the three images would be superimposed and a single bright image would be seen. In the normal eye the near point is 10 in or 25 cm from

155

the eye. For a near-sighted person the near point may be much less, while for a long-sighted one it can be much more than this. To focus an object properly, it must be at least as far away from the eye as its near point. As age advances the near point tends to recede. Watch Grandad reading the paper without his glasses. To find your own near point, look through the three pin-holes at the single one seeing the pattern of three images and then slowly take the single-holed paper farther from the eye until the three images just merge to become one. The position of the single-holed paper gives the position of the near point for that eye.

Again, returning to the original lens experiment using the card with two holes in it—if the diameter of the lens is great, the two holes can be farther apart and the duplicate images will also be farther apart for a given error in focus. In other words a large diameter lens will give a greater blurring effect than a smaller lens of similar focal length for the same error of focus.

Inexpensive cameras are often of the box type having no arrangements for focusing. The camera is made so that distant objects are in focus, but the lens is of such small diameter that it is not until an object is less than perhaps 6 ft from it that the focal error causes serious blurring of the image. Such small lenses are simple and cheap to manufacture; they have great depth of focus, but a very good light or long exposure is needed to take a satisfactory picture. Fast cameras have large diameter lenses and can be very costly. Such cameras must be focused very accurately as they have such a shallow depth of focus, but they can take photographs with so short an exposure that a fast-moving object, such as a horse jumping, can be taken without movement showing.

Discarding any spectacles, the pupils are asked to hold a book 2 in from one eye and try to name the letters in the print. In a good light let them try again, looking through a fine pin-hole in a piece of paper held very close to the eye, the book still being only 2 in from the eye. Can they explain?

Point for discussion: How would you photograph a church interior where both near and distant objects are required to be in focus, given (a) a simple box camera and (b) an expensive camera having a large aperture lens?

Physics Lesson 3

The Law of the Lever

Object

To find out how to apply the law of the simple straight lever to cases where the lever is not straight and the forces are not at right angles to the lever.

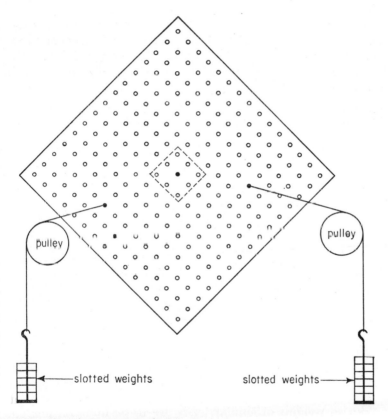

Fig. 29a Apparatus used with physics lesson on the law of the lever

The hardwood boss glued to the centre of the pegboard is drilled squarely through the central hole in the pegboard so that the steel knitting needle is a driving fit (drill $\frac{7}{64}$ in for a No. 11 needle). The point of the needle should come through and be protruding about $\frac{1}{16}$ in so that measurements can be made from it. A No. 11 needle runs freely in the nylon bush drilled $\frac{1}{8}$ in diameter.

157

Previous Knowledge

The law of the simple straight lever should have been found experimentally using pennies as weights distributed in two or more piles on either side of a metre rule balanced on a small prism or a round pencil, prevented from rolling by plasticine. The meaning of the terms 'fulcrum' and 'moment' have been taught prior to this lesson.

Apparatus

A disc or square (about 1 ft diameter or side) of peg board, mounted vertically on a horizontal (steel knitting needle) axis, running freely in a nylon bearing. The bearing could be a 1-in length of $\frac{1}{2}$-in diameter nylon rod suitably drilled and held in a heavy retort stand (see note below Fig. 29a for more details).

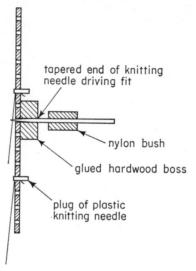

Fig. 29b Side elevation of apparatus to show construction of supports

Slotted weights or similar loads are to be hung on one end of threads each of which passes over a pulley and enters one of the holes in the disc. At this end of the thread a knot is tied and it is prevented from coming back through the hole by a plug of No. 7 size plastic knitting needle about $\frac{1}{2}$ in long or less.

A balancing weight in the form of a slightly tapered plug $\frac{3}{16}$ in diameter and $\frac{1}{4}$ in long is cut from a 4-in nail.

Method

Pupils are instructed to balance the freely mounted disc or square by plugging the balancing weight firmly into the appropriate hole. It is better that the pupils should do this themselves than to be provided with carefully balanced discs.

A slotted weight is hung on one end of a thread which is passed over a pulley. The other end is knotted and passed through a hole in the disc; it is secured there by one of the short plastic plugs provided. A second slotted weight is similarly attached to another point on the disc and the apparatus then allowed freely to settle in its position of equilibrium.

A necessary precaution is to see that the load-carrying threads run almost parallel to the face of the disc and yet foul neither it nor any of the projecting plugs.

A ruler is laid alongside one of the threads and a set-square slid along it until the side at right-angles to the one touching the ruler passes through the centre of the pivot. The perpendicular distance from the line of action of the force to the centre of the pivot (fulcrum) is noted together with the corresponding load value. The product of these two values is calculated and named, e.g. gramme-centimetre, the name of the load preceding the other to avoid confusion with the unit of work, e.g. centimetre-gramme. This product gives the moment of that force about the fulcrum.

The second loaded thread is similarly treated and the moment of its force about the fulcrum calculated.

It will be noted that one thread exerts a clockwise moment and the other an anticlockwise moment.

Three or four pairs of moments are similarly taken after changing the values of the loads and altering their points of attachment to the disc, and in each pair the clockwise and anticlockwise moments are compared.

Finally each group of pupils will conduct an experiment and compare the sum of the clockwise and the sum of the anticlockwise moments using three or more forces.

A study of the results shows that a system of coplanar forces is balanced when the sum of the clockwise moments is equal to the sum of the anticlockwise moments. This is called the *law of the lever*.

This result is always true and in no ways depends on the

shape or length of the lever, it is also independent of the angles at which the coplanar forces are applied.

It should be pointed out that an unbalanced lever provides an extra moment about the fulcrum and this extra moment must be taken into account. The moment of a balanced lever is zero since the distance of its centre of gravity from the fulcrum is zero.

The moment (importance) of a force about a fulcrum is the product of the force and the perpendicular distance between the line of action of the force and the fulcrum.

It will be seen that the straight lever is simply a special case of the above general law of the lever. Sometimes straight levers are divided into three classes depending on the relative positions of the forces and the fulcrum. These classes are of little importance except for examination purposes. The three types of lever are then stated giving examples of each. The forearm, itself being horizontal, while the hand holds a weight, provides an example of type three lever. The forearm, itself being horizontal, while the hand presses down on the table, provides an example of type one lever. The lower jaw and many other joints of the body provide similar examples, the type depending on the muscle in operation at that moment.

The lever is a machine and its purpose is either to magnify a force or to magnify a speed. In levering off a treacle tin lid with a spoon handle the purpose is to magnify the force exerted by the hand on the spoon. The hammer haft is a device for increasing the length of the forearm and thereby increasing the speed of the hammer-head striking the nail. Most examples of a lever used for increasing speed are more complicated, e.g. the cycle.

6. SCIENCE FOR PUPILS OF BELOW AVERAGE ABILITY

IN every secondary school there will be a number of pupils who may be described, for various reasons, as 'below average', 'less able', 'backward' or 'retarded'. All these children are individuals and have as much right to be given the best teaching as any others in the school. The teachers concerned must have sympathy, patience and understanding. If they regard the teaching of these pupils as a tiresome chore, to be avoided whenever possible, they are adopting an unworthy attitude. The work may be more difficult and frustrating and the results less apparent, but when the capability of the pupil is taken into account some satisfaction will be obtained. Pupils respond to enthusiasm and an adequately prepared lesson and properly taught will enjoy their science lessons with obvious pleasure and even excitement. It must be admitted that there are classes in some schools which have pupils who are very difficult to control. They may have a substantial proportion of anti-social pupils, particularly in densely populated areas. The science teacher does, however, have a subject which can be made interesting; nevertheless difficult situations can be expected. In any case, the difficult classes in a school should not be assigned in an undue proportion to newly qualified teachers; the head of the department should take his or her fair share and show by example how to overcome the various problems which arise.

The Syllabus

Some teachers believe in an approach through everyday things, analysing their scientific characteristics and dealing with each in turn.

In this way the bicycle could be taken as a starting point for a series of lessons on mechanics. Beginning with the wheel, its historical development could be traced from the roller, chariots and coaches to the present-day wheels with pneumatic tyres. The width of the tyres and the size of the wheel could be related to the terrain to be traversed. The purpose of the compressed air in the tyre could be investigated and also the action

161

of the valve, which leads to the study of pumps. The construction of the wheel could introduce elementary notions of stress and strain, and density when dealing with the material from which it is made. The movement of the wheel entails bearings and friction. The brakes bring in friction and also involve levers in their action. The framework shows the strength of tubular structure. In the seat the springs introduce Hooke's Law, though it is not suggested that it be studied as such. The pedals are another example of lever action and the chain and sprocket wheels can form the basis for discussion on the transmission of power through chain drives, belts and pulleys. When dealing with levers it has been found preferable to use the terms 'leverage' and 'pivot' instead of 'moment' and 'fulcrum'. The bicycle lamp can be used to introduce the study of electricity —indeed, it is used this way in the Electrical Development Association films—a lamp using dry cells for electrochemistry, and a dynamo lamp for 'the generation of electricity'.

This project may be thought to be a desirable way of dealing with the science to be taught to the below average pupil, but it is not really as easy as it appears and may not provide the pupils themselves with much in the way of individual practical work. In addition, when following a project through, the teacher may be asked to explain details involving concepts beyond the comprehension of the pupils and he, or she, must decide on the spot how far the matter raised can be taken. The range of projects must also be carefully selected so that all the science topics considered necessary are included in the scheme.

Some teachers do not consider it necessary to follow a systematic scheme of work with the lowest stream. They have a sequence of lessons, of course, but each lesson is complete in itself. The teachers feel that with these pupils it is not so much *what* is done in the lesson as *how* it is done. Is each child participating to the full extent of his or her ability? If this is so, then something useful has been achieved.

Other teachers believe in following the general science scheme of the average pupil, modifying it as necessary for each lesson given to the lower stream. This method keeps these pupils in touch with the work of the stream above, which is advantageous when there are possibilities for transfer. The following outline details such a scheme which has been followed by the lower streams at the school where a member of the committee teaches. It is provided as an example, not as a standard scheme for general adoption. Teachers would be expected to compile their own schemes according to their facilities, qualifications, and environment. It must be appreciated that the scheme which follows covers a good deal more ground than can be dealt with in the time available especially for the less able pupils. It is, however, better to have too much to do than too little. The teacher must decide how far he, or she, can develop each topic and modify the weekly assignment accordingly. Boys will probably spend more time on the physical and chemical topics, cutting down, but not entirely omitting, the biology. For girls the opposite action will probably be considered desirable. Our aim in teaching science is to provide an intelligent understanding, as far as possible, of the scientific phenomena met with in our everyday life. The omission of a substantial part of the scheme, e.g. one unit, would make our general science teaching unbalanced.

At the school concerned pupils work in pairs for science and care is taken to see that a 'weak' pupil is partnered by a more able one. Classes are usually less than twenty-four in number. In common with many other secondary schools, no laboratory assistance is provided and the science teacher is obliged to prepare all materials and apparatus in his spare time. A good deal of help, which is much appreciated, is given by the woodwork department.

For most of the outline, only the title of each topic has been given; details of several do appear but to provide details of them all would occupy more space than can be allocated.

First Year

Unit I. Air

1. The Nature of Air.
2. Air Pressure.
3. Measurement of Air Pressure.
4. Compressed Air.
5. The Air and Burning.
6. Making Carbon-dioxide.

7. Preparation and Properties of Oxygen.
8. The Air and Breathing.
9. Rusting.
10. The Bunsen Burner.

Unit II. Water

11. The Evaporation of Water and the Formation of Rain.
12. Our Water Supply.
13. Ice and Snow.
14. The Nature of Water.

Unit III. The Study of Living Things

15. Introduction: living and non-living things,
    plants and animals.
16. Signs of Life in Plants.
17. Seeds and Seedlings.
18. Food Materials for the Older Plant.
19. General Structure of a Typical Plant.
20. Introduction to Animal Life.

For the lessons on animals and plants the pupils should be taken to places where they can see the plants growing and possibly collect the smaller animals. Projects such as a collection of common flowers or one of trees' leaves, bark rubbings, drawings, etc., are worthy of consideration. It is very desirable to have a number of living things, plants and animals, for observation in the laboratory.

Second Year

Unit I. Heat

1. The Effect of Heat on Solids. (Bimetallic strips used as thermostats and fire alarms.)
2. The Effect of Heat on Liquids. (Thermometers.)
3. The Effect of Heat on Gases. (Hot air balloon.)
4. Convection Currents. (Ventilation, domestic hot-water system.)
5. The Conduction of Heat.
6. Heat Rays.

Unit II. Light

7. Rays of Heat and Light. (Pupils look forward to making for themselves such things as periscopes, pin-hole cameras and 'blob' microscopes.)

8. The Eye.
9. Colour.
10. Sound. ('Can' telephone; speed; echoes.)
11. Hearing.

Unit III. Biology (Invertebrates)
12. The Marvel of an Insect.
13. The Earthworm and Other Inhabitants of the Garden.

Third Year

Unit I. Mechanics
1. Measurement of Volume, Density.

In some schools this topic may be dealt with in the mathematics syllabus, but it would be beneficial to have the practical work carried out in the science classes in any case.

(a) Construction of a one-cubic-inch capacity box from paper or thin card.

(b) Using the cube to graduate a number of convenient vessels, e.g. Alka Seltzer jars, coffee jars; marking the graduations on strips of tape stuck on the sides of the jar.

(c) Construction of an overflow can—spouts can be made from metal pea-shooters provided by the pupils.

(d) Using graduated jars and overflow cans to measure the volume of common objects.

(e) Introduction to metric system. The metre, litre—constructed from 'tin' to show basic measurement. Meaning of common terms and abbreviations, including ml, the gramme (or gram).

(f) Idea of density, some common densities expressed in British and metric units (S.G. bottles will *not* be used).

2. Flotation. (Plimsoll line, hydrometers, submarines.)
3. Weight and Weighing Apparatus.
4. Levers.
5. Pulleys.

Unit II. Astronomy
6. This unit is brief and can be inserted when convenient in the scheme. In it the biographies of some of the early astronomers are dealt with and ideas from present-day space travel are brought in. Information about present-day developments is to be found in special articles in periodicals. It is useful to have

M 165

at hand a book containing biographies written in a dramatic manner with plenty of dialogue. One such book contains, amongst others, the lives of Copernicus, Galileo and Newton, each taking about 25 minutes to be read, thus allowing time in the lesson for quite a good deal of extra material to be interpolated.

Unit III. Chemistry

The chemistry done by the less able pupil will be considerably different from that done by pupils who are following a C.S.E. course. It must be essentially practical and very much of every-day application.

7. Combustion (formation of new compounds).
    Reduction (recovery of lead from lead oxide using blowpipe and carbon block, introduces smelting).

8. Some Common Metals.
Dramatic accounts of the discovery and use of the common metals:
    copper, tin, bronze; alloys.
    iron and steel; blast furnaces.
    aluminium.
    silver and gold.

Not much more than a descriptive treatment of the above can be given, dealing with the obtaining of the metals from their ores, and their uses, with some historical details. It is possible to obtain useful literature and films from the agencies of the industries concerned.

9. Rocks and Minerals, the Earth's Crust.
This is really an extension of the previous topic. Conventional geology is unsuitable for the lower streams, but some knowledge of strata is needed to deal with coal measures.

Weathering has created our soil and its nature is now to be studied, classifying it according to particle size. The amount of humus in the soil leads on to horticultural topics.

10. Hard and Soft Waters.
A simple method of comparison entails the preparation of a soap solution (soap flakes, methylated spirit and distilled water), a shaking bottle—the clip-on cap bottles as used for Eno's fruit salts are admirable, and a 'pipette' made from glass tubing with a ring cut from rubber tubing used as a level

marker. Equal amounts of various kinds of water are put into the bottles, equal amounts of soap solution are added using the 'pipette'. The bottles are then given an equal shaking, allowed to stand and the lathers compared. The softer waters will support a better lather. A softening agent such as Calgon added to hard water improves the latter considerably.
11. Acids and Alkalis (household uses).

Unit IV. Human Biology
Visual aids in the way of prepared diagrams are available from numerous sources, and there are excellent dismountable models in transparent plastic which can be obtained. The teacher must always bear in mind that this is a general science course and not a pre-medical one.
12. The Digestive System.
  The composition of foods- a balanced diet.
  Tests for starch, sugar and fat.
  Human dental structure and the teeth of animals; care of the teeth.
  Diagram of the alimentary canal—action in various parts of the system (this topic is admirably introduced by the Unilever films 'Nothing To Eat but Food' and 'The Digestive System').
13. The Circulation of the Blood.
14. The Skin (once again there is a very good film available from Unilever).
15. Movement and Support, Excretion and The Nervous System.
16. Reproduction in Mammals.

Fourth Year

Unit I. Electricity and Magnetism
Wherever possible individual work-sheets are provided, though it is realised that the standard of attainment of some of the weaker pupils is not equal to following printed instructions and then the teacher is called upon to explain fully each procedure.
1. Conductors and Insulators.
  Factors controlling the passage of an electric current through a wire. Resistance, Insulators, Heating effect, fuses, incandescence, lighting.
2. Magnets and some of their properties.

167

3. Electromagnetism.

Construction of a simple Morse sounder and model electric motor. The working of the electric bell and telephone.

4. How Electricity is Produced. I.

Simple cells and Leclanché (dry) cells.

Accumulators: observable features, not internal action.

5. How Electricity is Produced. II.

Dynamos (bicycle) and generators. Transformers.

6. The Household Electrical Circuit.

A demonstration board is very useful. There are many films available from the Electricity Development Association which can be shown to illustrate the above topics. They are, however, intended for general exhibition and the concepts dealt with, although generally well explained, are often beyond the understanding of the lower stream. Nevertheless, if the films are being used for the upper and middle streams the lower stream pupils may feel deprived if they do not see them.

Unit II. Fuels and Power

7. Coal and Coal Gas.

The geology of coal will already have been dealt with in the geography lessons. We are concerned with the heating effect and products of combustion.

Coal gas is made in a simple apparatus—reserved for use from year to year. There are Gas Council charts and leaflets to illustrate the lessons.

8. Oil.

There are many films, charts, diagrams and booklets issued by the oil companies to illustrate oil-bearing formations, and the processes of prospecting, extraction and distillation. Samples of crude oil and minerals are also available.

9. The Steam Engine.

The work of the pioneers of the steam engine could be dealt with briefly, though it may be thought more appropriate for the history lessons. Pupils should also understand the operation and uses of the steam turbine. A model can be constructed and coupled with a coil and magnet to provide an electric generator.

10. The Internal Combustion Engine.

Following the explosion of a gas and air mixture in a suitable tin, the driving force of the internal combustion engine can be discussed together with the other strokes necessary in the four-stroke cycle for the repetition of the explosion. Films and charts are available from various oil companies.

Unit III. Science and Health

Many of the boys and girls in the lower streams are from sub-standard homes, or have parents who do not bother to maintain satisfactory living conditions. These children need to be taught the rudiments of hygiene and sanitation.

There are books which provide interesting accounts of the pioneers in the fight against disease. The stories of Pasteur and Jenner make a useful introduction to the study of microbes. The development of a disease within the body needs to be discussed, and the methods employed to combat it. Then the ways in which diseases are carried should be dealt with, and the methods used to restrict the spread of disease. Some of the B.B.C. radio lessons cover these topics very well. There is little active practical work which can be done; most of the lessons will need to be discussion, illustrated with diagrams, filmstrips and films.

Notemaking

With the lower forms there is inevitably a small group of pupils who cannot read very well and who find it difficult to express their thoughts in writing. As a result notemaking must be cut down to a minimum. Copying material from the blackboard or elsewhere is not really of much value. Some thinking could be stimulated by requiring the pupils to complete sentences by filling in key words. Duplicated sheets with 'skeleton' sentences containing blanks for key words have been found useful. The pupils copy the whole sentence into their notebooks to provide a summary of the work done. Duplicated diagrams have also been provided which require the labelling to be completed as notes. This procedure has also been used for examination purposes though it has its limitations. It is obviously unsuitable for pupils who cannot read. When notemaking, these pupils could probably copy from the paper and be helped individually when filling in the blanks. It is, perhaps, relevant to mention that one second year boy who had asked for 'housefly' to be spelt for him was stuck in his writing because he had forgotten how to write the letter 'y'! According to *Half our Future*, the Newsom report, the method described above would appear to be in fairly general use, but it is pointed out that such pupils need more experience in expressing themselves and should be required to make more detailed answers, involving more practice in sentence construction. The science teacher is faced with the dilemma of dealing with a reasonable number of science topics or spending more time on notemaking with the increased demands on time for marking which is probably very meagre in any case. Some compromise is necessary. Teachers of English have been known to inquire about the topics their pupils have been studying in science lessons in order to provide them with subjects for composition.

Examinations

If examinations are considered necessary they should be as simple as possible. Practical tests would be very appropriate, but difficult to organise. An example of the type of paper used in connection with the preceding scheme is shown on page 171. In the lesson before the examination the class is given a paper from an earlier year thus preparing them for the style of the examination. The few pupils who cannot read the questions do as well as they can but could be tested orally later.

A Fifth Year Course

Pupils of limited ability do not as a rule stay on for a further year. No syllabus for a fifth year has so far been required in this school. If it were necessary to provide one, some of the work dealt within the fourth year would be postponed leaving time for a more detailed study of what was left, and the topics for the fifth year also studied more extensively, especially those in which a vocational interest appears. For boys more work in mechanics and electricity, for girls biology, particularly social biology. No attempt would be made to follow a C.S.E. examination syllabus. If any pupil in this stream showed promise of succeeding in such an examination he, or she, would be given special attention.

A Specimen Examination Paper

3.C. Boys   *Science Examination*   *One Hour*

PART I

Write the numbers 1 to 20 down the side of your answer paper and against them write the word or words you think belong to the numbered spaces below.

An object floats because it is less ___1___ than the liquid on which it rests. A block of wood would have ___2___ of its volume immersed in petrol than in water.

Soil contains decayed plant material called ___3___. Spaces in the soil are filled up by ___4___ and ___5___. Soil is broken up by ___6___. Mineral salts in soil water provide ___7___ for plants.

The rock or earthy material from which a metal is obtained is called an ___8___. The process in which heat is used to obtain the metal from it is called ___9___. A mixture of metals fused together is called an ___10___. Copper and tin fused together produce ___11___. Iron is an ___12___. In nature it is found combined with other elements such as ___13___ and ___14___. Until about 400 years ago, iron was smelted in small furnaces using ___15___. A hundred years ago ___16___ was very expensive but it is now cheap enough for kitchen utensils. This is because it needs large amounts of ___17___ to obtain it from its ore. The chief metals found as metals, not as ores, in nature are ___18___ and ___19___. ___20___ is one of the densest metals there is.

Some spellings which may help you:

alloy	aluminium	bronze
charcoal	dense	electricity
element	humus	hydrogen
iodine	nitrogen	oxygen
platinum	silver	smelting
sulphur	water vapour	weathering

PART II

Write the numbers 21 to 40 on the other side of your paper and opposite them write the word or words you think belong to the numbered spaces below.

If a 4-lb weight stretched a spring one inch, the weight stretching the spring $1\frac{3}{4}$ inches would be ___21___.

A bicycle needs ____22____ from time to time to keep it running more easily, the purpose of this is to reduce ____23____ .

Limestone, ____24____ and ____25____ are all forms of calcium carbonate, which when acted upon by an acid produce ____26____ . When heated in a kiln gas is driven off and ____27____ remains.

The garden needs ____28____ occasionally to counteract the acidity left after crops have been grown.

The water we get at home mostly comes from ____29____ . It is fairly ____30____ to make a lather because it contains ____31____ . In some areas rain-water is collected for washing purposes because it is ____32____ . Synthetic detergents often contain a chemical to make the water ____33____ and therefore easier to lather.

All living cells contain a substance known as ____34____ . To make more cells all animals must ____35____ . In the process of digestion, food enters the mouth where it is acted upon by the ____36____ , then proceeds to the ____37____ and then to the ____38____ .

Blood is pumped round the body by the ____39____ and carries ____40____ to be used in muscular action.

Some spellings which may help you:

carbon-dioxide	chalk	charcoal
chewing	dissolved	friction
hydrogen	intestines	iodine
liming	lubrication	marble
minerals	nitrogen	oxygen
protoplasm	quicklime	reproduce
reservoirs	saliva	stomach
water vapour	weathering	

Many teachers might prefer to have the pupils write the missing words into the spaces provided, and the whole, when completed, would be a connected prose account. This exercise then has considerable value as a learning aid as well as an assessment device. The marking would be just as simple, the more successful pupils would have an effort they would cherish while the less successful would probably find satisfaction in completing correctly a second copy for future reference.

172

7. THE RELATIONSHIP OF SCIENCE TO OTHER SUBJECTS

SOME relationship can be found between science and most of the other subjects taught in secondary schools. In this chapter three examples of the correlation that is possible are given. The correlation that can be achieved depends on the interest in the points of contact between the subjects that can be aroused and maintained by the teachers of the subjects concerned. It is unwise, however, to labour such relationships if the resulting interest shown or the knowledge gained by the pupils is not commensurate with the efforts required of the teachers of the subjects, for co-operative effort is the key to success in this field of school work.

The first example, written by a teacher with extensive experience of craft teaching, deals with the inter-relation of craft and science. Many science teachers may feel that the technical details of some of the points of contact are beyond their capabilities but it is hoped that teachers will consider how far they can use these ideas in correlating their science teaching with the craft teaching in their school. This section also contains a list of tools which will be particularly valuable in schools which are fortunate enough to have a laboratory technician, or a science teacher, who is interested in apparatus construction. The pupils, both boys and girls, can also be encouraged to make use of these tools in the making of apparatus and models with a scientific bias. The list is fairly extensive but good work is not possible on many occasions without the correct tools, but a smaller selection is possible if the work is limited in scope.

The second section deals with the correlation between science and housecraft (or domestic science) and is to a certain extent a symposium by a member of the committee who has had considerable opportunity for observing the teaching of both subjects using the links suggested. This is one approach which can help to dispel the idea that the physical and chemical sciences are not for girls.

The third and final section will have a greater appeal possibly to the non-urban school and is, in the main, the result of practical experience obtained by a teacher who taught both science and rural studies for many years, until a specialist in Rural Studies was appointed to the school. The correlation still goes on but the additional teaching time allows both subjects to be widened and deepened.

The teacher reader should bear in mind that these ideas are practical, useful and well worth while but they will lose their impact and lessen their usefulness if they do not arouse some enthusiasm and interest in both teacher and taught.

Craft

Scientific principles are in themselves insufficient. It is important that the child's knowledge and experience should be extended by the conscious application of the principles outside the laboratory.

Several school subjects are concerned in the main with the application rather than the teaching of principles. Amongst these subjects are those which in a boys' school, are usually grouped together as the technical subjects department, for example, woodwork, metalwork, and technical drawing with its related graphical solutions to design problems.

One occasionally meets the pupil who claims to have 'done' specific gravity in the laboratory but does not readily appreciate its importance in the craft-room in, say, the testing of reclaimed metals for purity or for estimating the proportions of two constituents in an alloy, i.e. lead and tin in soft solder. Similarly he might also have an academic understanding of oxide formation but not yet realise how important the possession of such knowledge can be as an elementary guide to temperature estimation in the hardening and the tempering of the steel centre punch he has made.

The teaching of scientific principles is, of course, not merely taught so that the pupil will better understand his school craftwork any more than school craftwork is limited to providing opportunity for the application of scientific principles. The two together do, however, provide unrivalled educational opportunities for the integration of theory and practice. An area in which joint activities could take place would be an advantage and would allow closer co-operation between teachers engaged in teaching the subjects. The interchange of ideas might also, with advantage, take place during syllabus preparation, the possible points of contact being discussed by teachers concerned and tabulated in a supplementary outline.

Many visual aids and sectioned working models common to both laboratory and craft-room provide a visible link between the two and help the pupil to appreciate the dependence of workshop on laboratory. It is true that craftwork teachers often refer to the underlying principles of a craft 'as the occasion arises' during the progress of the craft lesson. This is satisfactory so far as it goes but all children do not appreciate principles so readily. To them the principle, when they are out of the science laboratory, is not so obviously an integral part of their practical work. They, therefore, require a stronger emphasis than the reference to principles 'as the occasion arises'.

The craft teacher in consultation with his science colleague will know when he can safely assume a principle is known by the class. It might not be desirable for the craft teacher to attempt the introduction of new scientific principles as this could easily cut across the science syllabus. Often a principle is applied in craftwork long before it is even touched upon in science. This affects craftwork little while at the same time providing examples which the science teacher can draw upon when appropriate to his syllabus. Craftwork provides so many opportunities for the application of the same principle that integration does not suffer on this count.

The suggestions that follow are not given as being in chronological order but are given as points of contiguity between science and craft. The list is by no means exhaustive and its use will depend upon the syllabuses involved.

Science	*Craft Integration*
Nature of oxidation. Effect of thickness of oxide layer on observed colours.	Hardening and tempering small tools made of tool steel.
Demonstration of strength of aluminium oxide. (1) Changes in physical and chemical properties of steel on heating and quenching. (2)	Temperature changes noted by observing changes in tempering colours.
Examination of microscopical structure.	Preparation of heat treated and polished specimens of metal.

175

Science	*Craft Integration*
Effect of carbon content in steel. Carburising compounds and organic salts.	Carburising and case-hardening mild steel.
Alloys of lead and tin. Melting points of alloys. Simple bench test for high or low lead/tin ratio. (3)	Soft soldering.
Specific gravity tests for proportions of lead and tin in samples of soft solder. (4)	
Bronze formation on copper bit.	Care of soldering 'irons'.
Conductivity of copper compared with iron. Preparation of zinc-chloride flux. Capillary attraction.	Application of flux.
Electrolytic action and corrosion. Strength of soft soldered joints compared. (5)	Cleaning off in running water.
Generation of heat and static electricity. Heat and temperature. Centrifugal force. Conversion of rotational to peripheral velocities. Spark appearance.	Buffing and grinding.
Catalysts and chemical reaction. Synthetic resins. Identification of adhesives. (6) Penetration into material. (7)	Joining of materials, using adhesives.
Shrinkage in direction of annual rings compared with radial shrinkage. Comparison of rates of shrinkage, and moisture absorption in different timbers. (8) Chemical seasoning.	Reversal of boards when edge jointing, to counteract twisting.

176

Science	Craft Integration
Galvanic action. Nails in 'jelly battery' using indicators to locate poles. (8)	
Zinc as 'sacrificer'. Rapid corrosion of aluminium by amalgamating metal with mercury.	Use of metallic zinc based paints to prevent corrosion.
Stains of timber. Chemical action between timber and metals. (10) Colouring of metals.	Chemical colouring of materials.
Demonstration of electro-chemical action to clean dirty cutlery, using aluminium and hot trisodium phosphate/solution. (11)	Plating and anodising.
Making Hershel's light sensitive paper: solution (a) ferric ammonium citrate (green) $2\frac{1}{2}$ gm in 10 ml water, (b) potassium ferricyanide 1 gm in 10 ml water. Treat white paper with solutions (a) and (b) (mixed 50/50) in subdued light. Hang up to dry and keep in the dark.	Preparation of blueprints for both craft and science departments.
Expansion and contraption of metal at all temperatures. (12) Choice of rivets or nails to reduce galvanic action. Corrosive effect of timber on metals. (13) Strength of riveted and nailed joints.	Riveting (hot and cold) and nailing.
Comparative merits of standard woodwork joints. (14) Simple tensile or compressive tests to compare standard joints with glued joints.	
Biology of the tree trunk. Underlying considerations determining cutting of logs into boards.	Choice of timbers for strength and decorative effect.

177

Science	*Craft Integration*
Thermal action of certain substances.	Addition of temperature raising chemicals to dry off the dross.
Specific gravity tests for purity. Effect on specific gravity of method of production, i.e. cast, rolled, electrically deposited.	Pouring molten metal into ingots.
Densities of materials. Weighing machines and weighing procedure.	Weighing of alloying elements copper and aluminium.
Order of melting. Solid and liquid solutions. Specific heats.	Preparation of the stock alloy 25 per cent aluminium and 75 per cent copper by weight.
High-temperature measuring with instruments and other aids.	Temperature measurements.
Calculations involving proportion.	Addition of aluminium to stock alloy to give required working alloy.
Mechanical advantage. Levers. Couples. Cutting actions of tap and die. Lubricants.	Screwcutting (hand).
Simple and compound gear trains. Cutting action of lathe tool, compared with tap and die. The helix and inclined plane. Thread forms. Indicator and chalk marks. These operations lend themselves readily to integration as regards the many aspects of mechanics.	Machine (lathe). Turning in chuck and between centres using normal lathe accessories.
Solids of revolution.	Taper turning and form turning.
Balancing. Rocking couples.	Turning on face plate.

178

Science	*Craft Integration*
Production of heat. Coolants and specific heats. Nature of cutting action. Speeds and feeds. Action of the reduction back gear. Turning moments.	Drilling in lathe and drilling machine.
Nature of light. Polarised light.	Preparation of Perspex models to illustrate stress patterns set up in well designed and poorly designed components.
Penetration of stains. Stains of timber due to insect pest attack, fungal attack and natural chemical contents.	Staining and polishing and general wood finishing.
Reaction of timber with the stain or polish used and possible corrosive action on metal with which the timber is in close contact. (16)	Care in choice of fastening, i.e. cut joint. Metal screws or nails.
Inclined plane and wedge. Inertia of blade. Absorption of energy. Consideration of grain direction in plane body. Pure cutting action. Friction.	Many common workshop tools illustrate basic mechanical principles in their construction, use and adjustment, e.g. wooden plane.

Individual projects may be devised from the beginning with integration as the main themes.

Ease of metal flow and pattern withdrawal.	Oscillating cylinder steam engine. Design of frame and preparation of pattern.
Diameter of bore and length of stroke.	Piston and cylinder.
Determination of flywheel dimensions and drawing of diagrams.	Flywheel.

179

Science	*Craft Integration*
Turning moment diagrams.	Throw of crank.
Balancing, etc.	
Determination of horse power and efficiency.	

The diagrams and other calculations may be dealt with as deeply as considered desirable.

Optics.	Compound Microscope: A good
Preparation of slides.	project for two or three boys in-
Finished microscopes used in the	volving little accurate machin-
laboratory and workshop.	ing as the components are
	mainly 'as cast'.

Notes and Bibliography

The following is an outline of some of the experiments and a list of books which have been found to be of great value in the formulating and carrying out of an integrated scheme of work. The numbers are those referred to in the text.

(1) *Demonstration of strength of aluminium oxide.*

Suspend an aluminium strip or knitting needle from a clamp. Pass a Bunsen flame up and down the strip until the metal melts. The molten metal will flow down, inside its oxide envelope, and hang suspended in a bag of oxide.

See Edwards, W. H., *Aluminium in Metalwork and Science* (Science Club).

(2) Chapman, W. A. J., *Workshop Technology*, Volume 1.

(3) If the solder is held close to the ear and bent double a creaking sound, the tin cry, may be heard depending on the amount of tin present in the alloy. Lead betrays its presence by the greater density of the line when the solder is used as a pencil.

(4) The test is made by calibrating a beam to read the specific gravity of both copper and aluminium as in the classical account of 'Archimedes and the Golden Crown'.

See Edwards, W. H., *Aluminium in Metalwork and Science* (Science Club).

(5) Simple stressing frames, based upon moments, may be constructed to apply tension, compression or shear forces.

(6) Timber Development Association, *The Identification of Wood Glues* (Research Report C/RR/B).

(7) Wood shavings taken from a glued joint are examined, with a hand lens or microscope, and the results compared.

(8) Timber Development Association, *Timber Seasoning* (T. D. A. Red Booklet).

(9) Points of high stress become the anodes and points of lower stress the cathodes during corrosion. This may be illustrated by placing nails or treated metals in a jelly electrolyte consisting of an agar-agar salt solution with suitable indicators to locate the anodic and cathodic areas of the metal. An extremely interesting booklet, *Corrosion in Action*, and a film is available from the Mond Nickel Co. Ltd.

(10) Timber Development Association, *Stains in Timber* (Timber Information Leaflet 44).

(11) If aluminium scrap (milk bottle tops) are placed in a hot solution of tri-sodium phosphate it will be found that tarnished or dirty cutlery may be cleaned. This is due to an electro-chemical reaction.

   See Edwards, W. H., *Aluminium in Metalwork and Science* (Science Club).

(12) Armytage, George, *Metalwork for Schools and Colleges* (Oxford).

(13) Timber Development Association, *Timber Properties and Corrosion* (Information Bulletin C/1B/4).

(14) Croid 'Joint Cards' from Croid Ltd. Tests may be carried out in the stressing frames.

(15) Coker, E. G., and Filon, L. N. G., *Treatise on Photo-Elasticity* (Cambridge).

(16) Wood shavings, taken from stained or contaminated timber, are examined with a hand lense or microscope. See also the following booklets from the Timber Development Association: *The Examination of Timber* (Technical Leaflet T.B.L.4); *Timber Pests* (Red Booklet); *The Acidity of Wood* (T.D.A. Research Report C/RR/1);

181

Acidity and Corrosive Effects of Redwood and Whitewood (T.D.A. Research Report C/RR/7).

Apparatus Construction

Apparatus making can be a very worthwhile aspect of craft education in the school and children should be encouraged to build and improvise their own apparatus. In this way they will not grow up with the feeling that their scientific thinking must be limited by the apparatus available. When a special piece of unorthodox apparatus is required the person requiring it is often the only person who can make it or supervise its making.

To carry out this work it is essential that at least a basic tool kit is available. Improvising apparatus is one thing but it should not be necessary to improvise on tools, otherwise crudity caused by this economy will eventually result.

A suitable bench adaptable for both woodwork and metalwork is a first requirement. The size of the bench will of course depend upon available space. A suggested size would be about 5 ft × 3 ft. For bending sheet material a piece of angle iron let into the edge of the bench provides a sharp working edge. If funds permit, a suitably insulated hand or bench electric drill is an asset and saves much valuable time.

The equipment need not be excessive as the methods of construction are not of primary importance. After all, if a simple ray box is required there is no particular virtue in using dovetails when a perfectly neat and functional job can be produced by nailing the joints. Construction time can also be saved by making use of standard component parts such as pipe fittings; employing constructional kits, etc.

Care of tools is important and a suitable racked cupboard is ideal. Electrical equipment used by children should, in the interests of safety, operate at 110 volts a.c., provided by a suitable transformer having the centre tap of the secondary coil connected to earth (the maximum voltage that can give a shock is then 50 volts a.c.).

Suggested Tool Kit

Additions can be made from time to time according to personal requirements.

Article	Size and Description	Suggested Number
Abrafile frame and assorted blades	A very useful tool for cutting irregular shapes from wood, metal, etc.	1
Bradawls	Several small sizes with fast tangs.	3 sizes should suffice
Bench hook	A good quality bench hook will save the bench surface from saw-cuts and also help to hold the timber securely whilst using the tenon saw or chisel.	1
Brace joiners	10-in swing ratchet.	1
	Set of screw ended bits $\frac{3}{4}$ in to $\frac{5}{8}$ in.	1
	Expansive bit.	1
Callipers	6-in outside spring.	1
	6-in inside spring.	1
Chisel, cold	$\frac{3}{4}$ in, $\frac{5}{16}$ in and $\frac{1}{2}$ in cross cut. A variety of small sizes for awkward jobs, and for cutting grooves.	1 of each
Chisels, firmer	$\frac{1}{8}$ in to $\frac{3}{4}$ in.	
Centre punch		1
Combination	A useful tool, if funds permit, for squaring materials, marking angles and finding centres of round objects.	1
Dividers	6-in spring. 9.	1
Drilling machine	Breast 0 in to $\frac{1}{2}$ in.	1
	Hand 0 in to $\frac{1}{4}$ in.	1
Drills	$\frac{1}{16}$ in. to $\frac{1}{2}$ in in stand, with countersink. Several smaller sizes from $\frac{1}{16}$ in to $\frac{3}{16}$ in.	1 set: 6 of $\frac{1}{16}$ in 6 on $\frac{1}{8}$ in 3 of $\frac{3}{16}$ in
Folding bars	10-in. (Used for making sharp folds in rectangular tinned plate boxes and similar operations.)	
Files	A good variety of files of all shapes and cuts well repays its collecting. A full list of available files would be beyond the scope of this book; however, for general use a 10-in smooth cut, second cut and bastard cut, hand safe edge, are recommended.	

Article	Size and Description	Suggested Number
Gouges	¾-in and ½-in. (Useful for gouging out concave shapes in wood and soft materials or for cutting grooves.)	
Glass cutters	Interchangeable wheel type suitable for general use.	1
Glass cutter's T-square	A blackboard T-square with a piece removed from the stock at the end of the blade to allow the cutter to pass completely across the glass being cut.	1
Hammers, engineers' ball pein	½ lb.	1
	1 lb.	1
	1½ lb.	1
Mallet, joiners	4-in.	1
Magnetic link	A special tool for holding components in their correct spacial relationship whilst soldering.	1
Marking gauge		1
Nail punches	Assorted sizes.	3 sizes
Number stamps	⅜-in numbers.	1 set
Oilstone and oil can	Fine and medium grade for sharpening chisels, etc.	1
Pincers		1
Pliers		
Combination	Electricians' insulated.	1
Round-nose		1
Circlip	A useful tool in both cranked and straight forms for gripping circlips in instruments.	1
Rules	Rustless steel, 12-in.	2
	6-in.	1
Screwdrivers, cabinet	10-in.	1
electricians'	6-in and 8-in.	1 of each
watchmakers'		1 set
Smoothing plane	Steel body; 2½-in blade.	1
Soldering bit	Electricians', with cored solder spool, 8 oz.	1
Spanners box	⅛-in to ½-in B.S.W.	1 set
	Adjustable 8-in.	1

184

Article	Size and Description	Suggested Number
Stilson wrench	12-in.	1
Saws,		
tenon	10-in.	1
handsaw	22-in.	1
hacksaw	10-in rigid frame.	1
fretsaw		1
miniature		
hacksaw	Picador or Eclipse type.	2
Hacksaw blades	10-in soft 24 t.p.i.	1 gross
Scriber		1
Tin snips	8-in straight.	1
(non-nip type)	8-in curved.	1
	12-in cranked.	1
Taps and dies	$\frac{1}{8}$-in to $\frac{1}{2}$-in B.S.W.	1 set
	It is cheaper to buy the taps and dies loose than in a fitted box.	
Taps and dies	0, 2, 4, 5 and 6 B.A.	1 set
Try-squares	4 in. (More than one useful for supporting small units whilst glue is setting.)	4
	6 in.	1
Tank cutter	For cutting discs in metal, etc. (It	1
(adjustable)	is worth obtaining a good quality one.)	

Supplies to be Used with the Tool Kit

Article	Size and Description
Aluminium angle	$\frac{3}{4}$ in $\times$ $\frac{3}{4}$ in.
Brass rod	$\frac{3}{4}$-in diameter.
Brass rods	Assorted sizes.
Brass strips	$\frac{3}{8}$ in $\times$ 18 s.w.g.
	$\frac{1}{8}$ in $\times$ $\frac{3}{16}$ in.
	$\frac{1}{2}$ in $\times$ $\frac{1}{16}$ in.
Brass sheet	18 or 20 s.w.g.
Copper sheet	18 or 20 s.w.g.
Copper tubing	$\frac{1}{8}$-in inside diameter.
Case hardening compound	It is often necessary to harden points, etc., on apparatus.

Article	Size and Description
Cotter pins (split pins)	Assorted sizes. Used for holding joints together whilst soft soldering. Pass pin over metal to be joined to ensure close contact.
Wet and dry emery cloth	No. 150/240.
Glass paper	Medium.
Glass	18 oz and 24 oz.
Machine oil	
Nuts	$\frac{3}{4}$-in brass, B.S.W. 2 B.A. 4 B.A.
Perforated zinc	
Poly (vinyl) acetate	
P.V.A. synthetic resin or similar	
Rivets	$\frac{1}{2}$-in × $\frac{1}{8}$-in aluminium (and $\frac{1}{8}$-in aluminium washers). $\frac{1}{2}$-in × $\frac{1}{8}$-in copper.
Resin-based flux	If cored solder is not used.
Screws	$\frac{3}{4}$-in × 4-in B.A. csk. head 1$\frac{1}{2}$-in × 4-in B.A. csk. head $\frac{3}{4}$-in × 2-in B.A. cheese head) } plus washers.
Soft iron, solid bar	Not always easy to obtain.
Soft iron binding wire	Readily obtainable.
Steels, mild	$\frac{3}{8}$-in × diameter. $\frac{1}{2}$-in × $\frac{1}{8}$-in strip. $\frac{1}{2}$-in × $\frac{1}{16}$-in strip. $\frac{1}{4}$-in diameter rod.
Tinned plate	x and xx. Tinned plate is sold in grades denoted as x, xx, etc. x is thinner than xx. It may also be ordered in terms of s.w.g.
Tinmans' soft solder	

There are numerous books dealing with the production of home-made equipment and the equipment or apparatus required will vary according to the individual master. However, almost all include the following topics: the marking and cutting of the material, the preparation of the joints, the assembly, and painting or treating with other surface finishes if required.

The section on integration with other subjects outlines many of the possibilities existing in the school for integration between craftwork and science. If to this we add models which can be used by both the craft and the science teachers (models which are carried from one room to the other and used by either teacher), a link is forged between theory and practice which young minds might more readily appreciate.

How far one goes with these topics, of course, depends on several factors, not the least important being the abilities of the children concerned. However, it is possible to plant seeds which will one day bear fruit and, in many cases, it is better to explain than to ignore what is going on in the environment of which the child is an integral part.

Housecraft

There are immense opportunities in the fields of science teaching and housecraft teaching for co-ordination of these two subjects: the integration of the science course and of the home economics course will greatly enrich each other and lead to a comprehensive and rewarding curriculum for the pupil.

The introduction of properly correlated and integrated courses in science and housecraft into the school curriculum will ensure that girls of average ability will leave school with a sound training in modern home economics and a lively interest in the development and use of new domestic materials and appliances. This can only be achieved successfully if there is the closest liaison between the members of the staff in the departments concerned. There must be a 'give and take' attitude concerning the order and the content of the syllabus and a mutual and lively interest in the project as a whole. A school time-table is subject to many hazards, day by day and week by week, so that in many instances the timing of the various projects will be difficult. If, however, there is a sense of purpose, an attitude of goodwill and a determination to achieve co-ordination in the departments concerned much can be accomplished.

At present the extent to which such liaison exists is indeed very varied. In a few schools these two subjects are developed side by side, but, in far too many there is little or no attempt at integration. Perhaps the domestic subjects teacher fails to realise that home economics is becoming more and more scientifically based and that it is, therefore, very desirable that the scientific basis should be studied. Equally, perhaps, the scientist fails to realise the true nature of the discipline of home economics and is equally unwilling to make his or her contribution.

If one looks at one simple example—the nature of the advertising media which are now used in respect of domestic appliances and the apparent scientific evidence which the advertisers use—it becomes clear that there are immense opportunities in the laboratory, both in science and housecraft lessons to test some of the claims made on behalf of this or that machine or commodity.

There are, of course, some girls who will, throughout their lives, prefer merely to press a button and hope that all is well. On the other hand, for those girls who wish to apply a more sophisticated approach there will be an opportunity to make certain that home aids and machines are operated on a sound basis of a knowledge of the simple sciences and techniques involved. Such an approach will save hours of frustration and unnecessary expenditure and give a sense of purpose and direction.

Fields of Study

Syllabuses vary enormously in content and order but, so that some comprehensive pattern may be studied, a typical housecraft syllabus for a girls' comprehensive school of about 1,100 pupils has been used as the prototype. It is intended here merely to indicate possible areas of study and no attempt has been made to describe particular experiments. Most of the practical work involved is available in textbooks or in the Association for Science Education publications.

1. COOKERY

This subject provides a wide field of practical work in the science laboratory.

Food: a simple study of nutrition, the main constituents of everyday foods, the Calorie, food calorific values.

Chemical tests for these constituents.

Experiments with sugars, sugar candy, caramel, barley sugar, flour, eggs, milk and cheese—the lactometer.

Acidity and alkalinity of various substances using universal indicator, e.g. in vinegar, salt solution, lemon juice, milk, lactic acid, citric acid, Domestos, bicarbonate of soda, cream of tartar, salts of lemon, grapefruit juice, liver salts, toothpaste, benzoic acid, treacle or syrup.

Simple idea of pH value using $pH=7$ (neutral).

Viscosity of syrups.

Egg testings, coagulation temperature of egg white.

Chloroform test for the mineral matter in flour.

Alcohols and alcoholic beverages.

Esters (organic salts) as flavours.

The use of raising agents—comparative experiments with:

(*a*) sodium bicarbonate
(*b*) sodium bicarbonate and tartaric acid
(*c*) baking powder
(*d*) cake mix

Add water to each, test if necessary and observe the rate of liberation of carbon-dioxide.

Carbon dioxide—mineral water and wires.

Fermentation process—jam and yeast.

Breadmaking process—dough with and without the addition of yeast.

Correct method of making sauces and custard—breaking down the starch grain.

Inversion of sucrose.

Cooking of fruit—effect of acid on sugar.

Food preservation, enzymes, canning, fruit bottling, vacuum sealing, dehydration of foodstuffs under reduced pressure.

Preservatives in fruit juices. Food additives, sweeteners, saccharine.

Colouring of food.

Change of physical state—latent heat simply.

Finding the melting point of sugar, steaming food, 'solid' carbon-dioxide, 'Kepcold', depression and elevation of freezing points, freezing mixtures and ice-cream, iced waters.

Effect of heat on meat fibres, effect on proteins (mention of amino acids).

Osmosis:

(*a*) experiment with potato and carrot cubes;

189

(*b*) salt to extract juice from meat.

(*c*) crisping lettuce in plain water;

(*d*) crisping potato chips by pre-soaking in salt water.

Emulsions and emulsifying agents: glyceryl monostearate, mayonnaise, creams, ice-cream, furniture and other polishing creams.

Colloids very simply: gels, gelatine, jelly and jam.

Distillation—wines and spirits.

Evaporation: milk and butter coolers, refrigeration, deep freezing.

Humidity—food storage.

Efflorescence and hygroscopic effect on biscuit, and salt crispness, and icings.

2. LAUNDRYWORK

This branch of housecraft also has very many scientific applications in both physics and chemistry, with material suitable for all ages and abilities in the secondary school. (For suggestions for work in this field, refer to the notes on laundrywork science in *Science Teaching Techniques 12*.

3. DRESSMAKING AND NEEDLEWORK

In the larger school these two subjects may be in the charge of different specialist staff, whilst in smaller schools the same member of staff is responsible for both housecraft and needlework. The work on textiles is applicable to both these departments.

There is an admirable simple practical course on textiles outlined in *Textile Fibres* by Kemp, Oman and Pheasant (Whitcombe and Tombs).

Additional experimental work could be done on the elasticity of natural and synthetic fibres and on the insulating powers of materials, the waterproofing of materials using a silicone spray, production of drip-dry and permanently pleated materials, cake cup linings.

4. PERSONAL HYGIENE AND GROOMING

Structure and care of the skin—cleansing.

Comparison of soaps (acidity and alkalinity).

Study of cosmetics—nature of these products and effect on the skin.

Preparation of some cosmetics (recipes given in the chemistry section, chapter 3).

Care of the hair: some simple hairdressing science experiments; effect of bleach and perming lotions; science in the hair-dressing salon; simple physics in the fields of heat, light and electricity.

Growth of bacteria cultures after infection with dirty combs, fingers, etc.

5. HOUSEHOLD EQUIPMENT

The term is used here specifically for all appliances. Many of the electrical and gas appliances will be examined critically during the laundrywork course but there are many others which could usefully be studied.

Electrical: the vacuum cleaner and dustette, spin-drier, floor polisher, juicers, mixers, radiators and convectors, cooker, washing machine, irons, hair-driers, water heater, refrigerator, blankets and warming pads, toaster, a thermostat, oven thermometers.

The simple techniques of connecting a plug and mending a fuse.

The heating efficiency of types of electric hot plates.

Reading the meter and costing electricity.

Electrical faults and precautions.

The Electrical Association for Women produce useful charts and leaflets of several appliances. A visit at the end of this part of the course to the local showroom is usually found to be most profitable and enjoyable.

Gas: the cooker, boiler, fires and radiators, poker, refrigerator, storage heater, geyser, thermostat.

Efficiency of types of gas rings; gas pressure.

Reading the meter and costing gas consumption.

With some groups a simple study of coal gas can be made. This should not be too exhaustive otherwise it can be a boring topic. Again the gas showrooms can be visited and some attractive pamphlets and films are available.

Solid fuels: merits and demerits of open fires, under hearth draughts, closed stoves, central heating.

Oil heaters: convector and radiant types compared, care and maintenance, safety precautions when in use.

Cooking utensils: advantages and disadvantages of the varying materials from which these are now made, e.g. restrictions on using aluminium, non-stick frying-pans and saucepans, pyrex and pryosil glass, pressure cookers.

Steamers, latent heat transfer.

Other utensils: vacuum flask, insulated bags and beakers.

Action of foods, fruit juices on metals (copper, iron, aluminium, zinc, tin, lead.

Rust proofing, plating, lacquering. Prevention of corrosion in metals.

Contamination of food and water by metals.

6. FURNISHINGS

Materials in the home: flammability (ignition point), effect of acids and alkalis, thickness.

Heat resistance or absorption: suitability for various domestic uses (transference of heat considerations); heat resistant mats, oven cloths and gloves.

Plastic materials: effect of excess heat, acids and alkalis. (Insert experiments.)

Colour: scientific understanding as a basis to appreciation and design.

Metallic finishes: dull and polished surfaces, rust and corrosion.

Floorings: a scientific survey of the suitability of carpet, lino, rubber, plastic, tiles, wood, concrete, matting as flooring or floor covering; types of underlay.

Design of chairs to suit different postures.

Heights of working surfaces to suit posture and prevent tiredness.

Lampshade materials: variation in light transmission and durability.

Light fittings: function and efficiency, prevention of eyestrain.

7. CLEANING MATERIALS

Household soaps, soap powders, soapless detergents, scouring powders and pastes.

Surface abrasion, resistence to chemical action.

Wax polishes: content and necessary properties, silicone polishes, making a polish.

Metal polishes: chrome, brass and silver polish; silver 'dip'; 'Long Life' polish; a home-made silver polishing cloth.
Car polishes, 'Windolene', barrier creams.

8. HOUSE CONSTRUCTION
Damp walls and their prevention: damp-proof courses, rising damp.
Double windows.
This part of the course could be linked with the study of modern house design in the art department.

9. PESTS
Recognition of common animal and insect pests: cockroach, silver fly, ants, housefly, blowfly, flour weevil, woodworm, fleas, lice, bed bugs, etc.
Rats, mice and household pets as carriers of disease.

Bibliography

1. SOME REFERENCE BOOKS FOR THE TEACHER
FOX, B. A., and CAMERON, A. G. *A Chemical Approach to Food and Nutrition* (University of London).
RANKIN, W. M., and HILDRETH, E. M. *Intermediate Domestic Science*: Vol. 1, *Food and Nutrition*; Vol. 2, *Textiles in the Home* (Allman).
H.M.S.O. *Manual of Nutrition* (H.M.S.O.).
BICKNELL, F. *Chemicals in Food and in Farm Produce* (Faber).
BOGERT, L. J. *Laboratory Manual of Chemistry* (W. B. Saunders).
TINKLER, C. K., and MASTERS, H. *Applied Chemistry, Parts 1 and 2* (Lockwood & Son).
SANDERON, I. *Science Applied to Housecraft* (Edward Arnold).
POUCHER, W. A. *Perfumes, Cosmetics and Soaps*. Three volumes (Chapman & Hall).
DAVIDSON, A. *Waxes and Polishes* (Hill).
DAVIDSON, A. *Polishes and Cleaning Materials* (Hill).
DAVIDSON, D. M. J. *Floors and Floorings* (Crosby & Lockwood).
ALLCOTT, A. *Plastics Today* (Oxford).
COOK, J. GORDON. *Your Guide to Plastics* (Merrow).
TOOTAL BROADHURST & SON. *Handbook of Textiles* and *Notes on Textiles* (Obtainable upon request).
A. BOAKE ROBERTS & CO. Booklet of cosmetic formulae and information leaflets (obtainable upon request).

HARRY, R. G. *Principles and Practice of Modern Cosmeticology* (Hill).
HARRY, R. G. *Cosmetic Materials* (Hill).

2. BOOKS FOR THE PUPIL
DAVIS, B. *Science Cooks the Dinner* (Brockhampton).
JOSLIN, I. C., and TAYLOR, P. M. *Everyday Domestic Science and Hygiene* (Macmillan).
HOLT, J. M. *Housecraft Science* (Bell).
KEMP, J., OMEN, E. A., and PHEASANT, J. A. *Textile Fibres* (Whitcombe and Tombs).
I.C.I. FIBRES DIVISION. *Facts about Man-made Fibres* (obtainable upon request).
KILGOUR, O. F. G., and MCGARRY, M. *Introduction to Science and Hygiene for Hairdressers* (Heinemann).
LEE, C. M., and INGLIS, J. K. *Science for Hairdressing Students* (Pergamon).
Electricity in the Home (also titles in *Gas, Water* and *Coal* in the same series (Educational Productions).
ELECTRICAL ASSOCIATION FOR WOMEN (various pamphlets obtainable upon request).
GAS COUNCIL. (Publications obtainable upon request).
PLASTICS AND RUBBERS DIVISION, SHELL CHEMICAL LIMITED. (Publications obtainable upon request).

Many other books are available, some more elementary and others more advanced, and it will be for the teacher to select and use material appropriate to the age and ability of the group.

Rural Studies

Rural studies in secondary schools take many forms. In schools where facilities exist and the environment is suitable there may be a complete range of activities including animal husbandry, beekeeping and an extensive area devoted to growing crops. In other areas with similar requirements schools may be associated with neighbouring farms or farm institutes.

Science with a rural bias may be the only form of science taught in the school. Should it be so, it will be necessary to include much of the general science in chapter 4 of this book. Where science is taught separately from rural studies, or whatever name is given to it, there should be a close link between the teachers concerned in order to correlate one scheme of work with the other. The problem is simplified if one teacher is responsible for both subjects, but the work required to maintain both aspects of his teaching in good order and to make adequate preparation for his lessons, will be a heavy load for the teacher.

In rural areas the general science scheme should be given a suitable bias. The topics air and water, which form a common starting point for many science schemes are equally important in town and country and there may be little variation in the teaching. The factors affecting plant growth (excluding fertilisers, which are dealt with under chemistry) can be dealt with in much greater detail, indeed, in a country school the simple experiments found in the first-year schemes of many urban schools, may have been done years before. Some more elaborate ones are needed, e.g. the investigation of plant structure using microscopes and more detailed work on plant propagation. An earlier introduction to chemistry may be desirable in order to understand the requirement of a plant in the way of nutrients. Thus a series of plants growing in solutions can be set up and the effects of missing elements discovered. Many books contain details of such an experiment but *Science in the School Garden* by Mary A. Johnstone (Macmillan) contains the description of a successful experiment which was previously published in the *School Science Review*. A variation of this experiment employed tomato plants instead of the usual tradescantia and pupils were found to be intensely interested in their development.

The other customary experiments with plants, the 'tropisms', should be demonstrated effectively and it is worth while assembling moderately elaborate apparatus for this purpose as it should be used each year.

Chemistry has a prominent place in agriculture and horticulture owing to the importance of artificial fertilisers and the use of lime. It has been found convenient to resume the study of chemistry—following an introduction to it in the first year when dealing with air and water—with an investigation into combustion such as Lavoisier's discovery of the increase in weight which occurs when oxidation takes place. Thus, through the burning of sulphur the scheme leads to acids and compounds. Some idea of molecular construction, atomic and molecular weights is desirable, in order to estimate the proportion of useful elements in the various fertilisers. Acidity entails *pH* values and it is not really beyond interested secondary pupils to understand the need for such a classification and how to estimate it using a suitable indicator. The making of lime and the uses of limestone must be dealt with and a relation between the *pH* value of a soil and the amount of lime needed to render it again suitable for crop growing is readily understood. Some useful information about fertilisers and lime is contained in *Fison's Fertilizer Book*, copies of which may be obtained gratis.

The study of insects and other invertebrates such as the earthworm form an interesting section of the scheme suitable for the second year. *The World of Small Animals* by T. H. Savory (U.L.P.) is a useful book to have on hand; so is the Young Farmers' Club booklet *Garden and Farm Insects*, and there are several other valuable books, including A. D. Imm's *Insect Natural History* (Collins' New Naturalist Series). Special attention might well be given to the honeybee and there are several practical manuals on beekeeping. *The World of the Honeybee* by Colin G. Butler (Collins New Naturalist Series) and *The Social Insects* by O. W. Richards (Macdonald) provide additional information.

The work in mechanics can be related closely to rural activities, the diameter and width of wheels are chosen to suit the ground over which they travel. Applications of levers and moments can be found in agricultural implements. Use is made of pulleys and the block and tackle, gears and chain drives. Machines of various kinds can be found to illustrate almost any aspect of the subject. The increasing mechanisation gives considerable scope to the study of its fundamental laws. The internal combustion engine is met at an early age; many boys and even girls being allowed to drive tractors in the fields long before they are old enough to drive a motor vehicle on the public highway.

The study of the soil, in addition to the chemistry side already mentioned, also entails learning about its formation and mechanical structure. Experiments dealing with this are to be found described in *Lessons on Soil* by E. J. Russell (Cambridge), *Simple Experiments in Biology* by C. Bibby (Heinemann), in *Science Teaching Techniques III*, in an article written by D. F. Bergin (Murray), and in several other books.

The next stage in biology could well be the study of vertebrates, dealing with some typical animals. The various systems should be dealt with in turn, more attention being paid to digestion and reproduction. The dissection of at least one animal should be undertaken. Keeping animals in school provides useful information concerning their feeding and rate of growth, and attention is drawn to the book *Animals in Schools*, by J. P. Volrath, published by the Universities Federation for Animal Welfare and John Murray. Farm animals are not dealt with; in schools where such animals are kept specialised literature should be available, including Y.F.C. booklets. No difficulty should be met when concerned with the study of reproduction in mammals, the examples at hand are so many and varied and the results of selective breeding are to be found in the best herds and also in crops. Milk could be investigated more thoroughly, finding its fat and mineral content, and possibly visiting a milk-testing laboratory.

The general principles of electricity can be taught in much the same way as in the general syllabus, special attention being paid to its heating effect, the working of motors and the generation of electricity and its transmission. The study of biology should not be terminated before dealing with man and disease, and the interdependence of living things. Recently attention has been drawn to the harm done to nature by the indiscriminate use of insecticides and other chemicals used on the soil; the older pupils will be able to consider this question reasonably.

Science Out of Doors (Longmans) is the title of a report made by a distinguished study group set up by the Nature Conservancy in 1960, to examine the role of field studies and their relation to school education and to science teaching in general. It deals with the facilities needed and gives details of countryside centres.

A useful symposium on field studies compiled by Miss P. J. Nicholson appears in *Science Teaching Techniques III* and mention should be made of the *How to Begin your Field Work* series by Miss V. E. Ford initiated by the Association of Women Science Teachers and published by John Murray.

Other useful books include: Fisher, G. D., *The Teachers' Book of Nature Study* (Chambers). Buchsbaum, R., *Animals Without Backbones* (Pelican, 2 vols.). *The Oxford Junior Encyclopedia*, Vol. II: *Natural History*. Knight, M., *The Young Field Naturalist's Guide* (Bell).

The weather plays a big part in rural activities and a study of its main features is an essential part of either rural science, geography or general science. An excellent description of the place it can be given in science teaching is to be found in *Science Teaching Techniques II* in an article written by E. R. Franklin. (Some of the earlier volumes of *Science Teaching Techniques* are out of print but should be available in the libraries of the local Institute of Education or Colleges of Education.)

8. LABORATORY ORGANISATION

IN the secondary school the young science teacher may have to take responsibility for his subject, and for the laboratory, without the invaluable guidance of a senior science master who knows from experience the many pitfalls which beset work in a laboratory. Much of the material in this chapter is meant to help the young teacher, and, so far as it is possible, to take the place of the assistance which a more experienced colleague could give him. It is realised that the science teacher, in comparison with his colleagues, carries additional responsibilities. He has a practical laboratory to care for, materials to provide, check and replace, and services of gas, water and electricity to maintain.

Preparation for the Demonstration Lesson

When it is possible the pupils should perform experiments themselves. Even with a demonstration experiment pupils should be encouraged to play an active part. If lessons are to run smoothly, pupils must be kept busy all the time. This involves the preparation, beforehand, of the apparatus needed for all the lessons of the day, whether for demonstration or individual work. This should be done either the night before or upon arrival at school at a sufficiently early hour in the morning. If apparatus has to be assembled when the class is in the laboratory, not only is valuable time wasted but there is every probability that discipline will become slack and in a practical room that may lead to danger. The assistance of a laboratory technician will enable the teacher to work more efficiently. It is also assumed that interest in what is to be done will have been aroused by some indication, perhaps at the end of the previous lesson, of what is to be expected.

It is a good idea to have a separate tray for each lesson of the day ready in the preparation-room. A spare set of parts, particularly those which are liable to break, such as glassware, lamps for ray apparatus, etc., should be ready in case of accidents. Experiments should always be tried out before the start of the lesson. There is nothing worse than experiments which do not work; the teacher may 'get away' with the occasional one, but he needs to be a very strong disciplinarian when failure is the order of the day.

The demonstration experiment is meant to drive home some particular point—to help and not to hinder the development of the idea. Unnecessary refinements of the apparatus which make the experiment more difficult to follow or which distract the attention from the essential points should therefore be avoided. The apparatus should always be as simple as possible, consistent with the needs of the experiment. It is frequently worth while to make it up in the preparation-room or workshop. For example, the electrolysis of water is much more likely to be understood if the apparatus consists of two test-tubes inverted in a funnel of water than if the complications of Hofmann's apparatus are introduced: or again, the use of large quantities with the lever balance will avoid the difficulties involved in the use of a chemical balance.

Some lessons will have a number of demonstration experiments and therefore need several pieces of apparatus and a certain amount of other visual material. It is probably best to confine the apparatus on the demonstration bench to that in use at the particular time, having the remainder ready in a convenient, readily accessible place. If, however, it is desired to have everything for the lesson ready on the bench from the start, it should be arranged in the proper sequence and not in a haphazard fashion. Such parts of the other visual material— diagrams, charts, etc.—which are not needed at the time should be covered up so that they do not distract the attention from what is to be seen.

Consideration must also be given to the arrangement of this type of lesson so that, as far as possible, there are no unnecessary periods of waiting during the experiment, e.g. water should be ready boiling if it is needed at the start, or heating should be begun sufficiently early if it is needed later. Some pauses cannot be avoided, and during these the pupils must be kept busy if discipline is to be maintained, either by a spirited discussion of what is being done or by writing notes or making diagrams. The beginner is well advised to consider carefully the questions which he can use to keep the class alive and active during these periods of waiting. (Incidentally it makes talking easier if Bunsens are controlled so that they burn quietly.)

It is essential that all pupils shall be able to see clearly the details of the demonstration. This is more easily arranged in a square laboratory than in a room which is long and narrow. In rearranging the pupils they should not be too close to the demonstration bench in case of an accident. Some may sit on the tables so that they have a clearer view. It will help considerably if definite places are allocated, for example, along three sides of a rectangle, so that at a given signal the pupils know where to go and can easily move there without undue commotion. The arrangement must be such that pupils are neither behind the demonstrator nor even on the same level at the sides. The essential point is that *all* must see, and the teacher is advised to put himself in the place of the most distant or most awkwardly placed pupil so that he is absolutely certain on this point. Easy visibility also depends on the apparatus itself. It is advisable to use large articles where possible, e.g. a 15-cm funnel where children would use a 7-cm size, and in some cases it may be helpful to raise the apparatus on a box. A well-lit object is more clearly seen than a badly-lit one, so a judiciously placed lamp may be needed. The background is important, e.g. dark objects show up better against a light background (why not wear a white overall?). A use may also be found for a steel framework to hold apparatus in a vertical plane—this can be purchased from the scientific instrument firms. A small mirror near the apparatus is sometimes useful to enable things placed horizontally on the bench to be seen, and the possibility of the use of projection methods should not be forgotten. It is worth remembering that diagrams on the blackboard should match the pupil's view of the apparatus, and the oral directions should be in terms of 'your' right or 'your' left. In all work with Bunsens, whether demonstration or individual, there is a real danger when the Bunsen flame is used in bright sunshine, as the flame becomes invisible; it is better to use a slightly luminous flame.

Sometimes demonstrations will be of a kind which only a few can see at a time, or in which only a few take readings at a time, using the combined work of the class to obtain the data. Here again it is essential for good discipline, and for preventing a waste of time, that the remainder of the class should be fully occupied, e.g. with written work or reading. Even though many

201

of the points which have been stressed may seem obvious, it must be emphasised that these are mistakes which are made every day—and the culprits are not always beginners but sometimes experienced teachers.

Preparation for Individual or Group Working

Whatever method of organisation is decided upon, the first essential is that apparatus should be easy to find. Most of the material used by the pupils will be in drawers or cupboards in the laboratory itself, and for ease of working there should be 'a place for everything and everything in its place'. One method which gives satisfactory results is to number the cupboards and drawers and to have a wall diagram showing their disposition and the major items which each contains. In addition to this the teacher keeps and maintains a book of all apparatus in alphabetical order, showing quantities and where each item is kept, and leaving spaces for the entry of new apparatus as it is received. This book enables him to find, without difficulty, any article which may only be used at infrequent intervals; whilst the wall diagram will enable anyone to find the more commonly used pieces of apparatus.

In the secondary school, science classes tend to be large and the amount of time spent in the laboratory tends to be small. Whilst it is important that pupils should learn to use a laboratory and its apparatus properly, it is not considered advisable that they should all fetch what they need from the cupboards, as this leads to a considerable amount of unnecessary movement and possible waste of time. The method which is now suggested has the advantage that every pupil has the responsibility for looking after apparatus at some time; that the apparatus is ready for use when required; that it can be easily checked before being put away; and that the person responsible for any untidy arrangement in cupboards is known. Monitors are chosen from each class and they are changed at intervals so that everyone has the necessary experience of dealing with apparatus. Only the monitors for the time being are allowed to use the cupboards. Before a lesson, the teacher gives them a list of the apparatus needed. They are responsible for getting it from the appropriate place and for putting it out in groups on a convenient side-bench. In order that it can be easily checked and easily carried it is advisable to have a number of boxes, racks and trays available. These can usually be made up in the school workshop to suit different items of equipment, e.g. a base with circular depressions to carry explorer compasses, racks with holes lined with cotton wool to take thermometers, etc. The wall diagram of the cupboard contents is mainly to help the monitors to find what is required and to replace it in its proper home. During the course of the lesson the pupils collect the apparatus from the groups which have been put out, and later return it there—but only under direction. The monitors then replace it in the cupboards after the teacher has checked it—and this method makes checking easy. It should perhaps be added that all apparatus must be clean before it is finally put away.

If cupboards are provided in the pupils' benches, some teachers may prefer to keep individual sets of apparatus in them, e.g. Bunsen, tripod, gauze, etc., care being taken not to mix iron and glass ware. If this is done, the class should thoroughly understand that complaints of apparatus missing or broken will only be accepted at the commencement of the lesson. Experienced teachers will know that there are certain items which tend to disappear from the laboratory more easily than others, e.g. small test-tubes, compass needles, magnets, lenses. A more careful watch needs to be kept on these; it is advisable to lock up the laboratory when not in use, and all poisons must always be kept securely locked up in a special cabinet—preferably in the preparation-room.

Grouping of Class

The simplest arrangement is for the whole class to be working the same experiment, being grouped usually in pairs or sometimes in threes for the purpose. For suitable topics when the supply of apparatus demands it, it is possible to use larger groups of six or eight children working in pairs on three or four simple experiments all related to the same principle, and pupils going from one experiment to the next so as to cover them all. In this case written instructions are necessary.

Whenever pupils work in groups there is a real need to see that each member of the group is taking an *active* part in what is being done. The tendency is nearly always for one of them to do most of the work whilst the others look on, or just take down observations. The teacher must see that the experiment is broken down so that each member of the group has a definite part to play in the actual manipulation, and he must go round the groups to see that this is being done, as well as to help with any difficulties which may arise.

Instructions to Pupils

Whatever method of giving instructions is adopted, they must be as short as is consistent with what has to be said, must be clear and to the point. They must enable the child to carry out the experiment, the purpose of which has been made absolutely clear by the preliminary discussion. At the same time, whilst pupils must know what to look for, they must not be told so much that they know what the result is to be. If the experiment is to be worth while there must be enough detail for the pupil to be able to carry it out effectively, yet at the same time the need for real thinking and active observation must remain. The preparation of such instructions is a difficult task, particularly for the young teacher. If he has no one to consult, he will be well advised to notice the reactions of the class to what they are told—a spate of questions relating to what has to be done will be evidence that instructions are not sufficiently clear.

The blackboard can be used providing the details are not too lengthy, but it has the disadvantage that in many laboratories half the class will be working with their backs to it. Instructions given orally can be satisfactory when few points need to be mentioned, but 'modern school' pupils in particular have only a limited ability to remember the steps in the necessary order. For the older pupils it is advisable to plan the written work on the blackboard. For this a sequence such as the following is suggested:

(1) Aim of lesson . . . (heading)
(2) Apparatus . . . (labelling diagram)
(3) Description of experiments . . . how it was done . . . what was noticed, etc.
(4) Results and conclusions.

In the modern school, section (3) will usually be short, and it is a good thing occasionally to dictate a short description as a model. It cannot be too strongly emphasised that habits of neatness and care are often 'caught' from the teacher. It is a good plan to get a pupil to tell the class what has to be done after the teacher has gone through it. Where instructions are more numerous it is probably best to have them typed. Not only are they available for reference throughout the experiment, but they permit of far greater detail and they force the pupil to read with comprehension—or, perhaps more correctly, they provide the need and interest necessary for the understanding of what is being read. Illustrations should accompany the written word, particularly to help pupils to know what new pieces of apparatus look like. In the case of younger and more backward pupils it will often be necessary to give the instructions for one operation only; let them finish this, and then proceed with further details, breaking the experiment up in this way into a number of parts which can be easily followed.

Discipline

As in all lessons, the most important aid to discipline is to keep the pupil busy: the main difference in a lesson in the laboratory is that a certain amount of noise is unavoidable, as is a certain amount of movement. The noise should be that produced by quiet conversation about the work which is in progress; the movement should be reduced to what is really essential. The test of good discipline in the laboratory is that when the teacher speaks to the class, the class immediately pays attention. As has already been emphasised, good planning and preparation are of the first importance.

Lack of discipline manifests itself in the interference with apparatus, taps, etc., as well as in the ways which apply in any subject. From the start a strong line is necessary, and it must be made obvious to every pupil that one of the main rules applying to the laboratory is 'No fooling here'. The co-operation of the pupils is more likely to be willingly given if they are given reasons for the restrictions—a warning of the dangers involved and of the care which is necessary.

Requisitioning Apparatus

It is not possible to do more than give a few general hints on this matter to guide the inexperienced teacher. The procedure is the same, whether he is concerned with equipment of a new laboratory, or with additions to what is already in stock with such replacements as have become necessary. The first essential is to go carefully through the scheme of work and to decide on what experiments are practicable. Those which, because of difficulties of manipulation, cost of apparatus or possible danger, will have to be carried out as demonstrations should be marked. The next step is to write down the apparatus needed for each experiment and thus to find out how many of each article are needed, remembering that there must be sufficient to allow the class to work in pairs for normal purposes. In the case of glassware and other breakable apparatus an addition must be made to cover possible accidents during the year. This then gives the list of apparatus to be ordered for a new laboratory, or indicates what extra is needed in the case of one which is already equipped. It is most important to remember that each item must be carefully specified, giving details of material, size, or voltage required, etc. It is desirable from the point of view of easy requisitioning and stocktaking to keep the variety of sizes of beakers, etc., as restricted as possible, e.g. the beakers which are most generally useful are of 250-ml capacity. It is also advisable to order in quantities such as dozens or half-dozens.

Requisitioning is made easier if catalogues are available. Regular advertisements of firms dealing in scientific apparatus appear in the issues of the *School Science Review*. When catalogues are used, teachers will find that re-ordering is made much easier if the articles have already been marked, e.g. sizes of corks, glass tubing. Even experienced teachers find it difficult at the time of making out a requisition to recall some of the pieces of apparatus for which they have felt a need during the course of the year. It is an excellent plan to have a notebook hanging up in a convenient position, so that as a need is noticed it can be entered in the book—and the same procedure should be followed for breakages. Similar notes should be made when it is seen that stocks of any particular item are getting low.

Local education authorities differ considerably in the extent to which science teachers are allowed to order particular types of apparatus. Whilst the bulk purchase by the local education authorities of the more generally used common items, which are then supplied to teachers, can be quite satisfactory, it should be recognised that there are occasions when special sizes or shapes are needed by an individual teacher, which may only be obtainable from a particular firm. It should always be possible for the science teachers to order selected items for which they have a need. It would also be advantageous if local education authorities and headmasters allowed the science teacher a certain amount of petty cash for local purchases. Not only would it enable the teacher to collect together bits and pieces with which to improvise apparatus, but it would also be to the authorities' benefit since such improvised apparatus is frequently less costly than any roughly equivalent item obtained 'through the usual channels'.

Safeguards in the Laboratory

The need to take precautions in the laboratory is the same in the secondary school as in any other kind of school. It is essential, as has been emphasised in the section on 'discipline', that pupils should learn the care which is necessary, when dealing with apparatus and appreciate the dangers of lack of care in using taps, switches, etc. They must know that any negligent behaviour will be regarded most seriously. In order to avoid accidents teachers must be ready to use the main taps and switches provided. In laboratories where both mains and low voltages are available the plugs should not be interchangeable; if they are, they should be altered. Teachers should know what dangers are likely, and what should be done in case of emergency. Details are unnecessary here as much has already been written on this subject. Every science teacher should have in the laboratory the pamphlet *Safeguards in the Laboratory* published by the Association for Science Education. The Ministry of Education Pamphlet No. 13, *Safety Precautions in Schools*, published by Her Majesty's Stationery Office, contains chapters on 'Precautions in the Use of Electricity' and 'Further Precautions in the Science Laboratory'. In *The Teaching of Science in Secondary Schools*, published by John Murray, there is a comprehensive chapter on 'The Science Teacher and the Law', and another on 'First Aid in the Laboratory' (Chapter XI), whilst pp. 116–20 also deal with precautions which should be taken. The Department of

Scientific and Industrial Research have published *Safety in the Chemical Laboratory* (H.M.S.O.). Accidents *will* occur even in the best-regulated laboratories. It is most important that the teacher should reduce the possibilities of accidents to a minimum by a clear understanding of the part he has to play, and that he should have sufficient knowledge of first aid to enable him to cope with minor mishaps. The books recommended above will give him the necessary information.

Material for Biology

It must not be forgotten that biology is the science of life and that, wherever possible, live material should be the basis of the teaching. But it may not always be possible to use living specimens at the time when they are actually available, so preservation and storage should be considered. Such material can be saved and stored:

(*a*) *dry:* cardboard boxes (e.g. convenient size is 10 in × 6 in × 4 in,
or jam jars are suitable for dry seeds, fruits, shells and insects.

(*b*) *wet:* in 4 per cent formalin (i.e. 96 parts of water to 4 parts of the 40 per cent industrial formalin) or 50/50 alcohol (industrial spirit) and water
e.g.   (*i*) stems: marrow and sunflower stems up to $\frac{1}{4}$ in diameter
    (*ii*) roots: creeping buttercup, pea seedlings
    (*iii*) leaf: London pride
    (*iv*) seaweeds in salt-water formalin.

Animal dissections yield hearts, lungs, kidneys, which can be stored in 4 per cent formalin. Bones—jaws, skull, limbs—can be preserved by burying for several weeks if the weather is warm, then washing, and finally bleaching with hydrogen peroxide, and varnishing.

Seeds which are suitable for experiments and which can be stored in jam jars with loose covers include grocer's peas, beans, wheat, barley, grass, radish and maize.

One of the main reasons for preserving stems is for cutting microscope sections. Whilst the method of doing this is best learnt by watching an expert, the following simple method is effective:

(i) *Material:*   the stem, root or leaf if not sufficiently rigid is held between slips of carrot or elder pith.

(ii) *Razor:*   a *new* safety razor blade with one edge. Cut a number of sections.

(iii) *Transfer:*   to a watchglass of water with a small paint-brush, select the thinnest and place on a 3 in × 1 in glass slide.

(iv) *Mountants:* water *or* 50 per cent glycerine in water *or* warm glycerine jelly (in order of perman-ence). Glycerine jelly slides keep for weeks, and if ringed with stove black they are permanent. To melt the glycerine jelly, stand the bottle in a tin of warm water. For mounting, allow one drop of the mountant on the end of a glass rod to fall on the section, lower a cover-slip by one edge first on to the slide and then allow it to drop by its own weight.

Much useful information on the subjects of preserving material and cutting sections is to be found in such books as *Elementary Microtechnique* by H. A. Peacock (Arnold), *Practical Plant Anatomy* by C. J. A. Berkeley (U.L.P.), and *Biological Staining Methods* by G. T. Gurr (published by George T. Gurr Ltd., London S.W.6).

9. TEACHING AND LEARNING AIDS

Visual and Aural Aids

EDUCATION is intimately concerned with communication between groups and individuals, a process which depends upon speaking and hearing; but we might well recall that man depended upon sight long before he felt the need for speech and that the alphabet was derived from a picture sign language. In recent years the tendency to verbalism has increased and the teaching of science with its emphasis on experiment (thought and discussion put to a practical test) offers plenty of opportunity to the teacher to restore the balance. *The most effective aid to learning in the laboratory is the handling of apparatus and materials by the pupils themselves; all visual and aural aids should be used to supplement this fundamental concept.* 'Attempting to learn sicence without performing experiments is like attempting to learn to swim without water' (Dr J. F. Kerr to Yorkshire Branch A.S.E., 1964).

The next most potent teaching aid is the blackboard; often—perhaps more appropriately—called 'chalkboard'. In addition there are pictorial aids in the way of coloured drawings, photographs, prints, charts, maps, diagrams and posters, each of which has its own particular use as the occasion arises in the progress of the lesson and for temporary display on the walls of the laboratory or classroom. Other aids include the 'flannelgraph' and similar devices for holding prepared drawings and sections of drawings on a more or less vertical background. There is also the help to be gained from the study of working models, educational visits and a school museum. Finally there is the considerable scope provided in optical projection by means of slides, filmstrips and films; the science teaching programmes broadcast by B.B.C. (Sound) and the television series provided by both B.B.C.-TV and Independent Television.

The first part of this chapter deals with the simpler and more universal aids, later sections deal with the more complex and expensive equipment.

TEACHING AIDS WHICH DO NOT DEPEND UPON OPTICAL
PROJECTION OR ELECTRONIC APPARATUS

The Chalkboard

The chalkboard, when well used, has an astonishing power
of attracting and holding attention, and is the greatest aid to
teaching yet invented. All trained teachers will have had
instruction in its use, and it is not proposed in this section to do
more than deal with a number of points which are of particular
importance to science teachers.

Science rooms or laboratories may well be of greater length
than the ordinary classroom and in consequence the science
teacher should ensure that his, or her, work on the board is
easily readable from all parts of the room. Diagrams should be
kept simple and clearly defined and the teacher should not
disdain the use of the board ruler, set-square, compasses and
even cut-out templates of some of the more difficult drawings.

The style of writing and drawing adopted by the teacher will
be reflected by the pupils in their notebooks and they can hardly
be blamed for untidy work and ill-formed handwriting if the
example they see on the board is no better. A clear, legible
style of writing and printing, without flourishes should be used.

Many rooms are fitted with prepared cloth boards which can
be moved over rollers top and bottom to present fresh writing
areas. Usually there are four sections available and it is very
convenient to have one section painted white for use as a screen
for films, etc. Another section may be ruled into squares for
graph work; if this is done the ruling should be comparatively
inconspicuous as it will often be found that this section will be
needed for general work. These revolving boards can be as
much as eight feet wide; which is about the limit for ease of
handling.

There are other styles of chalkboard in common use; one
consists of a pair of painted wooden boards supported by cords
passing over pulleys near the ceiling; other types are of painted
wood or linoleum fastened to the wall. A type of 'board' which
is not very often seen nowadays is one made of a large sheet of
heavy glass, frosted on the room side and black on the other.
There is no difficulty in cleaning away previous chalk work and
in use the chalk glides smoothly over the surface leaving a

uniform line. Another type of chalkboard is made of steel covered with a vitreous material with a matt finish. The writing surface is stated to be excellent and it is understood that paint may be used for semi-permanent diagrams, erasing it subsequently with carbon tetrachloride. The steel base offers the teacher the facility of holding prepared diagrams to the board by concealed magnets. Portable boards include the old-established blackboard and easel, the framed rotating board and the endless roller board is also made in a portable frame. The rotating board made of cloth can be installed with a steel support for the writing surface, thus allowing magnetic attachments to be applied. Whatever the type of board available, it should be kept as clean as possible and free from the smear of erased chalk. Repainting is essential from time to time and many L.E.A.s have a renovation service which deals with all the boards in a school at regular intervals.

For use with chalkboards, or independently, there is a range of prepared diagrams, usually in white ink on a strong black cloth. These are intended to be chalked upon and the chalk marks subsequently erased. One series is advertised from time to time, with illustrations, in the *School Science Review*. The sheets can be pinned to suitable chalkboards or other penetrable surfaces. It has however been found advantageous to prepare a support of hardboard, mounted on a framework, to which the illustrations are held by bulldog clips.

The Flannelgraph

The 'flannelgraph', as its name implies, originally consisted of a sheet of flannel suspended in a vertical position to which outlines of diagrams from blotting paper were attached. Various materials are now used as back-cloths—flannelette, milk straining cloth and specially prepared fabrics in several colours, together with accessories from most visual aids suppliers. The reader who intends to develop this side of his, or her, teaching is strongly advised to obtain the visual aids catalogues of local or national firms which contain many more details than can be given here.

Plastic materials have been developed for use in a similar manner to the flannelgraph. Adhesion depends upon the pressing into close contact of two very smooth surfaces. The adhering material may be a soft very smooth plastic with a highly polished surface, available in red, blue, sky, green, yellow, black, white and clear. It is also possible to obtain 'stickers' which are small pieces of 'P.V.C.' treated with a self-adhesive backing which when placed on the backs of cards or similar materials will enable them to be used as symbols in conjunction with diagrams or backgrounds constructed of the appropriate material. It is stated that the plastic sheet will adhere to almost any type of smooth polished surface and can be peeled off at will, as often as desired, without affecting its adhesive properties.

A similar visual aid consists of a black plastic background 40 in × 30 in mounted on wooden rollers, and the illustrations to be applied to it are made from card with a special surface. Blank card is available in black or white and there are sets of cards prepared for special purposes, e.g. the life history of the swallow-tail butterfly. In use it has been found advantageous to provide a firm backpiece for the plastic background, as in the case of the outline blackboards.

Visual aids of the flannelgraph type can be used effectively to illustrate atomic structure and chemical combination, the anatomy of flowers and even of animals, and the imaginative teacher will find many other applications.

Three-Dimensional Models

To make three-dimensional models of atoms, cork balls half an inch in diameter have been used. They can be painted with poster colour to represent electrons, neutrons and protons so that the structure of some of the simpler atoms can be conveniently demonstrated. The cork balls are obtainable from Avern and Buchnall (Corks) Ltd., Iberia House, 16 Manor Grove, S.E.15. Balls of three-quarters and one inch in diameter are also available and have been used to represent atoms in molecules. Wooden balls have also been used for this purpose, suitably painted and connected by short lengths of curtain spring, for which a $\frac{9}{64}$-in hole in the ball needs to be drilled.

Wall Charts and Posters

There are many commercially produced wall charts available for the science teacher who has space to display them. A comprehensive list is given in the Catalogue of Wall Charts (2s 6d) published by E.F.V.A., which names the chart, states its size, publisher and cost. In addition, a few lines of description are provided. The A.S.E. publishes and distributes to members, from time to time, lists of teaching aids in physics, chemistry and biology.

Nevertheless, many science teachers prefer to make their own wall charts and diagrams. To be successful they must attract attention, though to do so they do not need to be of as high a standard of production as the commercial type. The teacher should, however, aim to produce a worthwhile illustration. A very good method is to use yellow poster colour on black card, with bold lines and not too much detail. Another excellent method is the use of fluorescent colour on white or pale coloured paper. There is a tendency when making wall diagrams for them to have so much detailed work put in to them that the essential message is obscured. Useful information about the preparation of wall charts, etc., is given in the National Committee for Visual Aids in Education booklet, *Classroom Display Material* by Alan Vincent, a geography teacher. The various drawing material catalogues list many items required for making effective diagrams and are well worth studying.

The National Organisation for Audio Visual Aids
A brief outline of the constitution and functions of the various sections of this organisation is given below.

(a) THE NATIONAL COMMITTEE FOR AUDIO VISUAL AIDS IN EDUCATION (N.C.A.V.A.E.), set up in 1946 by local education authorities and teachers' organisations determines a national audio-visual aids policy which incorporates the views of L.E.A.s and teachers. There is a Central Committee of Teachers' Audio-Visual Aids groups, set up in 1951, to provide direct representation of teachers at the policy making level.

(b) THE EDUCATIONAL FOUNDATION FOR VISUAL AIDS (E.F.V.A) is a non-profit making company, governed by a Council of Management with ten members, five of whom are appointed by N.C.A.V.A.E.
E.F.V.A. publishes catalogues of visual material which give details of films and filmstrips made by all producers who prepare material specifically for teaching purposes. All the material listed is available from the Foundation Film Library,

which is controlled by E.F.V.A. The catalogue is in eight parts of which Part V (*Physics, Mathematics, Astronomy and Chemistry*), Part VI (*Nature Study, Botany, Zoology, Hygiene and Health*) and Part VII (*Agricultural Science, Industrial Processes and Crafts*) are of most value to the science teacher.

(c) VISUAL EDUCATIONAL NATIONAL INFORMATION SERVICE FOR SCHOOLS (V.E.N.I.S.S.), offers members all the publications of N.C.A.V.A.E. and E.F.V.A. during the year, including *Visual Education*, which is published monthly. In addition to the two booklets already mentioned, *Wallcharts* and *Classroom Display Material*, there are the following teachers' guides: *The Tape Recorder in the Classroom* by John Weston, *Colour Photography for Education* by J. Newsome and *Film Projecting—without tears or technicalities* by Margaret Simpson. There is also a technical service maintained by E.F.V.A. which concentrates on the problems of audio-visual aids in the classroom and may be referred to for advice should a teacher be in need of it. Further information regarding the above organisations may be obtained from The Secretary, National Committee for Audio Visual Aids in Education, 33 Queen Anne Street, London W.1.

Many popular science books have illustrations which are of excellent teaching value. It is possible in some cases to have photostat copies made of a size suitable for wall display. Application should of course, be made to the publishers, and it will probably be found that the price per dozen copies offers a substantial reduction for each print than when purchased individually.

A stand made of perforated hardboard, very frequently used in shops, is of considerable value for mounting a collection of objects for display. On one board of this type is displayed a variety of insulating materials. The same board is also used to display raw materials and finished products in glass manufacture, and similarly with regard to soap. Special fittings are available to hold objects on the board but string and lengths of birdcage wire were used on the apparatus described. The raw materials were obtained from manufacturers or brought by the pupils.

THE SCIENCE TEACHERS' SPECIAL FORMS OF VISUAL AIDS

The visual aids described so far are in common use by all

215

teachers but science teachers use many more examples and the number available is very dependable upon the amount of time the teacher is allowed for their preparation and whether he or she is assisted by a laboratory steward. Any demonstration is, of course, a visual aid, but it is not in this chapter proposed to enumerate the very long list of demonstrations of which accomplished science teachers make use.

In planning a special visual aid; thought should be given to a number of factors.

(*a*) Does the importance of the idea or principle to be illustrated justify the work involved in preparing the visual aid?

(*b*) Will it be of value in subsequent years, and how often?

(*c*) Are suitable materials available?

(*d*) Is adequate and convenient storage room available? Arising from this will be the need to design a visual aid which can be stored easily.

In addition to the wall charts produced commercially, several firms market teaching models, e.g. the eye, the ear and a plastic skeleton. Catalogues of the laboratory furnishers also show demonstration models of such things as a central heating system. The limited budgets of most county secondary schools, however, rule out expensive purchases and there is a good deal of satisfaction to be gained from the construction of a model for a few shillings in the school science-room or workshop. It is, however, recognised that few schools can afford to grant their science teachers the time needed to prepare many models. Laboratory assistance is therefore urgently required, and it is to the credit of several local education authorities that the need for competent help in secondary schools has been recognised and steps taken to provide it.

Educational Visits

A visit to a near-by pond or stream is, of course, an educational visit, but the term is generally reserved to describe a journey for a special purpose for which preparation beforehand and follow-up work afterwards are planned. Such visits include public utilities—electricity generating stations, gas works and waterworks, and visits to industries such as a steelworks, blast furnace, coal mine, chemical works, etc., depending on the environment of the school. To be of most value the pupils must be 'primed' so that they observe the details of greatest use to them. This may be done by a suitable questionnaire which the pupil is required to complete during the course of the visit.

Museum visits can be made where circumstances permit. The Science Museum and Natural History Museums at South Kensington are the leading museums of their kind in the country and are worthy of making a considerable journey to visit. In addition to the museums, institutions such as the London Zoo are well worth special visits. Careful preparation is needed and the teacher is advised to make himself, or herself, aware of recent changes. Information about other museums may be obtained from 'The Group for Educational Activities in Museums' Hon. Secretary: Mr. G. McCabe, Schools Museum Officer, Museum and Art Gallery, 45–46 Dock Road, Newport, Mon. *Science Teaching Techniques III* contains a useful article on the use of museums by Miss J. Palmer. An article on museum worksheets appears in *Science Teaching Techniques X* In addition to the recognised museums, large organisations occasionally send travelling exhibitions on tour. One of these showed 'The World of Oil' using beautifully constructed models and diagrams; another dealt with nuclear power.

School Museum

A collection of objects of scientific interest may be put together to form a museum. Care should be taken to see that each object is adequately labelled. Finding suitable accommodation to display a collection of this nature is probably the biggest difficulty. Many local education authorities have a collection of museum exhibits which is available on loan to schools.

Science Fairs

Science fairs have been very popular in the U.S.A. for a number of years. In this country the British Association for the Advancement of Science has introduced them at some of their meetings. Basically they provide an opportunity for schools through their pupils to display science projects and similar activities. An important feature of the annual meetings of the

217

Association for Science Education is the exhibition of members' work—new experiments and demonstrations. At local meetings of science teachers the host school often provides a display of work which is generally a very popular attraction.

ELECTRONIC TEACHING AIDS
Sound Broadcasting and Television
    For many years the B.B.C. has broadcast science lessons addressed mainly to secondary modern schools, or their predecessors. In a book of this nature it is inappropriate to provide details of the annual programmes and the reader is advised to write to the School Broadcasting Council for the United Kingdom, 3 Portland Place, London W.1, for such information. Two series that have been offered were 'General Science' intended for pupils of eleven to thirteen years of age, and 'Science and the Community' for pupils of thirteen to fifteen years. The two series together were intended to provide a comprehensive background to a four-year general science course. For each programme a pamphlet of notes, which gave the content of each broadcast, background information and suggested ideas for preparation and follow up, was issued each term, in advance, for teachers. A well-illustrated booklet for the pupils was also issued each term. These were, and are, exceedingly valuable visual aids and are worth obtaining even though it may not be possible to listen to all the broadcast. The booklets will serve to enrich the science teacher's lessons just as well as they would the broadcaster's. When one has amassed a number of sets of these booklets it is as well to have a card index showing the topics covered by each pamphlet in order to save time when the need arises for them to be used. Permission is given to record school broadcast programmes, provided the recordings are used only within the school and are destroyed at the end of the school year. It may be useful to observe that the programmes continue throughout the term but repeat for a week about midway to allow for half-term breaks. Teachers on holiday could therefore listen to a broadcast then in order to assess its suitability. Brief details are usually to be found in the current *Radio Times*. The *Annual Programme* is issued during the preceding summer term.
    Considerable efforts have been, and are being, made to pro-

vide acceptable science teaching by means of television broadcasting. High level conferences are held from time to time and research is carried out by institutes of education and other organisations. However, the basic principles of science teaching, which have already been stated, cannot be reconciled with the passive watching of a television screen. Nevertheless, where a lecture is all that is needed, the cameras can provide views which are denied to many of the audience and pupils can be shown places inaccessible to them as a class. As in the case of sound broadcasting, pamphlets for the teacher and booklets for the pupil are issued each term in advance. They contain many suggestions for practical work. The difficulties encountered when prescribing a course of practical work on a national basis are that no two secondary schools can be expected to be identical in equipment and circumstances. Schools in different areas may well have markedly different aims and their science syllabuses differ accordingly, even adjacent schools in the same county may vary appreciably in their science teaching. The syllabuses set out in this book are not intended as standard syllabuses to be followed by all secondary modern schools. It is for individual teachers to select for detailed study those parts of the syllabus which are most appropriate for their schools and to deal with the remaining parts as fully as circumstances permit.

The difficulties which arise in having a programme of lessons at a fixed time every week will be obvious to all teachers, many of whom work to a six-day time-table. Even at schools which follow a five-day one, interruptions to it caused by organised visits, school activities and outside pressures often make continuous viewing of the programme impossible.

The survey carried out by the S.M.A. Secondary Modern Schools' Committee disclosed that many such schools did not provide sufficient time for science teaching, some as little as five per cent of the time-table. Under these circumstances, if television lessons result in even less time being devoted to practical science teaching the effect is to be deplored. A scheme to broadcast science lessons out of recognised school hours would probably be welcomed by many pupils and science teachers themselves. (The extension of the school day advocated in the Newsome report could be used for viewing.)

Most science teachers would reject the allegations that they are 'hidebound, firmly attached to traditional forms of teaching and hostile to the introduction of new techniques', a view expressed by M. Dieuzeide, Head of the French School Television Service.[1] The well-attended meetings of the S.M.A. and A.W.S.T., now amalgamated to form the Association for Science Education, and other groups of science teachers, provide abundant evidence of the desire of science teachers to learn new methods and techniques.

One of the objects of our science teaching is the development of the ability to discriminate between truth and falsehood. Television teaching with its inevitable lack of response from the pupils may tend to encourage the acceptance, without question, of statements which issue from the television screen. This might be particularly harmful when looking at advertisements, many of which are of doubtful scientific veracity.

Where there are few teachers available and limited facilities for secondary education, as in the southern part of Italy and the Italian islands, television teaching can achieve a remarkable success.[2] 'Telescuola' is operated under the supervision of the Italian Ministry of Education. The demonstrators are selected from qualified teachers with experience in the type of school for which the transmission is intended. They are given special training and usually have a small group of typical pupils in the studio whose reaction to the lecture can provide the teacher with evidence of its suitability, difficult points and the rate of assimilation. Where the pupils in the studio are primed to ask questions, it will relieve the monotony of a lecture, and it may also encourage viewing pupils to feel they are taking a more active part by identifying themselves with the pupils in the studio.

In a booklet entitled *After Five Years* (published in September, 1962) by the Schools Broadcasting Council of the United Kingdom, the progress of B.B.C. school television broadcasting is reviewed. As far as science is concerned, there have been three regular programmes: 'Science and Life', 'Nature Study' and

[1] DIEUZEIDE M. *Teaching through Television, a report on science teaching by the use of television in schools,* paragraphs 72(c), 79 and 80. (O.E.E.C.)

[2] Radio Televisione Italione (RAI) *School Broadcasting in Italy,* an account of Telescuola.

'Discovering Science'. 'Discovering Science', which is direct teaching, has been the most popular of the group; being watched either wholly or in part, by about 10 per cent of secondary modern schools in 1961-2, and by almost as many primary schools. It was intended to 'provide a basic course for the first year and to be used by the less qualified teachers of science who would be glad to have such guidance and assistance. . . .' The same programme has been repeated for several years and its main points are as follows: Autumn term—Unit I: Air; Unit II: Heat; Spring term—Water; Summer term—Unit I: Simple Physiology, Unit II: Life Histories.

A new series began in 1964-5, 'Science Session', designed for lower streams in secondary modern and junior secondary schools. The topics dealt with were:

Autumn—Records and recording; food and diet.

Spring—The motor cycle; your health.

Summer—Electricity in the home; good looks.

It is not always possible to provide enough science teaching in a school and a television series of this nature could help with junior classes and, in some schools, the lower streams of the more senior forms.

(Twenty minutes continuous television teaching does, however, present problems when dealing with those pupils whose rate of perception is slower than average. Too much can be crowded into the time available and the lecturer can too easily move from one basic idea to another without knowing whether pupils have grasped the first one. The limited vocabulary of the lower streams in a secondary modern school adds another restriction to the lecturer's freedom to express himself. It is understood that the producers of all B.B.C. programmes have had some teaching experience, but not necessarily in secondary modern schools.)

The Independent Television Authorities also provide science lessons, but the programmes are liable to vary from region to region. A.T.V. (Midlands) in 1963-4 broadcast two series: 'The World Around Us', age group ten to twelve, science alternating with history; and 'Science and Understanding', age range fourteen and over, dealing with some of the fundamental concepts of both biological and physical sciences and the part these play in the world today. Further information

221

regarding any I.T.A. teaching programme may be obtained by writing to The Independent Television Schools Broadcasting Secretariat, at 4 and 5, Grosvenor Street, London W.1.

It is essential for some preparatory work to be done by the teacher and the class before the lesson is 'viewed', and unless the suggested 'follow-up' work is also carried out, the amount of the lesson that is retained in the pupil's mind is greatly reduced. This is where the pupils' pamphlets and the *Teachers' Notes* are so useful, and it is false economy not to obtain them beforehand (the demand is so great that early application is desirable).

Closed circuit television is employed to relay the lecture or demonstration of a science teacher to other groups. The connections between units are usually by wire. In this way additional groups of pupils in adjacent schools or the same school could follow a lecture course given by a selected teacher. A detailed report of closed circuit television is contained in the January and February 1965 issue of *Visual Education*. The report is also issued separately.

The Use of Tape Recorders

Any teacher considering the use of a tape recorder in school is strongly advised to obtain the N.C.A.V.A.E. pamphlet *The Tape Recorder in the Classroom* by John Weston. The use of a recorder for repeating sound broadcasts has already been mentioned. Its other uses are rather limited, although there are advantages, when teaching sound, in having musical notes by various instruments readily available, especially if an oscilloscope can be obtained to demonstrate them visually.

VISUAL AIDS USING OPTICAL EQUIPMENT

The presentation on a screen before a class of an illustration demanding attention is an invaluable aid to teaching, provided the illustration is carefully selected and the subject matter is closely related to the work being done. There are numerous pieces of apparatus available for the purpose including filmstrip and slide projectors and film projectors. Their use in most cases requires a room to be darkened though there are daylight projection screens for use in rooms without such facilities. It is probable that science-rooms will have an efficient 'black out' system but some remarks concerning daylight projection will be appropriate as it may happen in some schools that other rooms are used for science teaching. Daylight projection equipment consists of a cabinet containing a translucent screen, shaded to some extent by panels which can be opened forward at the sides and top. The picture is projected from the rear, or from the side using a mirror which corrects the lateral inversion of the picture. The cabinet should be placed in a shaded corner of the room in such a position that all pupils can have a good view. Consideration, of course, should be given to the position of the projector and its manipulation—it would be awkward to have the screen in the left-hand corner of the room and have to squeeze between the cabinet and the wall to deal with the projector. If possible the whole apparatus should be placed so that it does not interfere with writing on the chalkboard.

Although a complete blackout is not essential when using a projector it is desirable to have the room as dark as possible. The visual perception of the image depends to a large extent on the contrast between the image and the dark area adjacent to the screen. In terms of illumination it should be 100:1 or more. In particular, photographs with a dark background suffer most from low contrast and the picture is rendered difficult to distinguish if rays causing stripes of light are allowed to fall on to the screen from the side or above. Colour films require a good contrast to be seen to their best advantage.

The illumination of the screen depends on three factors:
(1) the power of the source of light,
(2) the distance between the projector and the screen and
(3) the focal length of the projection lens.

Modern projectors usually contain the most powerful lamp that the projector can be designed to use. Increase in power brings with it the need to dissipate the heat produced and therefore a mechanical cooling system, usually an electric motor driving a fan. In addition the reflector mirror and condensers in the lamp chamber must be arranged as efficiently as possible so that the maximum proportion of the light produced by the lamp illuminates the film or slide. Some of the latest projectors claim a very much higher percentage of light output compared with similar projectors of a few years ago. Science teachers will not need reminding that the screen illumination will be reduced in inverse proportion to the square of the distance it is away from the projector. The focal length of the lens determines the size of the picture, a shorter focal length will make a larger picture than a lens of longer focal length for the same throw. The intensity of illumination is reduced by increasing the area. However, the manufacturers of projectors have given careful consideration to the needs of schools in the design of their apparatus and it is generally found that lenses of 4-in focal length are used for filmstrip and slide projectors and 2-in lenses for 16-mm film projectors.

The size of the image is generally described in terms of its width, and usually the image fills the screen. There is a useful guide as to the effective distance pupils should be placed in order to see distinctly all details of the illustration. It is that they should be no more than six screen widths distant. The lenses fitted to most projectors (2-in focal length for 16-mm film and 4-in focal length for 35-mm filmstrip/slide) produce an image in approximate accordance with this proportion, so that the matter arranges itself as long as no pupils sit behind the projector. The brightness of the image, as far as 16-mm projectors are concerned, is dealt with in B.S. 2954 (1958). The average 16-mm projector can be expected to illuminate adequately a screen 5 ft 6 in wide, and tolerably, a screen 7 ft wide. The latest projectors, with lamps of 1,000 W and 1,200 W, can be used to provide images up to 10-ft 6-in wide with adequate illumination. These figures assume the use of a matt white screen. Better results can be obtained with the beaded screen, but this requires the viewers to sit closer to the axis—those viewing from an angle of 30 degrees or more from the normal (from the centre of the screen) do not get as good a view as with a matt white screen. Other screens are available, each with their own particular properties. In general it can be assumed that where the throw is short a matt screen should be used so that the class can be spread more widely in front of it. In a long room, beaded and similar screens are advantageous.[1]

Darkening a room brings with it certain disadvantages. To draw the curtains usually requires the window to be shut, or it may be, the curtains themselves close the means of ventilation. Without extractor fans the atmosphere in the room may

[1] Alan P. Howden, 'Performance of Projection Equipment in School', *Visual Education* (September, October, November, 1962).

become quite oppressive, especially during the warmer weather. In colder weather the warmth may not be as noticeable but the atmosphere will become stale and ripe for the spreading of air-borne diseases. Under such circumstances the blackout should not continue any longer than is necessary and lengthy programmes should be avoided. Some benefit may accrue from the spraying of the room with an aerosol disinfectant.

The Filmstrip Projector

The filmstrip projector is probably the most common of all the projectors used in school today. They generally have lamps ranging from 300 W to 1,000 W, though there is one design which uses a paraffin-oil pressure lantern. The lower wattage lamps are cooled by convection but those projectors using lamps of 500 W or more, need mechanical cooling. A typical school projector is a blower-cooled model which gives ample illumination in a normally-lighted room and maximum definition over the whole picture area. Most makes have slide carrying attachments included, or available at a small extra cost. The filmstrip itself is a length of 35-mm film with a number of illustrations printed on to it. 'Single-frame' illustrations measure 24 mm × 18 mm and in use the film carrier is vertical. With 'double-frame' pictures the carrier is used horizontally. A mask is required when single-frame pictures are used. It is removed for the double-frame pictures. The number of pictures, or frames, on a filmstrip varies, some are as few as 12, others may exceed 40. The longer filmstrips, with the necessary explanation or discussion may well become boring. Between 20 and 30 frames is probably the most suitable number to use in one lesson.

When using filmstrips the teacher is advised to view the subject matter and read the notes which are provided with many of them beforehand. A pointer is a useful thing to have in order that the teacher may avoid entering the illuminated area to indicate an item of particular interest. A light 4-ft bamboo garden cane serves very well. The teacher probably wishes to speak about each illustration as it appears, so he or she, must then walk from the projector to the screen or somewhere near to it, in order to address the class from the front. Then the walk back to the projector leaves the picture on the screen for the pupils to reconsider it with the teacher's remarks in mind. The filmstrip projector is very simple to operate and a responsible pupil could be allotted the task of moving the frames onward. If a rear projection screen is employed the teacher's place is at the side and no delay need occur from frame to frame.

As with other forms of visual aids, filmstrips may be used to introduce a subject, deal with current sections of it or be used for revision. The latter use is probably the most desirable, as it enables the teacher's work to be extended—pupils will be shown material outside the school and also another teacher's approach. Filmstrips are cheap to make and are produced in considerable numbers. Any science strip should be considered from the point of view of being up to date—a preview service is generally available for the intending purchaser. Even in such simple topics as air pressure and expansion obsolete information is sometimes included, e.g. Jordan's glycerine barometer and Harrison's compound pendulum, hardly illustrations of value in secondary modern schools. As filmstrips are so cheap each school usually has its own library, though some authorities may prefer to keep a comprehensive stock in a visual aids department.

Where a 35-mm camera is available, filmstrips can be produced by the teacher. Article No. 232, 'How to make Film Strips and Miniature Lantern Slides' by C. H. Bailey, in *The Science Master's Book, Series III, Part IV, Experiments for Modern Schools* gives instructions and the booklet *Colour Photography for Education* by J. Newsome (N.C.A.V.A.E.), deals very thoroughly with the making of slides. There are also several firms which will produce filmstrips or slides to the customer's requirements. For the details of filmstrips available, the teacher is advised to consult the relevant sections of the E.F.V.A. catalogues already mentioned, which contain objective descriptions but no appraisals. In many cases the date of production is also given. Comments on new filmstrips are usually to be found in the educational periodicals including the *School Science Review* and *The Science Teacher*. In any case, it is useful to have the catalogues of the more noteworthy producers and their addresses will be found at the back of the current E.F.V.A. catalogue.

Nevertheless, it is felt that there is scope for the production of a series of filmstrips especially designed for use in secondary modern school science teaching. The syllabuses described in this book indicate the subject matter to be dealt with, but it is to be hoped that the producers will seek the advice of experienced science teachers in such schools before embarking on the project.

Nearly all filmstrip projectors are capable of being converted into 2-in × 2-in and 35-mm slide projectors. There are other sizes of slides—$2\frac{3}{4}$-in square and the original, and still useful, $3\frac{1}{4}$-in square. The 2 in × 2 in is so called because it is enclosed in two 2-in transparent squares. It is mounted so that the actual size of the slide is 40-mm square. A loss of illumination is generally found at the corners, which are sometimes masked, but otherwise the whole slide is evenly illuminated. This slide requires its own size of camera and film. The popularity of 35-mm cameras has brought into common use, slides made directly using positive film, many of them in colour. The slides are usually mounted on 2-in square frames but their size is 36 mm × 24 mm. Whilst it may reasonably be considered that a library of slides may be of more use than a number of filmstrips because the slides may be used in greater variation, it must be realised that the number of slides equivalent to, say, twenty filmstrips may be as many as five hundred, and this involves storing properly and cataloguing. Slides which are of the $2\frac{3}{4}$-in square size require their own projector attachment and are not in common use in schools. Nevertheless the teacher will realise the greater the area of the slide, the brighter the image will be for the same lamp and throw.

Filmstrip and slide projectors are so simple to use that it is possible to allow small groups of pupils to employ one, using a miniature screen, e.g. a piece of white card, if it would be beneficial to them for some special project. Normal teaching practice would ensure that their work did not take second place to the operation of the projector. A questionnaire based on the filmstrip or series of slides would be one answer.

In addition to the projection of filmstrips and slides the instrument can be used to project actual demonstrations. The composition of solids, liquids and gases can be shown on the screen in the following manner, devised by F. W. Kaye and exhibited at the S.M.A. meeting in 1958.

A transparent sided box is made to fit the slide carrier supports, the base of the box is flexible and of strip iron or steel. Underneath the base is an electromagnet working on low-voltage alternating current. About fifty mustard seeds are placed in the box and the projector set up in position. When the current is switched on the flexible base vibrates. The amount of vibration can be increased and the mustard seeds flung about indiscriminately all over the box and their images therefore at random over the screen. The limited vibration of the seeds represents solid state. A greater movement, but not allowing them to leave the confines of the box, serves to represent liquids and the vigorous movement when seeds are apparently ejected and lost to view indicates the gaseous state.

Many demonstrations of this nature have been developed. In Article No. 231 in *The Science Masters' Book, Series III, Part IV, Experiments for Modern Schools*, W. E. Pearce describes the use of the filmstrip projector as a science lantern. It gives numerous examples of the adaptation of the projector to demonstrate physics experiments. The work entailed does, however, require considerable manual skill and much spare time on the part of the teacher, or else a capable laboratory assistant.

The $3\frac{1}{4}$-in $\times 3\frac{1}{4}$-in Slide Projector

This instrument is still not to be despised. If one is available good use can be made of it, and it may be possible to obtain a second hand one for a few shillings. The larger size of the slides allows the science teacher to make his own by hand, e.g. diagrams and graphs. One method is to use suitable cellophane sheet for drawing on and have two pieces of glass to fit the slide carrier between which the cellophane is held. The two pieces of glass could be hinged at one side by adhesive cellophane strip. The instrument is also capable of being used effectively for demonstrations such as those described in the previous paragraphs.

The Overhead Projector

This is a comparatively new development and basically is a means of displaying on a screen behind the teacher material he, or she, is writing or drawing on a transparent sheet. The sheet is arranged to pass over a box in which a projection lamp with lenses and mirrors throws light upwards through the drawing.

A lens system and a 45-degree prism (or mirror) over the draw-ing at a height of about 20 in, projects an image on to the screen. The apparatus is rather expensive and it is necessary to place the projector about 6 ft from the screen to obtain an image of a useful size, e.g. 4-ft square. A 16-page booklet (price 2s) dealing with the overhead projector is available from E.F.V.A.

The later models of this type of projector are capable of throwing a picture the size of a normal chalkboard on to the wall behind the demonstration bench and it may well be that the better equipped laboratories, where demonstration lessons and lectures must be given, will have this projector as a standard fitment beyond one end of the demonstration bench. One immense practical advantage of this machine is that the teacher can draw upon the transparent diagram or picture while it is being projected and because of the mirror of 45-degree prism and lens system there is no lateral inversion of the image and 'mirror writing' is not required. Certainly any modern lecture-room in a school should have one fitted. Another import-ant point is that the teacher faces his class the whole time it is in use.

The Projection of Opaque Illustrations

So far the instruments described have been diascopes. Other instruments which produce an image from opaque drawings are known as episcopes. An epidiascope is a piece of apparatus designed to serve both purposes. An episcope does not produce as bright a picture as the diascope as it depends on the reflection of light rays from the illustration. Usually they are rather cumbersome but the advantage of being able to project a drawing or similar illustration should be apparent to every teacher.

The Microprojector

This is an instrument for throwing on to a screen the image of an object small enough to require a microscope for it to be seen. The great difficulty when using a microprojector is in obtaining sufficient illumination. The light falling on to, or passing through, the minute object will decrease greatly in intensity as it is projected on to even a moderately sized screen.

For this reason hoods are fitted to some projectors to provide a screen of about 6-in diameter. A small group of pupils can see the image quite easily. Many microprojectors, however, consist only of the objective lens system which limits their power of magnification. Attachments are available to fit several makes of strip or slide projectors converting them to microprojectors of limited range. The objects are usually mounted on microscope slides. There is also a range of filmstrips and slides made from microphotographs. The advantage of using a microprojector is that the teacher knows what the pupil can see and can point to structures, etc., that he wishes to be carefully observed; this is not possible with a microscope.

Film Projectors

The use of film to assist science teaching began nearly fifty years ago with silent films of 16-mm and 9·5-mm size. The 9·5-mm film has more or less disappeared from the educational scene to be replaced by 8-mm, and silent 16-mm films have become significantly outnumbered by sound films. In fact when a film projector is discussed at the present time it is understood to be a 16-mm sound model, unless stated otherwise. The film for such projectors is perforated along one side only and the other edge carries the sound track. The operating speed is 24 frames per second. In most projectors the sound track is optically operated but some of the more recent projectors have both optical and magnetic reproducing systems. With suitable film it should be possible with this type of projector to exhibit the film using the optical sound system and, with auxiliary equipment, record a special commentary using the magnetic system, in a similar manner to using a tape recorder, for a second showing of the film. Unfortunately such projectors are very expensive, costing about as much as would be required to furnish a laboratory with all the equipment necessary for a complete science course. Simpler and less expensive 16-mm projectors are, however, available. The latest information on projectors is contained each year in the August issue of *Visual Education* (which is the yearbook for visual aids).

Schools do not usually have films of their own available but need to borrow them from an agency or the L.E.A.'s visual aids library when required. Although there are about eight hundred different agencies offering films,[1] mostly on free loan, the number of films which can be classed as *science teaching films* is comparatively few. Many have a scientific interest but hardly justify science teaching time being allocated to them. They could be used, however, for showing to science clubs and at the end of term.[2] The majority of the films offered on free loan are produced by industrial concerns for advertising purposes or to promote good public relations for the firms, and the science teacher should choose his, or her, films with this in mind. It is therefore desirable to make a record of the content and suitability of each film as it is shown in order to make better use of it, if it is likely to be borrowed again.

The Petroleum Film Bureau, I.C.I., Unilever, The Gas Council and the Electrical Development Association offer useful films and their catalogues are worth studying. Sponsored films from many sources are also distributed by Sound Services and the Rank Film Library. Films from any of these organisations need to be booked several weeks in advance and it is a good practice to plan the film programme during the preceding term, booking accordingly. Even so, it may be necessary to accept alternative dates. Teachers should not need reminding that the prompt return of films is essential.

The Rank Organisation has now taken over the G.B. Film Library and is one of the few sources of 16-mm films on hire. Most of the old G.B. films are still available and the library now includes some Encyclopedia Britannica productions made in the U.S.A. Though their general standard of production is very good, they often exhibit disturbing peculiarities of American dress and diction. It is therefore highly desirable for a comprehensive range of films to be made which are in every way suitable for use in the schools of this country.

Whenever possible colour films should be made; black and white films appear drab and less interesting when pupils are accustomed to colour. The musical background, if any, should be very unobtrusive. Animated diagrams are invaluable to illustrate many scientific processes and should be used freely. They should, however, be of a high standard, comparable with

[1] See *Film User*, July, 1964.
[2] The extension of the school day advocated in the Newsom report offers another opportunity.

231

the animation seen so frequently in television commercial shorts and not of the simple type of articulated mechanisms associated with programmes for younger children. Ideally a project of this nature should not be left to private enterprise or benevolent industrial organisations. Several reports on the use of television in schools have suggested that some of the 'schools' television broadcasts could be released on 16-mm film for showing in schools. These would be welcome but, so far as is known, none has yet been made. It is, of course, not really using television but employing their facilities to produce films and the effort required would probably be better employed in making films in the first place. The advice of experienced science teachers working in secondary schools at the level for which the programme or film is designed should be sought by the producers.

The exact form in which a lesson using a film is to take is difficult to prescribe. The film may be introducing the subject, part of the lesson itself or revising it. The latter form is probably the more usual, but the teacher should remember that he is not bound to show the whole film. When the projector is set up before the class moves into the room it is perhaps as well to proceed with the film as soon as possible and set the pupils' minds at rest. The subsequent part of the lesson can then be used for discussion. Having some time after the film is an advantage in case there is a break in the film or some other delay. It may also be possible to rewind and show the film a second time, perhaps without sound, the commentary being supplied by the teacher, who can thus emphasise the points he wishes to stress.

Most films are about 10 minutes or 20 minutes in duration, though there are several which occupy the screen for 40 minutes or even longer. Some teachers prefer to group one or two films together and exhibit them in one period as revision for a number of lessons, but this is not considered a good general practice. Pupils generally welcome the showing of films to them and display considerable interest in the material exhibited. This is particularly noticeable with the lower streams.

Silent films are still available in 16-mm size though much less numerous than sound films. They are perforated along both sides and are operated at 16 frames per second. Although silent films can be shown on sound projectors which can run at the appropriate speed, *sound films* must *not* be used on *silent* projectors which have sprockets on both sides of the guide wheels. One set of sprockets would destroy the sound track. Continuous loop films are available for 16-mm projectors to illustrate repetitive processes such as the circulation of the blood and the action of an electric bell. Stands with pulleys are needed to support the film, although substitutes can be devised using ordinary laboratory equipment.

The popularity of the 8-mm cine camera has brought into use numerous 8-mm projectors. The range of films available for these is limited at present but the compactness of the projector and its cheapness are likely to encourage the production of teaching films for use with them. An 8-mm sound projector, providing adequate illumination for a darkened classroom, should be possible for about one hundred pounds. A special form of the 8-mm projector has been put on the market to show 'concept' films. These films are in cassettes and take about five minutes to show. The projector and screen are contained in a cabinet about the size of a large television set. To use the equipment the cassette is placed in position and the projector switched on. No film threading is needed and when the film has been exhibited it is ready for another showing. The films themselves are designed to illustrate one concept in science teaching and are mostly in colour but silent. They cost little more than filmstrips. The majority of the films so far produced for this projector are above the standard required for the majority of pupils below 'O' level. Of those which are suitable, some are poor in content though well produced. Teachers are therefore recommended to *pre-view all films before ordering*. The firm making the projector states that facilities are available to enclose the teacher's own 8-mm film into cassettes for use with the projector.

Closed Circuit Television

To some people, not usually educationists, the use of this medium is seen as the answer to the teacher shortage which may bedevil schools in this country for some time to come. To the real educationist however this teaching aid will enable more pupils to benefit from hearing and seeing the expert teacher at work in his particular field, and thus communicating his example, skill and influence to many more students than was previously possible. Those schools which have been fortunate enough to acquire a television camera for themselves and have used it as a serious teaching aid, have proved to themselves and others that, provided teachers will train themselves in the use of the equipment, the television camera and its receiver have a wider field of use than was at first envisaged.

Some authorities have decided to embark on a closed circuit television project to provide visual and aural material direct to linked schools in their area. If such programmes are to be fully used and to become of real educational value it behoves those teachers using this material to be prepared to spend time and forethought both in 'pre-viewing' work and activities and in 'post-viewing' follow-up work. Those of us whose knowledge of a particular branch or field of science is incomplete should be prepared to welcome any move along these lines to enrich our teaching and to widen the horizons not only of our pupils but ourselves. If the 'University of the Air' ever becomes a reality in this country then the well planned use of closed circuit television programmes in schools may have a large contribution to make to the attitude and the success of adolescents and adults in further education through this medium.

Programmed Learning[1]

Programmed learning is a set of techniques for ensuring that pupils learn what their teacher sets out to teach them. It is not tied to any theory of learning (though many of its advocates are adherents of 'behaviourism' or cybernetics) and it is not necessary to use machines as aids to presentation. The essential features of programmed learning are: that preliminary versions of the materials are tried out; a continuous record of the learner's activities is obtained which indicates where the teaching material may be defective; revisions are carried out on the basis of these records; and, finally, the whole process is repeated. When assessments of learning show clearly that the programme's aims have been achieved, i.e. most of the pupils have attained the required level of mastery, the programme is ready for use as a teaching instrument.

[1] The committee's thanks are due to G. O. M. Leith, Deputy Director of the National Centre for Programmed Learning in the School of Education, Birmingham University for this contribution on Programmed Learning.

A large amount of empirical work supports a number of guiding principles in the construction of teaching programmes.

(1) The programmer's aims (what pupils will be able to do on completing the programme) should be stated explicitly and in detail so that their accomplishment can be assessed objectively or unambiguously.

(2) An analysis of the teaching materials needed to achieve these ends must be carried out in such a way that no element of knowledge is omitted and the optimal order of topics is provided.

(3) The kinds of learning activities the pupil will have to undertake to obtain the required understanding, skills and knowledge must be determined. For example, distinguishing, repetition, forming categories, solving problems, making comparisons and drawing inferences are learning activities which require different sorts of practice.

(4) The teaching materials are prepared so that the learner is given frequent active practice which is constantly tested and he is given knowledge of his success immediately.

Most published programmes are written according to one of two patterns. Linear programmes tend to consist of a sequence of small progressive steps of instruction each of which requires the pupil to solve a problem by completing a sentence or expression. The learner reads all the steps or 'frames' and may be guided towards a solution of the problems by clues and hints. Branching programmes on the other hand present a larger amount of instruction at a time and ask for the correct answer to a problem to be selected from several alternatives. Mistakes in selection lead to remedial instruction in a 'branch' of the programme and ideally all the likely errors and confusions should be catered for. An analysis of learning processes involved in a particular task should be made to decide which type of programme to employ. The evidence suggests that conceptual topics can be learned equally well from branching and from linear programmes by fairly able children if they have adequate grounding in the prior stages of the subject matter. If, however, new concepts and categories are to be established or less able children taught, the linear approach is better. Many topics, clearly, need both methods at different points in their exposition.

The present trends in programming techniques are towards the integration of practical work and verbal instruction. Where it is beneficial to give concrete experience this is brought in as part of the task. A programme on volume, density and specific gravity for secondary modern children uses a set of standard sized cubes of different metals which are fitted into spaces in a block of wood, dropped into a displacement vessel and so on. The programme guides the pupil to form generalisations and draw conclusions on the basis of his experience. A similar approach is used in teaching magnetism and, in this programme, group work is undertaken—each member of a team of four being asked to carry out an operation in co-ordination with the others, all discussing their observations and formulating general statements which are then tested with the apparatus. A third method, in biology (which could be used equally well in other areas) is to give a general orientation and ask for a prediction to be made. Following this an experiment is set up, the programme amplifies the point of the experiment and by this time observations can be made to verify the hypothesis. In a similar way, contingency tables can be filled in or curves plotted as part of the programme of experiences. The implication of 'programmed' is that the examples of practical work have been proved by previous trials or have been improved until they genuinely teach.

It is not surprising that almost all comparisons of programmed teaching and 'live' teaching of the same subject matter show that learning from programmes is at least as great as from teachers and often greater. Moreover, the programme in many cases takes less time and gives the same amount or more retention.

Teachers will find it profitable to consider the use of programmes in one or more of the following situations:

(1) At the start of a course when pupils may have different levels of knowledge. The use of programmes will ensure that everyone begins with the necessary background.

(2) When the same material must be taught to several classes.

236

(3) In presenting a topic which has always given difficulty.

(4) For speeding up work to allow greater time for discussion or enrichment.

(5) When particular topics or skills ancillary to the main course must be taught.

(6) Where a course has been organised to make the best use of existing resources of staff and teaching aids, as one medium of teaching co-operating with the others, e.g. to follow up a film or TV lesson, or when flexible groupings have been arranged with large lecture groups, small discussion and practical work groups and individual assignments and tutorials.

(7) For private study or homework.

Teaching machines have become associated with programmed learning as a means of preventing the learner from looking ahead at the answers. The need for this measure of control has not, however, been demonstrated. Most of the experimental work (including some with below average secondary modern children) has shown that it makes no difference to learning should children see the answers before trying. If machines are to be purchased or hired it must be remembered that in almost all cases it is impossible to use programmes made for one machine in another even though they both use the same medium, e.g. 35-mm filmstrip. The range and suitability of programmes available for a machine is therefore an important consideration.

A national centre for programmed learning has been set up by the Department of Education and Science, in the School of Education of Birmingham University, which has the job of collecting and publishing information about programmed learning. The centre welcomes news of activities in programming and answers inquiries as well as regularly publishing articles, technical reports and reviews in *Visual Education*. A list of currently available programmes is given in the *Visual Education Year-book* and more fully documented lists will be published yearly in collaboration with the Association for Programmed Learning. A quarterly journal *Programmed Learning* is published by the Association as well as a Newsletter. *New Education* also gives space frequently to articles on programmed learning and U.S. Industries (G.B.) Ltd., issues *Tutor Age* free.

Courses on programmed learning are given by a number of colleges and universities and these are listed in the Department of Education and Science lists of 'one year and short courses for which secondment may be granted'. Many local authorities also run courses.

Two reasonably priced manuals of programming for teachers are:

LEITH, G. O. M. *A Handbook of Programmed Learning*; second edition, 'Educational Review Occasional Publications No. 1' (University of Birmingham).

LEEDHAM, J. and UNWIN, D. *Programmed Learning in the Schools* (Longmans).

10. WRITTEN WORK

OF the many problems which face the science teacher none is more difficult than that of the notebook work—the pupils' records of work done. *Why* should notes be made at all? What is their purpose? What kind of material should they contain? *How* should they be made—in class or at home, dictated or original composition, and so on? How much of the limited lesson time may properly be devoted to notes? How far must they be marked and corrected as English composition? These are some of the questions to which answers must be found.

Why Make Notes?

Most educationists would probably agree that in the secondary school, note-making is as much concerned with English as with science, the subject matter being used as a medium for the basic skill in the expression of ideas. There is much to commend this view, since in the secondary school the development of the fluent use of English is necessary yet difficult, and undoubtedly it is better for a pupil to write an account of an experiment than to write a composition on some arbitrarily chosen subject about which he may or may not, have ideas. But notes are in fact used also for other purposes, such as ensuring that by the act of writing the pupil has grasped the subject matter clearly. Moreover, before terminal or other examinations, many pupils are capable of using notes and glad to have them for revision.

If these premises be accepted, it follows that note-making in any form can have little value unless it demands

(*a*) an understanding of the subject matter, and
(*b*) an attempt by the pupil to transfer his thoughts to paper in word or diagram.

The second of these will be adequately done, unaided, by only a minority of the pupils; but one hastens to add that this is an important reason for giving all of them the opportunity for the exercise. The best pupils will produce well-written prose, but there will be many whose unaided efforts vary from those needing moderate correction to those which are the despair of the teacher. Beyond these again are the children who can cope only with diagrams. Herein lies one of the thorniest of problems—the pupil whose command of English is so poor is precisely the one who needs the most help, yet the science teacher just cannot afford the time needed for detailed correction. Some suggestions for solving the problem are given below.

It would be a gross mistake to judge the child's ability to comprehend by his ability to express; often the former is quite considerable although the latter is very weak. Thus in the course of conversation with the less literate pupils the teacher will often find that, if the subject matter is not beyond their reasoning ability, they have a surprising grasp of the facts. If he can find means for them to record this knowledge both they and he will have cause for satisfaction. Particularly with these children, anything which gives the child legitimate pride of achievement or sense of mastery is a valuable educative factor.

What Should Be Recorded?

A case for writing notes is not difficult to establish: it is less easy to determine *what* shall be recorded or *how*. As so often happens, the teacher must decide his policy in the light of all circumstances, including the opinions of his headmaster and his own standards. The following thoughts, therefore, can only be suggestions—not exhaustive or didactic, and intended to stimulate rather than instruct.

The material to be recorded may include:

(a) Written descriptions or diagrammatic records of individual or group work or class demonstrations.
(b) Notes on field work, often on a group basis. This is a special case of (a).
(c) Records of visits to factories, museums, etc.
(d) Summaries of facts and principles learned in a lesson or series of lessons.
(e) Exercises numerical or otherwise, on recent work.

In all the above it is intended that the term 'written work' shall include drawings. Points (a) to (d) all make very similar demands on the child's ability: to state something he knows now which he did not know before. The exercises suggested in (e) should be chosen to increase the pupil's understanding of the work being done. Occasionally records or summaries of prescribed portions of textbooks with the associated diagrams may be required of the pupil. Since the understanding of the printed word is a necessity in this age, this is not wasted effort. This could well be done in an English lesson if it can be arranged, or can be made an exercise for homework or private study.

Methods of Recording

(a) Original Composition by the Pupils

Experiments done by or for the pupils should not be too difficult to understand; granted this, oral work is then necessary to ensure that the essentials have been grasped. After this, if the pupils are told to 'write it up', the variations in style and effectiveness of their written English make this method of doubtful value unless it is carefully corrected by the teacher for inaccuracies of language, facts, and the interpretation of these facts into concepts.

In the main, if this type of recording is required, as for example in describing an educational visit or a process that proceeds in steps, it is best to give some kind of guiding lines for them to follow. For instance, an account of an experiment can be split up under the following paragraph headings: Title (aim), What was done? What happened? Conclusion. Pupils always need help with the formulation of conclusions for they do not always realise the significance of a result, even if it is a good one. These ideas will enable the weaker pupil to have some measure of success and coherence, while the more verbally efficient pupil will make an even better effort than he would unaided.

Since this procedure with the less literate pupils takes a great deal of time and effort which, in their case, could be better spent in studying more practical science, it is a method which should be used very sparingly with them.

(b) Diagrams

While diagrams will rarely be absent from the record of a week's work, they can sometimes form practically the whole of it (the technique of drawing is dealt with below); for example, the methods of reproduction of hydra lend themselves admirably to diagrammatic treatment. Where an experiment has been done which can be summarised in a diagram the writing to accompany it may be only one short sentence; for example, the title in Fig. 30 is sufficient explanation of the experiment indicated. Diagrams, like notes, should be the pupil's attempt to express what he has learnt, but here too he must be helped towards economy of effort, clear display of the essential factors, and elimination of irrelevant details.

(c) SENTENCE-COMPLETION

When the teacher thinks it appropriate, the pupils can make notes by one of the well-known methods which demand less ability in sentence construction. Thus sometimes one will give sentences with blanks to be filled in from the child's knowledge, or, instead of blanks, three or four alternative words may be given from which a correct choice has to be made; or two related lists may be given to be matched in pairs; or a series of deductions may be given after observations on an experiment and the children are asked to comment as to whether they are true or false. The difficulties here are two-fold; first, to ensure that the implied questions are not ambiguous, without merely repeating sentences used by the teacher in his lessons (in which case memory alone would be sufficient to enable a child to fill them in), and second, to ensure that the questions test something worth while—not, for example, merely a list of names; thus, the first of the following examples would be much more worth while than the second:

(i) The part of an electric lamp which glows is called the (x)—— and it is made of metal which is not easily ——. Inside the bulb there is no —— because if there were the (x)—— would ——.
((x) is the same word in each case.)

(ii) The space inside an electric lamp is a —— or it may be filled with ——. The part which glows is called the —— and is supported by ——. Current enters and leaves by the —— on the cap.

The first example requires knowledge and thought, the second little more than memory.

An example of ambiguity:

To make an electric current flow we need a —— (wire, conductor, switch, complete circuit, battery, etc.).

can be avoided thus:

A battery is used to —— the current round the circuit.

242

It will be clear that if such a method is to be used as an aid to note-making, a very great deal of care must be taken over the preparation of sentences; so much so that probably little less time is needed that would be required to mark ordinary notes.

(d) COLLECTIONS AND OTHER IDEAS

It may happen that the best way for the least literate children to summarise a topic is to make a collection: fruits, for methods of dispersal; samples of conductors and 'non-conductors'; foods, sterilised and sealed in test-tubes. Occasionally an actual experiment can be directly recorded in the notebook—for example, angles of incidence and reflection when using a ray-track apparatus directly on the book, by marking the positions of rays and mirror in pencil, and then measuring the angles. If pupils work in pairs, this gives an opportunity for each partner to measure the angle.

(e) NOTES

The term 'notes' can also include rough jottings made during a demonstration or oral lesson. If this note-taking is carefully watched and guided it can be valuable, but children are usually slow writers, so that undue time may be devoted to the practice, and attention taken from the thread of the argument; or, the pupil's mind is distracted, he seizes on inessentials and neglects what is vital. Where new words or particular points are to be noted, it is desirable for the teacher to pause while it is done. It is an excellent thing if every child can have two notebooks, one for rough and the other for finished work.

Diagrams

Diagrams have been mentioned several times above. These should be as simple as is compatible with full display of the desired features. It is not necessary that the diagrams should be formal, although that does not imply a lowering of standard, and the use of the ruler and compasses is to be encouraged. Drawings of chemical glassware, although unlikely to occur very often, should be subject to the usual convention; sectional elevation, liberally interpreted and diagrammatic, rather than pictorial, representation. (At the same time the artistic need not be forbidden to produce a good 'picture'.) For a diagram to be as complete a record as possible, explanatory notes and a title should be added, together with labelling where necessary.

Two of the commonest faults in children's drawings are that they are far too small or grossly out of proportion—a barometer tube may appear to be anything between a tenth of an inch and 6 in in width. Approximate dimensions should be given (e.g. 'about a quarter of an inch', 'half the width of the space between the writing lines', 'the thickness of your pencil'). Diagrams of apparatus look better if shown standing on a bench, suggested by a line and shading as in Fig. 30. For labelling

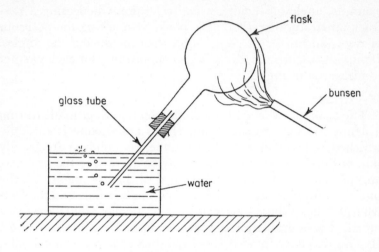

Fig. 30 To show that air expands when it is heated

parts of a diagram, some teachers insist on a guide-line (or a pair of guide-lines) being drawn in pencil, the lettering being added in ink, but probably it is best to reserve this method for those who cannot do a straight row of letters without it. 'The proof of the pudding is in the eating'—if the diagram is clear and the labels neat and horizontal it does not matter what technique was used. After the first few occasions it is unnecessary to label familiar items like stands, flasks, Bunsen burners. It is most important that the part to which each label refers should be unmistakably indicated. The guide-line for this purpose should end in either a dot, or an arrowhead (Figs. 30, 31) actually touching the part in question. If the end of the line can be sufficiently definite these may be dispensed with but most teachers use them.

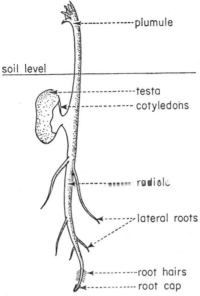

Fig. 31   Germinating broad bean

Standards of Work

It cannot be too strongly urged that the emphasis throughout must be on the development of the child, with the subject as a convenient vehicle. Therefore the *standard* of work is paramount: the highest standard of which the pupil is capable must be maintained and the pupil urged to feel pride and achievement in his or her work, the completed notebook becoming a valued possession. To encourage those who are less able with pencil and pen the teacher should try to get round the class and give help where necessary.

How Much Time for Notes?

It can hardly be disputed that the bulk of time allotted to science should be spent in active investigation—formal experiments, field work, visits, etc., and the less given up to ancillary matters the better. Thus the teacher whose classes normally write their notes outside class time can be satisfied that at least from that point of view he is making the best use of his time. In those schools where regular homework is the rule this presents no difficulty, but in others varying degrees of opposition may be met; classes unused to homework may be disinclined for it; sometimes home circumstances prevent it being done —often the boys concerned have part-time jobs which prevent them from remaining after school to do it; occasionally parents flatly refuse to allow it. On the whole, however, it seems likely that most A and B children could do the bulk of their work at home, after making a start in class.

In most schools the time given to science falls short—often far short—of the allowance recommended by the Association in its Reports. It may be only two periods per week—say 80 to 90 minutes. *That we offer advice to teachers working under these conditions is not to imply that we approve of such a small allowance.* Certainly in such circumstances 15 to 20 minutes is all that can legitimately be claimed for writing—and probably not every week. If three or more periods are allowed for science, the time for written work might be 30 minutes; or in general perhaps a quarter of the total time.

What is done if the notes and diagrams are not finished in the time suggested? One answer has already been given—that they be done in the pupil's own time, at home if the child has facilities; if this is not possible the choice lies between leaving the notes unfinished or devoting a part of the next science period to them, so reducing still further the time for the succeeding practical work. There is no satisfactory way out of this dilemma but usually the lesser evil is to tell the children to finish the notes, reminding them that opportunities frequently occur during school hours, and on the next occasion go on to new work at once. Then when the time for notes arrives again, the books can be checked to make sure that the work has been done or to see that arrangements are made for space to be left for subsequent completion.

Time can be saved, and the pupils with little ability to draw aided, by the use of duplicated complete or partially complete line diagrams. These are completed and the necessary captions inserted, with the correlated notes added below, by the pupils. If the diagrams are of a suitable size they can be stuck into the pupil's notebooks. When a flat-bed duplicator is available the diagrams can be printed direct on to the notebook page. Whenever a diagram is provided the pupil should be required to do some work himself.

It is obvious that whether books are marked or not every week, they must at least be inspected. Marks should not be given for unfinished work. The assessment of written work for marks—for term lists, etc., is difficult; if these are to mean anything they should convey an estimate of the child's progress in *science*, and not merely be a duplication of the marks he gets for his English composition. This is not to say that English should, or can, be ignored, but the content rather than expression will be what the teacher looks for. Where really backward pupils are concerned, a good deal more latitude must be allowed as regards expression than with the more able ones; otherwise the pupil will find his marks uniformly discouraging. Frequently one finds that a pupil who has the greatest difficulty in expressing his thoughts on paper, can in his own way, make clear to the teacher that he really has a grasp of the facts he has been learning. He should not be penalised for his lack of ability to write. Here again, of course, the teacher finds himself in a cleft stick—he can only give credit for the pupil's ability in science by ignoring his lack of ability in English.

11. THE SCIENCE LIBRARY

General Considerations

Science teachers as well as the teachers of English must be concerned with the need to encourage their pupils to become literate as well as knowledgeable. The craftsman must acquire the ability to use his mechanical tools, the scientist must be familiar with the use of the apparatus he needs for his experiments, before anything worth while can be produced or achieved. But neither can widen and deepen his knowledge of the subject without the ability to understand the written as well as the spoken word and to read with understanding, particularly when the pupil has left school. For this reason, despite the welter of visual aids and experiences which compete for the interest and attention of children and tend to mitigate our efforts in this direction, we must continue to encourage all, even the less able, to make the necessary effort to master the mechanics of reading and also to try to grasp and understand the subject matter, i.e. to read with comprehension. In science, as in any subject that requires technical terms, the child reader's difficulties are added to by the need to understand these terms. Fortunately an increasing number of authors are giving consideration to this point when writing for children, with the result that there are books available with carefully chosen and graded vocabularies with all technical terms explained as they are introduced. This is as important a feature in a science book for the average secondary school pupil as are clarity and simplicity of style.

Books for the younger and the less literate of the secondary school pupils should be chosen so that the format, type, illustrations and vocabulary are such that the book appeals by its looks as well as its contents. The present plethora of books written for the non-academic pupil enables the teacher to be ruthless in his desires for high standards in these respects. The field of interest, work, or knowledge that he wants to be covered will be found somewhere in these better books if he is prepared to search and to pay the cost. The size and quality of the type, the line spacing, and the quality of the paper used are important factors and the illustrations should be such that whether

248

diagrams, drawings or photographs they are 'easy' on the eye. Provided the author has done his part in saying something of import and value and has said it well, the interest of the child will be maintained if the book's appearance also satisfies the eye.

There should be plenty of variety in the science library and the titles can range from the simple book on popular general science topics to works of a more serious character which could be classed as 'study books'. Books on the history of science and biographies of scientists should not be neglected as pupils are stimulated by these more often than we think. Children at first are often more interested in persons than things or concepts.

It is unwise to place any restrictions on the choice of books chosen by a pupil to read. If it proves beyond him in reading matter and he is really interested in the subject he will be stimulated to further efforts towards obtaining a higher state of literacy, with corresponding benefits to his work in science as well as other subjects.

When the science teacher wishes to measure the comprehension of the pupil regarding the passage read, this is better done in co-operation with the English teacher during his library periods than by questionnaires submitted to a pupil on his own private reading. Providing books within his compass are available, he will come quite naturally to the science teacher for explanation of the things not understood if he is really interested in the subject, or the book, or both. A wise teacher will encourage this approach. (Testing for understanding of textbook reading comes within the science lesson itself.)

Situation of the Science Library

The science library should be in the science laboratories, or at a convenient point easy of access from the laboratories, so that the teacher can guide the pupil in his choice of book or by referring to a book in the library, place an incentive to the reading of it before the pupil. Then, too, books from the library can be used by the teacher during his actual lessons to show a picture or diagram, or an interesting page or two on the topic of the lesson can be brought to their notice.

Ideally, all these books together with a copy of each science textbook being used in the school should be duplicated in the school (lending) library, then the books of the science library itself will always be on their respective shelves for immediate use.

If financial considerations prevent this duplication of books, then the teacher must decide whether he wishes to be burdened with the oversight of the loan of books or not. If the latter, then all the science library books apart from the reference type will be housed in the school library and the teacher will need to 'borrow' them when he wishes to use them or show them to his class.

Another advantage in having the science library duplicated in the school library is that then the non-scientist can also borrow them from the main library and a pupil can read books of a lower level as revision, or of a higher level because he wishes to advance his knowledge faster than would normally be possible.

Choice of Books

The S.M.A. publication *Science Books for a School Library* reprinted and revised in 1959 covers all the secondary stages and would prove a useful guide in the setting up of a new library or adding to an existing one.

BUT *no* book should be added to the library without its first being seen and read, or at least being carefully examined, by the teacher. This can be done by sending for inspection copies or at publishers' exhibitions at meetings, etc. The environment of the school or the pupil or both may influence one's choice of book. Just as the dearest publication is not always the best, so the cheapest is not always a good buy on the grounds of length of life and quality of printing. Books with limp covers or paper backs can have quite a useful length of life if suitably re-bound or strengthened by additional transparent covers. There are some excellent paper-backed reprints of publications long out of print which are well worth purchasing. If the subject matter of the book appeals and the illustrations are first class, then the reading content of the book can be above the pupil's literate limits, provided the teacher is prepared to act as interpreter on occasions and the pupil knows that this help is forthcoming.

Books other than fiction have, in the main, a higher price.

Taking the average price per book as 13s then an initial grant of £65 would provide approximately 100 volumes which would be a fair nucleus for a beginning. Allowing for wear and tear (one education authority reckons that the life of a well-used and well-read book is 3–4 years), then a grant of about £20 per annum would enable this nucleus to be kept more or less intact and slightly expanded each year. If the school has a growing 'top', i.e. candidates for G.C.E. 'O' level and possibly 'A' level, then this figure would need to be increased by at least one-fifth. There is a great need for good background science books for these pupils to read to widen and amplify their work both in the laboratories and at home, and this work has of necessity to be more academic and stereotyped in order to achieve examination successes.

SOURCES OF BOOKS OTHER THAN BY PURCHASE FROM CAPITATION

House magazines, booklets and pamphlets from the large industrial concerns (e.g. Lever Bros., Chance Glass, Nickel Mond, Shell, Esso, B.P., British Iron and Steel Federation, etc.) are also worthwhile additions to the library, as are periodicals of a scientific nature. (The school fund might pay for the latter and if this is known to the pupils the monetary response is on occasions surprising.) Some local authorities allow their local public libraries to loan parcels of books for protracted periods to schools for special purposes. When the school is used as the headquarters of the local county library then some liaison with the local librarian might enable books to be made available from this stock on short- or long-term loan.

Many schools have established the tradition that on leaving school a pupil donates a book to the school library. Those pupils interested in science might donate to the science library.

PUBLIC LIBRARIES

When giving advice on the use of the science library in the school, attention can be drawn to the local public libraries and the special advantages of joining the latter because of the greater range of books available can be stressed.

The local county or town library may be prepared to work an exchange scheme (if they do not already do so) in which books are sent out on loan to schools. Several hundreds are sent out at a time and a similar number are returned, this exchange taking place two or three times in the course of the school year. It might also be mentioned that at intervals of two months a small crate of new books is sent out and in this way stocks can be increased. Generally speaking, a number of these books are on topics connected with science and it is well for the science teachers to be acquainted with the new titles so that they can be referred to when the need arises.

12. EXAMINATIONS

IT is not possible, or desirable, to summarise here all that has been written about examinations in the secondary school but a brief note of the examinations available to the secondary school pupil, together with some information about new methods of examining, may be of use to the inexperienced teacher. Examinations may be internal—tests set and marked by the teaching staff of a school, or external when the whole procedure is controlled by one of the various examining boards.

Internal Examinations

Some teachers think these are necessary and desirable but others claim that the continuous assessment of a pupil's work is a much more satisfactory method of estimating ability. It is fairly easy to substantiate both of these opinions but it is not intended here to discuss fully the pros and cons of examinations as such but rather to look critically at methods of examining in science subjects. Before this survey perhaps it would be useful to comment on the standard of written English expected in science examinations. The science teacher is as aware as any other subject teacher of the desirability of a good standard of both written and spoken English. This he should strive for throughout his teaching career but an ever-present problem in examining in science is to decide whether a mark gained for good scientific ideas should be reduced because of spelling errors and/or ungrammatical expressions. Obviously there must be limits to the kind of spelling error and phrasing which are acceptable but there is support for the view that a pupil's work in science should not be too heavily penalised because of a lack of ability in English.[1] The move towards the short-answer type question has considerably reduced this problem. Certain papers set for the Certificate of Secondary Education examination in science are nearly all composed of this kind of question and many of the Ordinary Level papers, and some Advanced Level papers, now have one section requiring short answers only.

[1] See Chap. 6, Science for Pupils of Below Average Ability, page 169.

There is, too, a very desirable move right away from the question requiring an essay-type answer and from that which tests merely the memorising of facts. Questions can be framed to give facts and data and ask the pupil to apply his scientific knowledge to solve a problem, or comment on certain phenomena. This type of question tests whether the pupil really has understood the science involved and is infinitely more desirable as an examination technique.

It should, however, be realised that these new methods of examining provide the teacher with some problems. Although the answers are more easily and more quickly marked, the setting of the paper will be a more lengthy and difficult task. The short-answer type of question falls roughly into the following categories:

1. Completion tests.
2. Multiple choice tests.
3. True–false tests.
4. Sentence discrimination.
5. Logical selection.
6. Reasoning tests.
7. Identification tests.

Questions in all these tests need to be carefully worded so as to be free from ambiguity and also framed so that only one answer is correct. In type 2 it is important that at least two of the possible answers are very similar so that the pupil has to think carefully before making the final choice. Teachers will find much of interest in *Examination Bulletins Nos. 3 and 4*, compiled by the Secondary School Examinations Council (now Schools Council for the Curriculum and Examinations) (H.M.S.O., 6s 0d and 2s 3d).

Specimen Questions

The following questions are not meant to be ideal samples but all have been used successfully by practising teachers. As a warning to the inexperienced, one unsuccessful question is quoted:

Complete the following statement:
When a liquid is heated. . . . .

254

Many answers are possible, e.g. boils, gets hot, expands, changes colour, evaporates, disappears, is sterilised, etc. It would be impossible to assess the merits of all these answers.

Many of the questions have actually been used by members of this committee, but it must be remembered that even if a question has been used successfully and without ambiguity in an internal examination in one school it is not necessarily suitable for every class of every school. Teachers place emphasis on different aspects of a subject so that questions that are easily answered by their own pupils might puzzle other pupils. It is very difficult indeed to frame questions which are universally understood, unambiguous, and also useful in testing some important part of the work.

How heat travels

1. (*a*) Heat travels through a metal by a process called.........
   (*b*) Heat from the sun reaches the earth by.................
   (*c*) A hot-water system works by...............
   Which of the above processes in *a*, *b*, *c* will *not* work in a vacuum?
   ....

2. From the list of words given, select words to complete the sentence.
   When a fire is lit in a grate, the air in the chimney gets
   ....and it...............and it...............
         cold; expands; sinks; hot; rises; contracts.

3. Complete the following diagram:

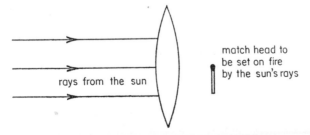

rays from the sun

match head to
be set on fire
by the sun's rays

4. In the hot sunny weather white clothes are more comfortable to wear than black. Why is this?
   ....

5. Some electric light filaments are enclosed in a vacuum. Name the process by which heat may escape when they are in use
   ....

The surface skin of water

1. We can show that water behaves as if it had a skin by........
. . . .
2. Name one insect which uses the surface skin of water..........
3. If you touch the inside of a tent while it is raining, the result
   is...............................because.............
   . . . .
4. Mark the positions of the water in the three tubes with their
   ends placed in water.

State two everyday examples where this kind of action is used.
. . . .

Water as a solvent

1. Underline the substances in the following list which are soluble
   in water:
   glass; common salt; copper; copper sulphate; brass; chalk;
   sand; washing soda; sugar; alum
2. Complete the following statements:
   Water + ... = brine
   Solute + ... = solution
   A solution in which no more substance will dissolve is said
   to be.............................
3. A mixture of sand and common salt is shaken up with water.
   State what happens in each case if
   (*a*) the mixture is filtered:
   . . . .
   (*b*) the mixture is distilled:
   . . . .
   (*c*) the filtrate is heated for some time, then left to cool:
   . . . .

4. Some clear water is gathered from a stream. What might be in the water to make it dangerous for drinking?...........

  How could this water be made fit for drinking?............

  ....,...

5. What is *observed* when hard water is shaken with

  (a) soap?.........................

  (b) washing soda?..........................

  How can this hard water be made soft?

  ....

Insect life histories

1. Select from the following list the food on which the stated insects feed.

  Privet leaves; cabbage; carrots; blood; water fleas; decomposing rubbish; fish; chipped potatoes; nectar

Insect	Food
Cabbage white butterfly	....
Cabbage white caterpillar	....
Female mosquito	....
Dytiscus beetle	....
Stick insect	....

2. Fill in the blanks in the following scheme for the life-history of a butterfly:

  Egg →   →   → Imago

  .... (Adult)

3. Name the labelled parts in the diagram of a butterfly:

  A ....

  B ....

  C ....

  D ....

  To what part of the body are the legs attached?...............

We think that perhaps readers might like to see what one of the committee has devised as a terminal test for the First Form D stream. Following are given two lists A and B. Pupils are given copies of list B and are asked to mark, underline or draw, according to the questions on List A, which are read out to them in order. (The spaces necessary for answers to questions 7, 9, 10, 15 and 18 are not actually shown in the list printed below.) Such an examination paper aims at testing scientific ability—neither reading nor writing; it serves to to encourage and fire with enthusiasm those youngsters who are lucky enough to take part.

SCIENCE EXAMINATION—FORM 1D

A—QUESTION PAPER

	Marks
1. Underline the gas we use when breathing.	(1)
2. Copy the one which is no use to us.	(1)
3. What happens to our breathing after exercise?	(1)
4. This is because we are:	(1)
5. What do we breathe with? Underline.	(1)
6. With what does a fish breathe? Underline.	(1)
7. Draw a diagram for an experiment to show that there is water vapour in the air.	(1)
8. What does this cause? (See Q. 7.) Underline.	(1)
9. Draw something to show that air presses.	(5)
10. Draw something to show how we use the pressure of the air.	(6)
11. What would happen to a diver if he did not wear a strong suit?	(1)
12. The three cubes represent 1 lb each of water, iron, cork. Put C on Cork, W on Water, I on Iron.	(2)
13. Put L on the least dense.	(1)
14. Put F on any of the cubes that would float on water.	(1)
15. Lead can be made to float on water. Draw a sketch to show how.	(4)
16. Draw a line across each outside sketch to indicate how deep the test-tube would sink.	(2)
17. Underline the name of the liquid in which it is easier to swim.	(1)
18. Draw the thing we use for heating in the lab.	(3)
19. Underline the two living things.	(2)

258

20. Draw in the part that grows first. (1)
21. Draw it as it appears a week later. (1)
22. Name the parts of the flower from the list at the side. (7)

B—ANSWER PAPER

1. OXYGEN   NITROGEN   CARBON DIOXIDE
2. ....
3. FASTER   SLOWER   THE SAME
4. TIRED   NEEDING OXYGEN   HUNGRY
5. HEAD   EARS   LUNGS   STOMACH
6. SKIN   LUNGS   GILLS   TAIL
8. SUNSHINE   DEW   DROUGHT
11. ....

12.
13.
14.

16.

salt   fresh   meths
water   water

17. FRESH WATER   SALT WATER

19. SMOKE   WORM   STONE   GRASS   WATER

20.

broad
bean
seeds

21.

259

22.

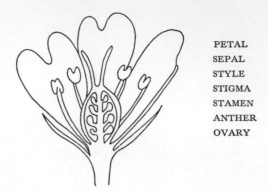

PETAL
SEPAL
STYLE
STIGMA
STAMEN
ANTHER
OVARY

Practical Tests

Opinions vary on the desirability and value of a simple practical examination. Some of the examining bodies set Ordinary Level practical examinations in science but others do not. The teacher must make the decision whether or not to set a practical test as part of a terminal or annual examination. A popular form of such a test is to set up a number of exercises around the laboratory, each one taking about three minutes to answer, and the candidates then move round at three-minute intervals. A number of the regional boards conducting the C.S.E. examinations are having practical tests of this nature. To illustrate this method, a set of specimen exercises is given below but very many more such questions can be devised.

Specimen Exercises

1. Take a little of each of the liquids A, B, C into each of three test-tubes. Blow the air from your lungs into each liquid in turn, through a drinking-straw. State what happens.

   Rinse out the test-tubes and leave them clean for the next pupil. Pour all waste liquids into the basin provided.

   (A = water; B = lime-water; C = water + 2 drops neutral litmus solution).

2. (Accumulator set up in series with ammeter and suitable resistance R.)

   Read the value of the current indicated by the ammeter, hence assuming the accumulator gives 2 volts, calculate the value of the resistance R.

3. Make a saturated solution of ammonium chloride in a test-tube and note the lowest temperature reached.
Wash out your test-tube and leave it ready for the next pupil.

4. (Flask fitted with stopper carrying about 18 in of glass tubing 3–5 mm diameter, dipping below water about 1 in deep in the flask.)
Warm the flask with your hand and note the result.

5. Put the iron nuts on the string in the boiling water, leave for a minute. Meanwhile pour 50 c.c. tap water into the can provided; take the temperature of the water, then transfer the hot nuts quickly to the cold water. Note the temperature reached and record the *rise in temperature*.

6. Find the focal length of the convex lens, D, by reading the distance from the white screen at which a *distant* object produces a sharply defined image on the screen.

7. (Half-metre rule pivoted at mid-point.) Using the 50-gm weight provided, find the weight of the object E.

8. F is an indicator in solution. Add two drops of this solution in turn to a little of each of the liquids in a test-tube. Note the results and hence state what you learn about the nature of K
(G is labelled acid; H labelled alkali. G = dilute HCl. H = NaOH (dilute). K = dilute H_2SO_4.)

9. Heat a *small* amount of the crystalline powder L. Test any gas given off with moist litmus. Describe *all* that happens. (L = ferrous sulphate crystals.)

10. Test cut slices of M, N, O to find out whether they contain starch. (M = potato; N = broad bean; O = onion)

11. The two dishes contain liquids P and R respectively. Some sultanas have been placed in each for some time. Looking at these sultanas, what conclusions can you form about the nature of P and R?
(P = water; R = sugar solution)

12. S is the underground part of a plant, look at it closely and decide whether it is a stem or a root. State your reason briefly. (S = a rhizome, e.g. mint or couch grass.)

13. Take a portion of the warm milk in a test-tube. Add about 10 drops of liquid T and keep the test-tube warm in your hand. Record any change noticed. What conclusion can you form about the nature of T? (Warm milk is kept in a water-bath at about 40° C. T = rennet solution.)

14. Which of the small animals V, W, X is an insect? State *one* good reason for your decision. (V, W, X could be, say, spider, centipede and ladybird.)

External Examinations

After prolonged discussion and much controversy the Certificate of Secondary Education is now an established and recognised examination although, regrettably, it has not emerged in the form originally envisaged in the Beloe Report. Fourteen Regional Boards have been set up and these make syllabuses and conduct examinations in a wide variety of subjects. Committees of these boards certainly include some practising teachers as members but, in general, these are external examinations and not internal as the Beloe Report recommended. It is appropriate, at this point, to mention that the long-established G.C.E. Boards have always encouraged schools to submit their own syllabuses for examination and the C.S.E. bodies are also offering this same facility.[1] In the past, comparatively few schools have taken advantage of this opportunity but it is to be hoped that the majority of schools presenting pupils for the C.S.E. tests will submit their own schemes of work for approval by the appropriate board. However, even if the teacher accepts the external syllabus there is no need for the work to be dull and frustrating—the syllabus should not control the teacher although the less experienced may find it a useful guide in planning his work. It must be emphasised that an examination syllabus is not a teaching syllabus.

Fear of external examinations very often springs from ignorance of the procedure normally adopted by the eight established G.C.E. bodies. As the great majority of subject committees members are practising teachers, it is obvious that the teaching staffs of schools can, and do, have a great influence on the content of syllabuses and examination papers. After the initial drafting by the chief examiner, the papers are very carefully moderated to see that questions are fair, unambiguous and relevant to the most important parts of the syllabus. There is usually much discussion with the examiners before the final draft is sent to print. The candidates' scripts are marked by a panel

[1] See *The Certificate of Secondary Education*, pages 7–9, paras. 4–9 (H.M.S.O. 1s 9d).

of examiners and every possible care is taken to ensure uniformity of standard as far as is humanly possible. Very detailed marking schemes are devised and standardising meetings held so that there should be little, if any, discrepancy in the examiners' standard of marking. The chief examiner is in touch throughout with his team of assistants and requires, at intervals, at least two batches of marked scripts from each assistant which he then marks quite independently—equivalent standards can thus be established. Examiners are, as a body, extremely conscientious and make every effort to maintain a constant standard throughout their period of marking. Their attitude to candidates is generous and not the reverse, as is so often implied. When the scripts have been returned to the Boards, marks are checked for additions and omissions and distribution graphs are drawn. An awarding meeting is held when the pass mark is fixed and borderline cases are re-marked. Each of such candidates is carefully assessed and school records consulted at this stage. Any school, on payment of a fee, may request a special report on their candidates' efforts, and this can be very helpful.

Presumably the newly established C.S.E. bodies will be adopting these techniques and procedures which have been adopted after many years of lively experiment. Already it has been officially decided that a Grade 1 pass in a subject in the C.S.E. examinations will equate with a pass at Ordinary Level G.C.E. Initially, science subject syllabuses of some C.S.E. boards, although intended for a different ability range, resemble very closely those of the G.C.E. boards. This seems very inappropriate and it is to be hoped that schools will devise new and exciting science programmes, more relevant to the pupil for whom the C.S.E. is intended.

The Science Panel of the London Secondary Schools Certificate Examination, inaugurated by the L.C.C. in 1962, held examinations in 1963, '64 and '65, and tried out and subsequently adopted two new methods in science examinations at this level. These are being continued in the C.S.E. of the Metropolitan Regional Examinations Board. These new techniques aroused much interest at the very successful meeting on the London Examination held at the Annual Meeting of A.S.E. at Birmingham in 1963.

Briefly these new ideas were:

(a) A paper in 'basic science' (called Paper I) consisting of about 20 open ended questions followed by some 80 multiple choice questions. The multiple choice type of question, while requiring reading ability because of its length, assists the pupil by its 'recall' factor. Some examples of this type of question are given below. (A word of warning here; although these questions are easy to mark they are far from easy to construct and their validity must be tested by pre-testing with other similar groups before use.)

Each of these questions contains an unfinished sentence followed by five words or phrases labelled A, B, C, D, E. One of these completes the sentence correctly. In the space provided write the letter which show the correct word or phrase.

(1) Water can be seen dropping from the exhaust pipe of a motor car on a cold morning because
    A. there is water in the petrol.
    B. it has been out in the rain all night.
    C. the combustion in the engine produces steam.
    D. atmospheric moisture condenses on the pipe
    E. hot air is coming from the pipe.

(2) To build up proteins the roots of most plants absorb
    A. oxygen.
    B. nitrates.
    C. carbon-dioxide.
    D. bacteria.
    E. carbohydrates.

(3) Oxygen may be obtained by heating *any* of the following *except*
    A. potassium chlorate.
    B. saltpetre.
    C. common salt.
    D. mercuric oxide.
    E. red lead.

(4) People wear snowshoes or skis in arctic regions because they
    A. lower the pressure exerted on the snow.
    B. make the snow slippery.

C. make it easier to grip the snow.
D. avoid melting the snow.
E. enable easily-seen footprints to be made.

(5) The way in which human beings differ from all other primates is that they
A. feed their young on milk.
B. chew their food.
C. have upright posture.
D. have hands that grasp.
E. have the power of speech.

(6) Iron will go rusty
A. in the presence of air alone.
B. if not magnetised.
C. in the presence of water alone.
D. in the presence of air and water together.
E. if it is heated in air.

(7) Some magnesium is caused to burn inside a sealed glass globe. The globe and contents would weigh
A. more before the experiment.
B. more after the experiment.
C. the same before and after the experiment.
D. more whilst it is still hot.
E. more after it has cooled down to room temperature.

(8) An element is a substance
A. which has all the atoms in it joined together.
B. in which all the atoms are of the same kind.
C. which has in it atoms but not molecules.
D. taking part in a chemical change.
E. which cannot be weighed.

(9) During photosynthesis in a green plant cell, all the following are essential for the production of starch *except*
A. oxygen.
B. light.
C. carbon-dioxide.
D. water.
E. chlorophyll.

265

(b) A 'practical examination' consisting of some twelve 'stations' where apparatus for short experiments or activities was set up. These tested the candidate's practical ability in science but not necessarily his facility to recall work previously done in the laboratory. The capabilities being tested were grouped under the following headings:

(i) Knowledge of the *name* and the *use* of common pieces of apparatus or materials likely to be used in practical experiments.

(ii) Ability to *perform* simple experiments from data given.

(iii) Ability to *solve* a simple experimental problem from the data given or the experiment performed.

(iv) Ability to *record* what is seen to happen or is visible in carrying out an experiment or performing a technique in practical work.

(v) Ability to carry out an experiment using the correct *technique*. This station was called the 'observed station' because the marks for this were awarded by the teacher at the time, as the result of watching the pupil at work.

An example of each of these types of stations is given below in three parts:

(a) the set-up of station,

(b) the examination question to be answered,

(c) the answer required and the marking schedule.

EXAMPLE (i) 'KNOWLEDGE OF NAME AND USE'

(a) The following items will be placed on the bench, each labelled with correct letter:

A. A clinical thermometer.	B. Evaporating dish.
C. Hydrometer.	D. A distillation flask.
E. Convex lens.	F. An empty petri dish.

(b) *Question:* Write down the names of these items opposite the appropriate letter. For what purpose would you use each of these items in an experiment?

(c) *Answer* (1 mark for each correct answer):

A. clinical thermometer; for taking temperature of human or mammalian body.

B. evaporating dish/basin; for concentrating a solution or boiling off water from a solution to obtain the substance dissolved. (Accept liquid solvent in lieu of water if explanation is clear.)

C. hydrometer or S.G. measure; finding specific gravity (density) of liquid.

D. distillation flask; for obtaining pure liquid (water) by boiling off liquid in vapour form and then cooling. (Accept 'distilling a solution to obtain pure liquid free from impurities dissolved in it'.)

E. Convex/converging lens; used as magnifying glass/camera lens/telescope/projector/binocular lens.

F petri or culture dish; used to grow colonies of bacteria on jelly (medium) out of contact with the air. (Accept description that means this.)

EXAMPLE (ii) 'PERFORM'

(a) A 6 in × ½ in hard glass test-tube with bung to fit. The test-tube has a painted band or mark 2 in from bottom.

Soap solution in a beaker and a dropping pipette with teat are provided.

(b) *Question:* Rinse the tube with tap water. Fill the test-tube to the mark with tap water (use top edge of mark as guide-line). Add soap solution drop by drop until a permanent lather is obtained. Write down how many drops were required. Empty test-tube before you move off to the next station.

(c) *Answer:* Teacher will have performed this experiment with the same materials and found the correct number of drops required.

3 marks for correct answer. 2 marks for error of plus or minus one drop. 1 mark for error of plus or minus 2 drops.

EXAMPLE (iii) 'SOLVE'

(a) Four dishes marked A, B, C, D, are placed on the bench. Each contains ¼ in– ⅜ in cubes of the following: Brazil nut in A, raw potato in B, hard cheese (as white as possible) in C, peanut (ground nut) (fresh) in D.

A piece of absorbent paper for each candidate. Container for used paper.

267

(*b*) *Question:* Which of these four foods does not contain fat?
(*c*) *Answer:* B (2 marks).

EXAMPLE (iv) 'RECORD'
(*a*) A 6 in × ½ in Pyrex test-tube with ⅛ in of ferrous sulphate crystals at the bottom is provided for each candidate. A test-tube holder is provided. A Bunsen (already lit) with a medium-sized flame adjusted so that the blue cone is just visible is provided for heating.
(*b*) *Question:* Gently heat the tube and its contents and record all that you see happen. Allow time for recording.
(*c*) *Answer:* Teacher will do experiment and give one mark to a maximum of four for each correct item recorded by candidate.

EXAMPLE (v) 'TECHNIQUE' 'OBSERVED STATION'
(*a*) A 'patient' (pupil/lab technician) is sitting down in front of the bench. On the bench is provided:
  (1) one clinical thermometer (or more, if possible) in
  (2) a beaker of weak disinfectant solution,
  (3) a sweep seconds hand clock (need not be a stop-clock).
(*b*) *Question:* Hand your answer paper to the teacher in charge of this experiment and then:
    Take the patient's temperature and enter the temperature in the space provided on your answer paper.
(*c*) The teacher will watch what the examinee does and award marks as per schedule:
  (i) Shaking down the thermometer after examining.   1 mark
  (ii) Placing it under the patient's tongue for 2 minutes.   1 mark
  (iii) Reading the temperature correctly.   1 mark
  (iv) Shaking down the mercury after use.   1 mark
  (v) Replacing thermometer bulb downwards into disinfectant.   1 mark

If the pupils have been taught to leave the thermometer in for the time period shown on the thermometer then this can be marked correct. The teacher in charge will check that the temperature entered is the one recorded by the thermometer if it has been left in the mouth for the correct time. If the patient's temperature is likely to be variable the teacher should check at intervals.

Note: The marking schedule could be varied to suit individual school conditions and the practical paper's design as a whole. The one quoted above is only an indication of what can be done.

268

The following documents are well worth studying. Some of the statements in them are provocative, but careful consideration of all that is said, and the suggested methods of procedure, cannot but be helpful in assisting the teacher-reader to improve his perspective on examinations as a whole:

(i) *Examinations Bulletins Nos. 1, 3, 4 and 5.*
These are of a general nature but much of the contents pertains to science.

(ii) *Experimental Examination Science, Examinations Bulletin No. 8.*
An account of two phases of an exploratory examination in science for C.S.E. carried out on the Schools Council's behalf.

All the above can be obtained from H.M.S.O.

It is well worth acquiring copies of syllabuses and the relevant examination papers from the local C.S.E. Boards apart from your own district. Their study will enable teachers to assess their own efforts in this field.

INDEX